MW00605456

The KnuckleHead's Guide to Escaping The Trap:
THE ABRIDGED TRILOGY

By Dr. Amir Whitaker Esq.

DEDICATION

To my family and friends back in Jersey. To the hopes, dreams, and aspirations of youth in environments where unfavorable conditions often prevent dreams from becoming realities. To the memory of those who have struggled to create a world with less struggle. To the ongoing struggle for equality, peace, and true justice. To the youth of Project KnuckleHead.

CONTENTS

PREFACE

Those of us born in the 1980s have witnessed significant shifts in our lifetimes. The prison population has quadrupled. Many states have started spending more on incarceration than education. Meanwhile, the cost of higher education and housing has multiplied, but salaries have barely budged. We were also born during America's longest and most expensive war—the War on Drugs. As we adjust to the rhythms of adulthood, we find it difficult to reconcile the principles that were drilled into us during our childhood—justice, freedom, and opportunity—with our current reality. I decided to write this book for our generation and for future generations, in hopes that they can avoid these pitfalls.

The KnuckleHead's Guide to Escaping the Trap is an abridged compilation of chapters from a trilogy, set to be released over the next few years.

The first part of the saga is *Origins*—a raw look into my adolescence and development. In retrospect, I've realized these experiences have had a traumatic, yet enlightening, impact on my life. The devastating consequences of mass incarceration, the War on Drugs, and the School-to-Prison-Pipeline are often exposed through endless statistics and numbers. My story is one of the many that personalizes these systems. Through sharing it, I hope to highlight the consequences of the traps at the individual, family, and community level.

At age 31, I realized that few things have impacted my life more than America's criminal justice system. This epiphany came after noticing that I was taking care of four generations: there were monthly bills for my grandparents, my mother's living expenses while she moved in with me, my brother's commissary that I occasionally loaded with money while he was incarcerated, and my niece who I helped take care of because her father was in a cage. The financial strain from the multi-generational impact of mass incarceration influenced my decision to move from Miami to Alabama. I left an office where I valet parked my car and enjoyed a high-rise view of the ocean for a small cubicle, sandwiched between colleagues, in a sleepy town in the Deep South.

The second book, *Million: Money on My Mind*, follows a

young Amir as he spreads his wings physically, mentally, socially, and soulfully. It includes a compilation of over a decade of my college journals, and the enlisted help of a celebrity narrator. Reading all of my old journal entries at once sparked another epiphany: my 12-year career as a professional student was actually a cowardly retreat from the world to escape my feelings of inadequacy and confusion. The inadequacy came from feeling underprepared to take on the challenges and injustices that awaited. The confusion arose from questioning whether the barriers I faced were the results of intentional oppression, or were merely consequences of history and circumstance. I grappled with the question of whether the system was broken, or was the result of a well-designed Trap.

Last, but not least, *Street Traveler* contains short stories about five of the thirty countries I have visited: South Africa, England, Guatemala, Japan, and Croatia. Throughout my travels, I have been searching for something, but I'm still not quite sure what. At times, I felt as if I were looking for evidence of the "One Love" Bob Marley sung about. Or maybe a place where darker people did not suffer more than everyone else. Regardless of what I was looking for, I am confident that traveling and seeing the world firsthand has critically shaped the person I've become. I am shamelessly addicted to traveling, and get an adrenaline rush just thinking about being in a foreign place. There's something about the newness, the unknown, and the unseen. I approached every trip with a belief that if I lived hard enough, there'd be no need to live forever.

This book would not be possible without the people who have been a part of my life throughout the years. Your love and patience are eternally appreciated. Special thanks to those who lent their support by proofreading throughout the process: Tiffany Krause, Nate Kostar, Vania Salgar, Marielle "Maui" Moore, Benjamin Chambers, and Kenneth J. Blakenship. I look forward to further developing the stories as I grow as a writer. Full editions of each book will follow, once I find a major publisher to pick up the series (or when I'm no longer working full-time as a civil rights lawyer, while also volunteering my time to run a national non-profit).

I'm not sure how the Creator managed to get this book out of me, but here it is.

BOOK ONE — ORIGINS

During the first 19 years of his life, Amir is engulfed in a war without realizing it. Poverty and the War on Drugs entrap his neighborhood in a cycle of addiction, incarceration, and chaos. Dominating the drug trade at age 15 brings the world to his fingertips—until he and his mother are arrested in a police raid. Amir struggles through the rest of his teenage years after being kicked out of school and lured back into the Trap. A battle to rise above an inner-city warzone plagued with drugs, violence, and death transforms him into a resilient young man—one difficult lesson at a time. Follow this hard-fought journey of a boy with an unrelenting desire to overcome the odds.

Chapter 1: Hunger

<u>Age</u>: 15 years old

<u>Hunger</u> (n) /hun-ger/- When being deprived of something leads to a great desire, craving, or appetite for it. Hunger causes all living things to resort to extreme measures. It brings about savage ways among even the most innocent.

For nearly one hundred years, the stack of bricks my family called home stood near the corner of 6th and Liberty Street on the west end of Plainfield, New Jersey. The front yard of overgrown grass and scattered shrubs is enclosed by the remnants of a burgundy picket fence. So few pickets remained, the yard looked as if it were laughing with a nearly toothless smile. Throughout the neighborhood, churches, corner store bodegas, and empty lots dotted every street.

My grandparents had six children, six grandchildren, and lived on West 6th Street. That, ironically, equated to 6-6-6, and was just another reason I believed this house could truly be hell on earth. But not even the devil himself wanted a piece of this house during the morning hours. Besides, this was a God-fearing home, sanctified by a life-sized portrait of Black Jesus hanging above the living room couch.

Out of the six children my grandparents had, four of them were still living here. However, they were no longer children—at least not as far as age was concerned. Now grown-ups in their thirties and forties, my aunts and uncles frequently added fuel to hell's flames. My cousins and siblings comprised the third generation of hell's demons living in the house. 6-6-6. Nana, Pop, and the two strangers renting out rooms brought the total number of people living here to 14. It was indeed hell, but my grandparents—Nana and Pop—were the two closest things to angels I had ever known in my 15 years on this earth.

I'm happier than a butcher's dog that I no longer live on 6th street. But while living around the corner over the past year, I find myself coming back to Nana's house quite often. There's something about this place that lures me back. As a matter of fact, there are two things: cable television and food. Mom is always too busy running the streets to cook at home. Sometimes, I wonder if she even eats. Our refrigerator is so empty, leftovers would be lonely. This morning all it contained was BBQ sauce, spoiled milk, three eggs, and a half-a-stick of butter. I think I've had as many BBQ-buttermilk-egg sandwiches as I can take. With the habits my mom has, food is the least of her worries. So whenever I'm hungry, I just go around the corner to Nana's house to dine in Hell's Kitchen. Despite the 14 people living in the house, there's usually plenty of food. Nana runs the food bank at our church that provides for people in need, and we're probably the biggest clients. In more ways than one, we are in need.

Nana is my favorite cook. She is the 5-star chef of the hood. Cinnamon, clove, and brown sugar flavors linger on your palate long after her sweet potatoes melt in your mouth. She bakes her macaroni and cheese until the combination of cheeses crystallizes into a golden, layered crisp on top. Her creamy, savory lima beans and rice are my personal favorite. You'll never see her measure ingredients or anything like they do on TV either. I guess she lets her soul dictate her measurements. As corny as that sounds, I can offer no other explanation. Her delectable dishes are single-handedly the reason why I'm a size 42 waist. I swear I would die if she told me she would never cook lima beans and rice again.

Pop can cook too. It must be a southern thing. Before my grandparents moved to Jersey fifty years ago, our family lived in South Carolina for a hundred years at least. Their culinary traditions and ingredients were passed down for centuries, and can be traced back to Africa. That's why Pop always throws vegetables like okra and squash into his deep-fried delicacies. My grandparents even grow vegetables right in the back of their house—another holdover from country life in South Carolina. We're the only people in the hood with collard greens, cucumbers, tomatoes, sunflowers and other plants and vegetables growing in the backyard. Sometimes we catch crackheads stealing our homegrown produce to sell so they can get high. One time, I thought about making a scarecrow to frighten them away. His name would be Osmosis: The Crackhead Scarecrow. He'd be dressed up as a cop or parole officer, since they are the only things that seem to strike fear into crackheads' hearts. He would come alive at night, round up all the fiends and drug dealers in the neighborhood, then transport them to a drugless island for a fresh start. Two birds, one stone. Osmosis: The Crackhead Scarecrow would save Nana and Pop's vegetables and rid the world of crackheads and dealers.

Indeed, there was always something mysteriously special about the food at my grandparents' house. Unfortunately, my aunts and uncles knew how to kill my appetite. When they were high, though, they were a bit cooler. But when they were sober for too long and needed that fix, they turned sour real quick.

"Ain't you got a refrigerator around the corner?!" one of them would say. Sometimes I could ignore them, but their words would gradually grow sharper.

"What's the matter? Ya Momma done smoked up her damn welfare check?" they'd say, as I peered into the fridge.

When they were at their worst, I wondered how "grown folks" could speak to a 15-year-old boy the way they spoke to me. There were days I'd rather starve than hear their mouths. But on other days, I loved them for the compassion they could show. After a while, I noticed that I woke up less hungry if I went to sleep without eating, as if my body was adapting to food deprivation. This actually helped me, since breakfast was even rarer than dinner was around here.

Breakfast was part of the reason why I decided to sleep at Nana's house. I wanted to watch my Japanese anime show, plus I figured I'd have a better chance of getting a decent breakfast if I woke up here. The temptation of food and cable cartoons made me temporarily forget how the mornings here were hell. Had I remembered, I probably would have preferred to starve and not watch TV.

And so my day begins on a couch etched in my earliest memories of this house. Once suede, its material has worn down to a smooth leather-like texture over time. Cigarette burns reveal the canary-colored foam cushioning. Pop puts the plastic covers over the cushions every once in a while, but like my patience for my aunts and uncles, the covers never last. Sleeping on plastic is uncomfortable anyways, especially when it's hot. As you sweat, your skin sticks to the plastic like a melted chocolate bar clinging to its wrapper. You have to slowly peel yourself off the couch to avoid ripping your skin. So I say, funk the plastic. I'll take the canary-colored cushioning any day.

As I wipe the sleep out of my eyes, I'm interrupted by my Aunt Leslie's screeching voice.

"I ain't steal no god-damn iron!" she says.

"Come on Leslie, nobody was over here this morning but you. I gotta iron Shante's clothes so she can go to school now. Shhh*t!" Nana responds.

Nana was cussin'. That only meant one thing—she was furious. She rarely cursed, but when she did, she would just attach "shhh*t" to the end of a sentence in a high pitch tone. This was a sharp contrast to the soft, mellow voice she usually spoke with.

"Damn yo' soul, Leslie!" Pop interrupted.

My grandfather, on the other hand, had a filthy mouth and a wicked tendency to "damn" people's souls. Despite their varying communication styles, my grandparents have strikingly similar physical appearances. As a kid, I wondered if this resemblance was the result of them spending decades around each other. Both are the same shade of chestnut brown, which has been passed on to me and many other Whitakers. They often make the same facial expression: a pouting mouth with squinting eyes. Pop's glasses are slightly thicker, while Nana's nose is a bit longer. Nana wears short curls that evolved from her Afro, while Pop sports an eternal salt-and-pepper hi-top. Both are very spiritual and never miss a Sunday at church.

Mornings like this are frequent here. Aunt Leslie was always ferociously trying to defend herself after being accused of stealing something. She had been caught stealing everything from packs of barrettes to hair grease, from clothes to washing powder. She was a skilled thief, who could find a way to sell the most random of items.

I remember once thinking my video games were lost, until visiting a friend's house and discovering that Aunt Leslie had sold them to the kid's parents. I also used to think my action figures and toys disappeared because they "died and went to toy heaven," as Nana would say. Of course, this was not the case—Aunt Leslie struck again. At one point, I tried burning my initials into my belongings to later identify them in other peoples' homes or deter my aunt from taking them in the first place. I tried to sabotage the hustle by telling people in the neighborhood not to buy things from Aunt Leslie, but nothing worked. She always took whatever she could get, and sold it for what she needed.

As I listened to Nana and Aunt Leslie bicker, I tapped on my foot to make sure my $25 of birthday money was still in my sock. I ran my fingers over my two-day old socks until I felt a slight lump. I was relieved—still there. I'm sure Aunt Leslie could have gotten to it if I was asleep just a little longer. One time, she stole a video game from under my pillow while I slept. Ironically, my dad had stolen the game for my brother and me in the first place. What goes around comes around, I guess. If there was ever such a thing as Karma, Aunt Leslie had a great deal of pain and anguish coming her way eventually. I remembered opening gifts one Christmas, only to get them stolen before New Year's Eve. She could be heartless and was capable of anything when she was trying to get a "blast" or "hit" of that poison. Other times she could be my favorite aunt, because of her sense of humor and willingness to go to the liquor store for us. Still, that poison brought out the worst in my aunty.

I can't even say crack no more, I just call it "that poison." And what a poison it was. A poison that ravaged not just individuals, but entire families and communities. A poison that could take a boy's Christmas toys away, pluck barrettes from a little girl's hair, and swipe vegetables from a struggling family's garden. A poison that was literally taking the food out of my mouth this morning. I know my fridge would contain more than condiments if my mom's addiction didn't consume so much. That poison was the reason why my four aunts and uncles were still living in their parent's house. It was the reason I witnessed sides of my parents that no child should be subjected to. Those inflicted with the misfortune of being addicted better pray they never get caught. That's when they toss you in a cage like an animal.

This morning I had to leave Nana's house quickly to escape the poison's wrath that was starting to seep in. I had long ago learned that if crack invades your morning, it messes up your entire day. Although I loved my Nana and Pop more than anything, and despite their charity and fear of God, the poison reigned supreme in their house.

As my grandparents and Aunt Leslie continued to argue, they were interrupted by the phone ringing.

"I ain't finished with you yet!" my grandmother warned Aunt Leslie, as she pointed her finger and placed her other hand on her hip.

"Hello!" she said, in the same tone she was just using with Aunt Leslie.

"Say what ... What happened?" her tone changed and her eyebrows raised. Her jaw dropped, and the house became the quietest it had been all morning.

"What you doing with a stolen car? Who else was with you?" she questioned.

I wondered who she was talking to. I did a mental roll-call of who was currently in the house and narrowed down who it could be.

"Leslie, it's yo' son. He done got hisself locked up. Riding in a stolen car. Says your brother is with him too, Mir-Mir," she said.

"Mir-Mir" was what most of my family and friends called me. I didn't like it, but at least it was better than Aunt Leslie's son's nickname.

"Pookie!?" Aunt Leslie shrieked, as her eyes opened wide. "Aww Lord. His probation officer was waiting for this!"

Pookie was Aunt Leslie's 14-year-old son, and my first cousin. We were always close growing up since I was only one year older. Both of us lived with Nana and Pop most of our lives, since our parents were victims of that poison. We were the tightest of the five Whitaker boys who were not actual brothers. There were five boys: me, my brother Jamal, Pookie, his brother Ray Ray, and our oldest cousin, Kwame. Aside from us five boys, there was my little sister, Shante. More times than not, our grandparents were left with the responsibility of taking care of the lot of us. They thought raising our parents in the 1960s and 70s was bad until they started raising us in the 80s and 90s.

When Pookie and I were together, we were always trouble. When we were just three and four years old, we nearly burned the house down experimenting with smoking cigarettes. Pop was so angry, he beat all six of us grandkids, and said there'd be more coming if we even thought about doing it again. His tactics were so effective, that I recited my ABCs aloud for years to distract me every time I thought about smoking a cigarette. His indestructible leather work belt was our biggest fear. The thinner belt he wore on days off would sting, but his work belt had the bite of a slave master's whip. If I planned to do something wicked, I made sure Pop was on his day off to avoid the work belt. Ray Ray even tried hiding Pop's work belt and once even tossed it in the garbage. But that thing was immortal and undying, like the killers in scary movies…and equally as dreadful.

Now with my brother, Pookie, and Ray Ray locked-up, three out of the five Whitaker boys were in jail. Ray Ray was already locked up behind some foolishness with a stolen car. So today, sixty percent of Whitaker Boys are in cages. Such statistics were shameful since we were all only between the ages of 14-19. We were young, reckless, and actively contributing to the hell my grandparents were going through. As if their kids didn't put them through enough hell already, now their kids' kids were repeating the cycle as teenagers.

Now that I think about it, I do remember Pookie and my brother having a car yesterday. A brand new 2001 Ford Explorer in candy apple red. They kept circling the block blasting Track 4 on the new Nas album.

Some of us have angels (the kingdom, the power)
Some of us have demons (the power, the glory)
Some of us have angels (greed, lust)
Some of us have demons (lust, temptation)

By the end of the day, I vowed that I would never listen to that song again.

They claimed they had rented the car for 3 crillz. Translation: $30 worth of poison. Must have been a shifty fiend who called the cops and snitched on them after smoking the 3 crillz they got to for the car. Some fiends can smoke that up in half an hour. I'm just glad I didn't get in the car when they asked if I wanted to roll out with them. I told them to wait on me for 20 minutes because my Japanese cartoons were on. As much as I love Dragon Ball Z, I would have never guessed it would save me from being put in a cage.

As Nana and Aunt Leslie switched from talking to Pookie on the phone, I wondered if I would be making a similar call home one day. I tucked away the worry and began to think about what I would do with my day. It must have been a school day because Nana was getting my little sister Shante ready for school. I was contemplating whether or not I should go to school myself. I have Spanish class first period, and I hated my teacher with a passion. She already made it clear she's going to fail me regardless of what I do or don't do, so I feel no need to go to her class. She's had it in for me ever since I started joking around and asking her what different curse words were in Spanish. I don't feel like dealing with her "mierda" this morning. I'll probably just skip her class and go to school second period, which gives me time to go home and change.

Although I attract attention every time I open my grandparents' fridge, not a soul in the house cares whether or not I go to school. I could stay on this couch all day, and no one would ask why I wasn't in school. Mom is out in the streets. Dad is in prison. Both of them dropped out of high school themselves, so they wouldn't care much anyway. Nana and Pop are so exhausted from dealing with the anarchy we cause in school, it's actually less of a headache for them when we stay home. Half of their six children dropped out of high school. I'm the only one out of the five Whitaker boys who hasn't dropped out. Shante has damn-near dropped out, since she misses a day or two out of every school week and is continually on the verge of being expelled permanently. Nana has to cook her breakfast, iron her clothes, and perform all sorts of acrobatics just to get her to go to school. Shante has always gotten V.I.P. attention as the only girl. She's 12 years old, and Nana serves as her personal maid. This makes us Whitaker Boys eternally jealous.

My attendance isn't the greatest either. With no encouragement to go to school, and no consequences at home for missing it either, it's a daily struggle to get out of bed in the morning. I've come to terms with the fact that I have to push myself. It's the only way for me to escape and not perpetuate. I have to be extremely self-disciplined to do simple things, like stay out of trouble and stay in school. Perhaps it will pay off in the future, but for now, it's a struggle. It's the worst when I wake up in my mom's house and it's as empty as our refrigerator. I immediately turn on all the televisions to drown out the sound of morning birds and help me forget that not a soul is in the house with me. I always think of that Wu-Tang lyric: "Life as a shorty shouldn't be so rough." Wishful thinking.

The only reason I made it this far in school is because I force myself to go every morning...well, most mornings. No alarm clock. No cheerful parents calling from the living room to wake me up. No breakfast on the table like on TV. Nana only cooks breakfast for Shante, not me. I'm one of the Lost Boys. If I don't wake myself up, nobody will. If I don't force myself to go to school, I'll miss class. If I don't sign my parents' signature on permission slips for field trips, I don't go. It's been like this since middle school. With everything else going on, no one pays attention to education. Nobody asks where I want to go to college or what I want to be when I grow up. Luckily for me, I'm always anxious to get out of whatever house I'm in—even if I have to deal with annoying teachers. My desire to leave home is often my strongest motivation to go to school. The resentment I have for my aunts and uncles and all the failure surrounding me keeps me going too. Aside from my grandparents, there are no positive role models in my family. I'm sure he unspoken hope and prayers of my grandparents also keeps me going.

The fact that most of my friends, as well as my family, have dropped out also makes going to school difficult. Each year that passes, there are fewer and fewer of us walking to school together. I still remember the first day of high school when our crew was 18 deep. Now, a year later, most days I walk to school alone. Sometimes I walk around the lunchroom for several minutes searching for my homies, feeling like a rescue worker ravaging through rubble for survivors. Most of the time the mission concludes with me finding a spot to sit in the corner in isolation and agony. Some days I stay home from school just to avoid this embarrassment and pain.

Last month I left my report card on the table to see if anyone would pay attention to it. It stayed there unopened for weeks, until one of my aunts finally threw it in the garbage. I normally didn't care, but this frustrated me because my grades were actually starting to improve. I yearned for someone—anyone—to say "good job."

Last year as a freshman, I got F's in more than half my classes. This semester I was only getting an F in that Spanish class. And it's not even that I'm that much better of a student this year. I just don't have a crew to act-a-fool with since nearly everyone I came up with dropped out of school. I'm starting to mature a bit and actually do my work instead of wasting time.

I often overhear other students in school talking about the colleges they want to go to. One time I heard a kid talking about how his mom wanted him to go to Rutgers University, but he preferred Howard University. I couldn't help but get a little jealous when I heard him talking. The jealousy wasn't so much directed towards him for wanting to go to college. That would have been hatin,' and the block had taught me wise against having a Ph.D.-Playa Hater Degree. Instead, I was jealous of his mother who seemed to be guiding him to college. I thought about how nobody in my family had ever told me to go to college—ever. Hell, at this point, nobody was even concerned if I went to high school. Most people probably assumed that I was destined to the same fate as my parents, aunts and uncles, and others before me. My mother only made it to the 10th grade and my father, the 11th. My goal was to go as far as I could.

With both parents running the streets, preoccupied with that poison, and cycling in-and-out of jail, the burden of raising us was with my grandparents. They never went to court to get full legal custody. We simply fall into their laps whenever our parents aren't around. If and when our parents managed to get their acts together, we would go back to stay with them. It was always fun at Nana and Pop's while it lasted, but I made sure I never got too comfortable. The more I got my hopes up, the more upset I would be when things fell apart again.

As a consequence of that poison, I'm forced to limit the emotions I feel for my parents. I can count the Christmases when my dad was out of prison on a single hand. I imagine this was painful for both of us; him being in a cage and not getting any better, and me being without the person responsible for showing me how to be a man. Still, whenever he was home, he did what was necessary for us to have a good Christmas. The greatest day in my life is still the Christmas we got bikes, and I taught my older brother, Jamal, how to ride. My father could be great when he was around. Unfortunately, that poison and the punishment from its use prevented that from happening regularly. As a small child, I eventually learned to accept this as my "normal." But I could never get used to the frustration of coming home to find out my dad had been as locked up while I was at school. Never getting the chance to say goodbye before he went away for a few months cut me deeply, every time.

Mom, on the other hand, is usually around, but can never hold a steady job or apartment. In fact, we have moved so much that my brother and I went to five different elementary schools. Between the three blocks of Section 8 housing that surround the Liberty Street Projects, we've lived in seven different places. Luckily, my grandparents lived nearby on 6th and Liberty Street, so we could always return to their house. And most of my friends and family were in the projects on Liberty (Lib-Side) or in the neighborhood. Still, I was always confused about us having to move so often, since we were on Section 8 and paid cheap rent. But Mom's I-can-do-better attitude combined with her addiction, made maintaining a job and paying cheap rent difficult. Just like Dad, Mom tried to do what she could during the holidays. Every Christmas she got a seasonal job at some fast food restaurant to try to scrape together money for gifts. Most of the time, she actually pulled it off. Other times, the streets deprived us of a happy holiday. Sometimes that poison literally took the food out of my mouth and the clothing off my back. Holiday presents were not immune to the poison.

"Back again, huh baby?" Nana would say with a smirk, when we returned to her place with garbage bags full of our clothes.

Because my grandparents were so family-oriented, they were always pleased to welcome us back. They'd always find a way to make space for us. So, of course, Nana didn't mind me sleeping on her couch this morning before school.

Despite my love for my grandparents, the calamity in their house this morning was becoming unbearable. It wasn't even 8 AM yet, and the house was down an iron and two Whitaker boys. Aunt Leslie looked like she was on "empty" too, and that's a distressing sight to see. Heroin, her current poison of choice, is one of the worst addictions to observe because it becomes physically debilitating. After a period of consistent use, the human body needs it to function in the same way that a car needs gasoline. When someone's on empty, that poison becomes the antidote.

As the time drew closer to the start of school, I took a quick shower at my grandparents' house. If I felt like it, I would stop at my house to change. If not, I had no problem wearing the same clothes as yesterday. I'm not significant enough for anyone to notice. I do it all the time actually.

After my shower, I walked into the kitchen with a growling stomach and noticed that, as usual, Nana had only cooked breakfast for Shante.

"I didn't know you would be here, baby. I can make you sumtin', if you give me a sec" Nana apologizes and offers.

"Nah, it's ok, Nana," I replied. "I'm just gonna go to school."

Seeing Aunt Leslie on empty reminds me of my mom on a terrible day. A runny nose, dripping snot into her mouth. Squinting eyes in a battle with light. Physical weakness causing her to drag one leg across the ground like a zombie. I have to leave this place even if I have to deal with my Spanish teacher's "mierda." I'll stop by the corner store and get two granola bars and a fifty-cent C & C soda. The inner-city youth's breakfast of champions. You can't beat it for a dollar.

"Come to the church after school," Nana requests. "We need your help unloading the truck for the food bank."

"I'll try," I say, as I grab my book bag and head out the door.

In my mind, I was already planning on taking the long way home from school to avoid passing our church. I knew I wouldn't be in the mood to unload hundreds of pounds of food by myself, since Pookie and Jamal were locked up.

And so I departed from the hell at my grandparent's place to seek salvation in the streets of Plainfield. If only the streets offered a warm welcome in return. Instead, their gritty greeting was discouraging. Potholes dot the streets, looking like the surface of the moon. Roads neglected by the city for years, crying to be repaved. Malt liquor cans, cigarette butts, broken glass: the streets' everyday attire. In fact, on the rare occasions the city did decide to clean things up, it left the streets looking strange, surreal, and naked. This was the natural habitat of "Painfield," the name of our city in its lowest moments.

Plainfield is one of America's oldest cities, but many of its historic houses have fallen into disrepair. The only exception in my neighborhood is the Drake House Museum. More than 220 years ago, America's first President—Mr. George Washington, himself—lived there during one of the most critical battles of the Revolutionary War. Today, it's across the street from Plainfield's largest housing project. Section 8 skyscrapers shade this house that existed before America was America. Now passing red, white, and blue police lights and the silhouettes of our city's scoundrels decorate the historic house's facade. It's on the same street as the "hoe stroll," the most popular strip for Plainfield's prostitutes. The Drake House always reminded me of a precious diamond buried in a heap of broken glass. You can easily miss it amongst the liquor stores, hoe houses, chicken joints, and housing projects. I wonder what George Washington would think if he saw Liberty Street today.

The brief encounter with my neighborhood's landscape made me not want to go home to change clothes. The decrepit atmosphere became even heavier after a few blocks. So it looks like I'll be rocking yesterday's finest: a brown and tan Guess shirt that my big cousin gave me, along with hand-me-down FUBU jeans from my Aunt Wanda. The clothes I have at home aren't much better. I'm long overdue for new school clothes. I'm still wearing the same threads from middle school. Nobody wears FILA's anymore, yet I'm still rocking the Grant Hill rookie sneakers from a few years ago. He got traded to the Orlando Magic, so I can't even hide the fact they're old kicks. Not to mention my ancient jacket which was already out-of-style years before I got it. But mom is running wild in the streets like never before with her new boyfriend, Bootsy, so I know not to look to her for fresh school clothes. And Nana doesn't take us school shopping anymore. When there was four or five of us in school, she didn't mind taking us to Shopper's World to buy us all clothes. We would even share them. I would get the black and dark blue jeans, Jamal would get the light blue and gray ones. Pookie was always much skinnier than us, so we couldn't share his clothes. Pookie's brother Ray Ray thought he was too cool for Shopper's World, but he would still wear the stuff when Nana bought it. And sometimes, all four of us would sneak into our oldest cousin Kwame's closet and borrow his clothes while he was at work. Doing this multiplied our individual closets five-fold.

That was back in the day. All four of the other Whitaker boys dropped out, and now I was the only one left in school. If I wanted school clothes now, I had to get them for myself. I'll be damned if I go into the 2001 school year sporting the same gear from 98'. To make things worse, all rappers talk about nowadays is "Bling-Bling" this and that. Now you can't even get a girl's attention unless you're wearing jewelry, along with the latest fashions. So next year when I go to the 11th grade, I will make sure I'm one of the flyest in the school. Maybe that will make the girl from my geometry class notice me. But for now, these hand-me-downs work like an invisibility suit—nobody notices my presence.

After walking a block or so, I encountered a victim of that poison who woke up on the wrong side of the bed. Then again, some victims never sleep, so it's hard to tell which is the case. It was Carol, a middle-aged woman who went to school with my mom. I always hear stories about how she "had it going on back in the day." She was a cheerleader captain and prom queen, among other things. Unfortunately, I never saw that side of her.

"You straight?" she asks me in a raspy voice.

Where I'm from, someone asking you if you're "straight" is another way of them asking if you have any poison for sale.

"No," I responded angrily. "Just walking to school a little late."

These streets have no mercy. I can't even walk to school without getting asked if I'm "straight." Part of the reason was that I look a lot like my brother, Jamal, who just started selling that poison before he got locked up. But, in general, we both looked like what most people thought drug dealers looked like: young black males. The police stopped and searched us so frequently, I'd leave for school a few minutes early sometimes just in case. Things like this always made drug dealing seem inevitable in my future.

"I don't know why you tell me the same thing every morning, boo," said Carol. "You need to get hip and get a couple bags to sell. You'd make $100 on your way to school."

She then let out a wheezing cough that buckled her body to within inches of the ground. Picking herself up, she nodded her head before continuing on to Liberty Street. From the looks of it, she was on empty too. I had left the house to escape this wretched condition, but it spills all throughout my neighborhood. There's no escaping.

I'd been contemplating ways to get money for school clothes for some time now. I figured all I needed is a good $250 for a school years' worth of gear. I can't ask Nana or Pop for the money because they are struggling while they wait on Pop's retirement check. I thought about asking my grandparents on my father's side, but it would feel odd asking that grandma since I only see her a few times a year during holidays. She would probably give it to me, but I don't want it to seem like I only reach out to her when I want some money. And Grandpa on my father's side is terminally ill. If he wasn't, I know he'd be happy to give it to me. I'd just have to work for it in his auto shop. I was trying to get a job at this burger joint, but that wasn't working out. I didn't have any work experience so they wouldn't hire me. I put in applications at a few other places, and they all said the same thing. "No experience, no job." How am I supposed to get work experience if no place will hire me BECAUSE I had no work experience!?

I arrived at school just in time to miss the endless metal detector line. This year marked the first time in Plainfield High School's history that metal detectors were installed to prevent students from bringing weapons to school. As a consequence, school sometimes started more than an hour late, because more than 1,600 students had to be filtered through the metal detectors and have their book bags searched. The line wrapped around our school building and spilled out into the street. Some days, I stayed home from school just to skip the agony of waiting in line to get into a building that I didn't want to enter in the first place. The funny thing is, I'd never seen a gun in school, and I'd never heard of a shooting happening on PHS's campus. The administration also decided to spend thousands of dollars of our school's money on a security system that put the school on lockdown. This explained why my favorite after-school program, The Game Room, was cut. Instead of the funds providing recreational time for students after school, they were used to ensure a screeching alarm could be triggered whenever someone attempts to exit the building before our 3:00 p.m. dismissal. We occasionally skip our classes, and know they want to keep us in school by any means necessary. Walking into PHS evokes childhood memories of visiting my parents in prison because of the maximum-security measures. It's a bit different from the high schools you see on

"Saved by the Bell" or "Fresh Prince of Bel-Air." Nah, this is Painfield.

My first-period Spanish class flew by thanks to the assistance of a substitute teacher. Afterwards, I headed to gym class, which was my favorite part of the school day because the few friends who haven't dropped out are in it with me. My boy, Chris, greeted me with an upwards head nod as soon as I walked in.

"You ain't getting dressed today?" I asked.

"Nah, I'm good," he responded.

I looked down to discover him rocking a fresh pair of double-soled Timberlands. They were the new limited-edition ones with the pearl white sole.

"Oh, I see," I said. "You don't want to change into your gym clothes because you want to sport your fresh pair of Timbs? Them silky dudes from the East End rubbing off on you?"

He smirked, and unknowingly licked his lips. He's known for doing this so much, we call him L.L. Cool Chris.

"Nah son, I'm just coolin' out today. Don't feel like getting all sweaty before work," he responded.

Chris was one of my closest dogs since 6th grade. He was one of the few people in the 10th grade that actually had a job...well, a legal job, at least. We depended on him to introduce us to the latest fashions. He stayed fresh.

"Yea, aiiight bruh," a distant voice said. "I'm trying to be like you when I grow up, daddy!"

It was my other dog, Sheek, joining us. He bobbed and weaved from behind and jabbed Chris with two gentle body shots at lightning speed. Sheek hit him twice before Chris's hand could rise to block the third one.

"Tssh Tsh," Sheek whispered, mimicking the sound of boxing gloves punching a heavy bag.

"If ya'll ain't getting dressed for gym, then neither am I. Coach Butler can lick my ba-"

"Aaayooooo!" came a scream from across the gymnasium.

Our fourth comrade, Nyce, was approaching. His tall, lanky arms spread out like a soaring hawk to signal he was there. He never did that to get our attention, especially since we were looking dead at him already. No, he just wanted every girl in the gym to look at him. Indeed, he was…" nice." While he was approaching in the distance, you could see something shiny dangling on his shirt.

"You see the new ice, son!" he said with excitement while grabbing his newly acquired bling.

"Why y'all not getting dressed today?" Nyce inquired.

"We tryin' to be cool like Chris," I responded.

He looked down at Chris's white soles that stood out.

"Oh, I see what you working with, daddy! Fresh Timbos on your feet make ya cipher complete," said Nyce. "Ya'll can stay out here and politic all you want. I'm getting dressed today so I can yam on dudes on the court. They talkin' 'bout moving me up to varsity next week!"

"Maaaaan, stop lying," Sheek interrupted.

"Swear to God on your Uncle Tug-Rug!" Nyce said, raising one hand in the air to swear while still holding on to his jewelry. "Coach told me they want me on varsity now."

While Nyce's hand was near his face, he couldn't resist the temptation of putting his thumb in his mouth. He was a 6'2, 16-year-old who still sucked his thumb.

"Since y'all wanna be cool, hold my ice for me. I'm bout to YAM on dudes!" he screamed.

He took his chain off, and all of our hands went out and reached for it. Sheek's lightning hands snatched it before the rest of our palms even fully opened. Nyce let out a muffled laugh before running to the locker room.

"See, that's why they call him Nyce," Chris said.

"I heard he robbing dudes now with them East End cats. I bet you that's how he got this," Sheek said while putting Nyce's ice around his neck.

I sat in silence. Jealousy for Nyce's bling briefly consumed my thoughts.

Instead of participating in gym, we chilled on the bleachers and people-watched like senior citizens sitting on a front porch.

"I heard Pookie and Jamal got bagged last night," said Sheek.

"Yup. They both already on probation too," I responded.

"Dayyum!" Sheek and Chris said in unison.

"The block will be hungry now without them," Sheek said, thinking out loud. "You know I got that work for cheap now too. Spend $25, and you can flip it for $50 on the street. Spend $50, you make $100."

He was talking about that poison. First Crackhead Carol, now one of my closest friends. Although I remained quiet, my blood was starting to boil. The reason I left home in the first place was to avoid that poison. Despite its overwhelming presence in my environment, I had been valiantly trying to avoid selling it. Naturally, it was the first thing I thought of when wondering how I was going to get that $250 for school clothes. I always felt like a nun in a sex shop.

"That poison has been taking clothes off my back and food out my mouth for years," I refuted. "I ain't f*ckin' round with it."

"Yeah, I was like that for a while, too," Sheek said. "Whether you sell it to them or not, fiends are going to get it any way they can. People like us deserve the money more than these other dudes. We young, but we gotta do for ourselves."

Sheek was in a similar situation to me. His parents' struggle with addiction led to a cycle of incarceration and neglect, too. Luckily, he had an older sister who recently took him in. But she had her own children and couldn't provide everything Sheek needed, and definitely not enough to keep up with Chris and Nyce. Still, Sheek was a roughneck who never gave a good-god-damn about what other people thought. It's one of the things that made us connect. He was much more liberated than me though. Sheek would wear the same clothes for three days with no attempt to hide it. Instead, he would proudly boast about how he could still have any girl he wanted despite it.

"How long would it take you to get the hunnit?" Chris asked curiously.

"Shhiiieed, if you grind it out, you can do it in less than an hour," Sheek responded.

"What?!" Chris and I screamed at the same time.

"It takes me at least a week before I make that much at that burger joint. And that's before taxes," said Chris. "I'm aiight with what I got though. Anything else would be greed. It ain't like I'm starving or anything."

I, on the other hand, was far too familiar with hunger pains. Chris had his job, Sheek had his hustle, and Nyce was doing whatever he was doing. I didn't have jack. Just the stark responsibility of clothing and feeding myself at the age of 15. An internal battle was being waged in my head. The pain and suffering I saw as a consequence of that poison battled against the laws of self-preservation. Sheek's last words echoed in my head and were the straw that broke the camel's back. I no longer gave a shhiiieed.

I dug in my sock and pulled out a sweaty twenty-dollar bill that was sticking to a moist five.

"Ewww, son! Nobody wants your funky feet money!" Chris said. He always hated anything involving feet.

"Money is money," Sheek responded, before taking it with one hand and grabbing my book bag with his other. "I'll be right back," he said, before dashing to the locker room.

Moments later, Sheek returned dressed for gym with my book bag on his back. His red, oversized basketball shorts were wrinkled like they were tied in a knot all semester. His white V-neck shirt was so tan, you could tell he didn't wash it with bleach or in cold water. But on his feet were a fresh pair of the newest Air Jordan's: high-top red and black number 11's, that looked too immaculate to walk on our gym floor. At $180 a pop, you would think they could enable flight.

"Coach was in the locker room, so I put on some of Nyce's gym clothes," said Sheek. "I put that work in your book bag though."

Instead of handing me my book bag he dropped it in the corner with the other bags.

"This dude think he Tony Montana," Chris remarked.

But Sheek was doing something we learned vicariously for years growing up around Lib-Side. Take the money all you want, but be as creative as you can when giving someone that work.

"I can't believe he is about to ball in a pair of fresh 11's!" Sheek said, as he darted off to join the basketball game.

While saying it, one of Chris's eyebrows raised as he pouted like a small child refusing to go to bed. Chris's feelings for footwear were similar to an environmentalist's feelings for trees. To him, seeing Sheek ball in a fresh pair of kicks was like someone chopping down a tree for no reason.

After retrieving my book bag, I discover a palm-sized bag with ten smaller bags in it. For the first time in my life, I had poison of my own. I vowed to myself that I would quit after making $250 for school clothes. Maybe a few dollars extra for breakfast for the rest of the school year. But I knew this was a game that was seldom ever quit. It wasn't a performance where you could bow and exit stage left after the last act. From what I'd seen, most of the players became trapped in the game. But for me, it was just a means to reach a goal. Once that goal was accomplished, I would no longer need the means, or so I thought. I'm too sensitive to the pain it causes and won't be able to endure perpetuating the cycle for too long.

With the newly acquired poison in my possession, I felt even more uncomfortable in the school. I would have gone home, but my last battle with our Terminator 2 security doors ended in me getting suspended. It would probably be easier if I laid low for the rest of the day than risk another run-in with the alarm system. After school was dismissed, I anxiously walked home. I felt that tingling sensation in my knees that you get moments before something exciting, or terrifying, is about to happen. I'd be lying if I said I wasn't nervous. I had been stopped and searched by the police countless times since the age of twelve. I was never guilty of anything. It's just the way the cops and "jumpers" operated in my neighborhood. I thought it happened in all neighborhoods, until Chris was subjected to the ritual when he visited me in my neighborhood. Chris's eyebrows were raised in shock the entire time. They slammed us on the unmarked police cars, ran their hands through our butt cheeks, made us take off our shoes, among other things. Chris nearly had a heart attack when the narcotic cops swiftly jumped out of their car to surround us. That's why they call them the "jumpers." Sometimes, they'd appear out of nowhere, almost like they came out of the ground or down from the sky. You would swear they had those Star Trek teleporter transmitters or something. Sheek and I just stood there like statues and waited for the humiliating ceremony to end.

If anything, dealing with jumpers over the past few years showed me how to be clever when hiding drugs. It also made me feel like a drug dealer already, since I was treated like one. As I placed the work I got from Sheek under my sleeve, I felt a self-fulfilling prophecy coming true. A part of my soul was disappointed knowing the cycle was repeating yet again. A conflicted part of me was excited about the thought of new school clothes.

For a second, I paused and wondered what I was going to do with the poison. It's not like anyone ever showed me how to sell drugs. There aren't instructional videos or books written on "Trappin' 101." Dad never sat me down and said "Hey son! Let me show you how to hustle that work!" Of course I'd heard what the rappers said, and I knew Notorious B.I.G.'s "Ten Crack Commandments" like the back of my hand (i.e., "never get high on your own supply"). Then suddenly, I realized it was something I naturally knew how to do from watching everyone else in my neighborhood do it all my life. It's like a baby watching everyone else walk. It's only a matter a time before the baby starts to mimic the movements. First crawling, then walking, and eventually running. But these streets move too fast to crawl or walk. You gotta to hit the ground running, especially if you wanna escape the jumpers.

Further along on my path home, I encountered Carol again. This time, I have something to ask her.

"You straight?" I ask awkwardly. I was almost confused myself, hearing this come out of my own mouth. My heart was pounding like the basketballs on the gym floor earlier.

"Oh, so you holding now, huh, little Tasha?" said Carol, remarking on my resemblance to my mom. "Let me get twelve nickels. I got a white boy waiting to pay double for them."

"I only have ten on me," I say. "But they are nice and fat so you can break them down into more."

In reality, I barely knew what my nickel bags of crack looked like, let alone their size. Nor did I have an idea of how large they should be. I didn't read Chapter 3 of the non-existent "Crack Dealer's Guide to Pushin' the Poison," which dealt with the portioning of crack into $5 bags. I was just doing what I thought was hustlin.' After Carol nodded her head in agreement to the deal, I shook my arm on the side and the small package I got from Sheek landed on the ground. You would have thought it was a mistake by the way neither of us acknowledged it.

Carol handed me a crisp, folded fifty-dollar bill in a motion that looked like a handshake to the untrained eye. It was one of the new fifties with the big face on it. I had never seen one before. The only other time I had a fifty-dollar bill was last Christmas when Grandma gave it to me in a card. Today, I got one handed to me with a swift motion of the arm. I couldn't believe I doubled what was left of my birthday money by simply walking home from school. It was the easiest money I had ever made in my life. The tingling sensation in my knees intensified.

As soon as I got home, I called Sheek up.

"Yo! Bring me another $50 worth tomorrow! The streets are starving, and I think we've got the recipe!"

Hunger (n) /hun-ger/- When being deprived of something leads to a great desire, craving, or appetite for it.

Hunger causes all living things to resort to extreme measures. It brings about savage ways among even the most innocent.

Chapter 2: Addiction

Addiction (n) /a-dik-shen/- An uncontrollable obsession leading to the endless pursuit of desires. Addiction is often rooted in adverse experiences, psychological state, and/or the chemical composition of the brain. It is often understood as an organic disease, social malfunction, and/or mental illness. Its wrath can afflict destruction upon the most disciplined and well-intentioned.

Within the span of a few weeks, I transformed the $25 I received for my 15th birthday into more than $3,000. First the $25 turned into $50, then $50 to $100, then $100 to $200, from $200 to $400, and so on. As simple as that sounds, that's just how it went. The block was starving, as was I—literally. We were a match made in heaven.

When my older brother, Jamal, came home from juvie, he claimed he saw a different person in me.

"Damn! Before I got locked up, all you did was watch Dragon Ball Z and play video games," he said. "Now you're out here huggin' the block."

The block of Fifth Street, also known as "5A," was starting to know my name. The local stray cat named "Streetz" comes up to me now and purrs at my leg. Stray dogs, that once viewed me as a stranger, have stopped barking when I pass. The sweet smell of one neighbor's freshly cut grass, combined with the stench of cheap wine and cigarette smoke from another neighbor's dwelling, have become second nature to my nostrils. The screeching of screen doors slamming shut is no longer disruptive. I've even learned to live with the interference of another neighbor's sound system with bass so strong, it vibrates the concrete. The jumpers now recognize my face, but I've discovered ways to stay a step ahead of them. I've got more stash spots than there are Pokémon.

Countless hours have been spent on this block turning my original $25 into $3,000. I skip Spanish class every day now so I can put in extra work. Sometimes I skip all of my classes, except gym with my boys or Mr. Johnson's geometry class. Mr. Johnson expects me to be there and do my best, so I have to deliver. With the exception of Spanish, I'm still passing every class. I've managed to achieve a balance reached by few: doing well in school while being embraced by the block. When in class, I give my teachers my undivided attention and complete all assignments.

Some would say I "hug the block," or compassionately spend excessive hours with it. They're right. I hug it as if it were a beloved mother, and I, its precious first-born child. We block-huggers often refer to "the block" as an animate object with a life of its own. So instead of saying "I put in work on the block," we'd often say, "I put in work with the block." As far as we're concerned, our block has its own soul — its own heartbeat and rhythm.

In my short time hugging 5A, I've watched the block embrace and destroy its own. There's no way to tell which side you'll fall on at any given time. For now, I'm just thankful to be on its good side. So many lives have perished here, leaving behind nothing but a limited legacy. If this block could talk, Lord knows the stories it would share. Who would it consider to be in its Hustla's Hall-of-Fame? Who has achieved the ultimate Street Glory that so many have died for? Perhaps the block would reminisce on characters like J-Live and his wild trips off angel dust. One time he jumped out of a second-story window, convinced he could fly. He still walks with a limp because of it.

I wonder what the block thinks of me, the 15-year-old who sits in his yard for hours reading books between crack sales. Is it as confused by me reading books as everyone else seems to be? It's funny. People act as if drug dealers are all illiterate. One time, the cops jumped out to search me, yelling "Hands up!" I complied with their orders and held a Maya Angelou book to the sky.

Sometimes crackheads came up to me in search of that poison, and I'd make them wait until I was finished reading a particular sentence.

"Come on, let me get two crillz!" they'd demand.

I'd raise one finger in the air while keeping my eyes locked on the book.

"Maaaaan forget you! Muthafu... acting like you the only person on the block selling!" they'd scream.

But because the block was in a dry season, I usually was the only person out there—unless they wanted to walk a block away to Lib-Side and multiply their chances of encountering the jumpers. I knew even if they walked away, they'd always come back. They had to get that poison. Each time they returned, I obnoxiously greeted them with a quote from something I was reading.

"What this grim, ungainly, ghastly, gaunt, and ominous bird of yore? Quote the Raven...nevermore...muthafu..! Twenty dollas please," I'd say.

The confused fiends would roll their eyes before taking the poison. But Edgar Allan Poe departed when I found my true block companion. Once my new partner kept me company, there was no need to do leisure reading while hustlin'. Our conversations were just as intellectual. After seeing me double my money a few times, Sheek wanted to get down with the operation. And he had an exclusive connection that I couldn't refuse. Since he was the one selling the wholesale crack to me, he got it for cheap. Even though I had to split my profit now, with the connection he brought to the table, everything balanced out. And he didn't mind grinding around Liberty Street in the projects where the money flowed like a waterfall. I figured two heads were better than one. We could watch each other's back and bleed the block together. So we formed like Voltron and excelled as one.

Sheek and I were always close, but grinding together brought us closer. He was my dog, my dude, and now my business partner. At times, I thought we were the only two people in the world who thought the way we did. We'd finish each other's sentences, knowing exactly what the other was going to say. It was as if our similar life experiences had given us similar visions, similar thoughts, and similar voices. We were two boys faced with the burden of becoming men at an early age. We were trying to make sense of the world while transitioning into the mentality required in the manhood years. In the process, a camaraderie developed similar to that of soldiers in war. And if you think about it, that's exactly what we were. Two soldiers in a war—a war in which we never knew who the real enemy was. All we knew was that we were comrades on the same side of the battle, and we had to stay at least two moves ahead of the enemy—the jumpers—at all times. We made moves with each other's welfare in consideration. Brothers in arms, indeed.

Night after night, we broke day with the block. Sometimes we stayed out there so long, we'd watch both the sunset and sunrise. Nothing compares to the lavender sunrises seen from my porch around 6 AM. It's the image I bring up in my head to calm me down when I'm angry. Sheek and I would sit there watching the sky and talking about the latest developments with chicks, sports, politics, music, or anything else. Sometimes we'd sit in absolute silence until someone seeking poison interrupted our peace. Aside from Sheek's heavy breathing and the occasional passing car, all I'd hear some nights were crickets calling through the darkness and birds chirping at the break of dawn. Because Sheek and I were both introverts, we could sit in silence and listen for hours.

The block was so tranquil between the hours of 3:00-6:00 a.m., it was shocking. It felt like Godzilla breathed fire and cause chaos on the streets all day, only to fall solemnly asleep in the middle of the night. We called it the "night shift," and it was the most serene, probably because most block-huggers refused to do it. If they did break day with the block, it was either on the 1st or the 15th of the month. Every hustler considered those two days to be sacred holidays. Fiends would flow endlessly during all hours then. It was a trapper's dream. From the 1st to the 3rd, you could catch some block-huggers, like J-Live, up for 72-hours straight. I was confident he didn't go in the house to bathe or change clothes. He didn't want to miss a single transaction, and I didn't blame him. The 1st and the 15th were like a Hustler's Hanukkah, a Block-Hugger's Bar Mitzvah. They are the most common paydays. Mazel tov, indeed.

Holidays aside, Sheek and I put in more work than any of the other youngins on the block. If we were in the mood after a long shift, we'd go to the local diner for breakfast in the morning before school. Like me, Sheek didn't feel a strong connection with school, so we cherry-picked the classes we attended. Together, we figured out a way to penetrate PHS's high-tech security system and its locked doors. We could figure anything out with our minds combined. We often talked about how we should use our dual mind power to find a way to game the system. Our mutual hatred for the system brought us closer together. We didn't quite know what the system was, but we felt its weight on us eternally. We felt like bastard children deprived of the innocence of a nurtured childhood.

Since we were a team now, we could expand our business enterprise. Together we decided to start hustlin heroin, or "dope," along with the crack we were selling. Indeed, crack is ugly, but dope is beyond hideous. If both drugs were poison, crack was pesticide, while dope was venom. Crack was child's play, dope was a grown man's game. Crack was a misdemeanor, but dope, a first-degree felony. Unlike crack, dope had that physical addiction. Fiends HAVE to have it after a while. Although it might not be preferred, a crackhead could go a day or two without crack. Dopefiends, on the other hand, may find it physically unbearable to spare a couple of days without dope. Their body requires the chemicals to function normally. If a fiend doesn't shoot-up or sniff dope in the morning, it could be hard for him to go to work or do anything productive. This is why those morning hours were the best time to sell dope. The lavender sunrises were often accompanied by platoons of dope-sick fiends, too far gone to notice the beauty in the sky.

Few sights mirror the sadness of dope-sick fiends. They reminded me of Michael Jackson's "Thriller" or "The Night of the Living Dead." Eyes cluttered with crust, faces drained of energy, as emotive as a stone, hair looking like the last comb on earth was made of kryptonite and they were Superman. Their scratchy voices uttering the two words that might bring them salvation from their suffering: "You straight?"

I'd usually just nod my head while gazing at my lavender sunrise. I couldn't even bring myself to make eye contact with them most times. They possessed the mythical stare of Medusa that would instantly turn me to stone. I hated seeing people in that condition. It reminded me of my mom on her worst days.

Regardless of her habits and imperfections, I always thought I had one of the greatest moms in the universe. It reminded me of one of Tupac's most famous lines;

"And even as a crack fieeeend, Mama, you always was a black queeeeeen Mama."

I was always grateful for my mom because I knew it could have been much worse. Many of my friends and family members' mothers were still living with their grandparents. At least my mom had her own place—most of the time. Of course, she wasn't that perfect TV mom who cooked breakfast in the morning and dropped me off at school. She wasn't one of those parents who gave their kids 9:00 p.m. curfews on weekdays and 10:30 p.m. curfews on weekends. The mom who forbade her kids from getting tattoos or put her children on punishment if they used drugs or alcohol. These were things I imagined most mothers would do—but not mine. To the contrary, I couldn't remember the last time my mom cooked me breakfast. She'd never had her driver's license, let alone a car to drive me to school in. When I wanted to stay home from school, she didn't question my decision or encourage me to reconsider it. She never asked to see my report card. At age 15, I could go anywhere, anytime, and not have to tell anyone. I remember laughing at this parental guilt-trip commercial that came on every night before the evening news for years;

"It's 10 p.m. Do you know where your children are?" it asked.
I'd laugh out loud and think, "It's 10 p.m., and I have no clue where my mother is."

A few days ago, I got my second tattoo without even thinking to ask for anyone's permission beforehand. It was one of those "jail tattoos" from a fiend for $20 worth of that poison. My mom didn't find out until I asked her for Vaseline to moisturize the tattoo. She gazed at it briefly, without uttering a word. No, I wasn't put on punishment for my decision to permanently decorate my skin at the age of 15. As a matter of fact, I haven't been on punishment since 4th grade, when I got into a fight at school. I no longer bother hiding the fact that I drink and smoke. Hell, she has been giving me cigarettes and liquor since I was 12-years-old. Above all, I wouldn't be able to sell drugs in front of her house without her support. She even brings customers to buy my poison. Some would consider her part of the Amir-Sheek team. That $25 birthday money would not have turned into over $3,000 without her assistance. When she found out I was trappin' from Crackhead Carol, she immediately started sending me customers.

Some would categorize my mother, Tasha Whitaker, as a neglectful parent—but it's more complicated than that. Despite her imperfections and hands-off approach, she raised me to be somewhat responsible. She instilled values like honesty, respect, and kindness that sticks most of the time. This is the reason I believe she trusts me enough to make my own decisions, or at least that's what I told myself in moments when I felt like she didn't care. Ultimately, she equipped me with a lens to understand and survive our street environment.

I was always considered a "Mama's Boy." One of the easiest ways to get me angry was to say one of those "Yo' Mama" jokes. I've put my hands and feet on a few people because of those jokes in my earlier years. But you eventually become numb to the joking. You had to have an extreme sense of humor to survive our reality. Being poor or black requires a lighter outlook on life as a coping mechanism. Surviving 400 years of American oppression, enslavement, and discrimination is no easy feat.

But despite our need for humor, there'll never be any shortage of angry black folk. My Uncle Jacob, for example, always seemed to get angry for no reason at all. Sometimes it was as if he was mad at me for being happy. There are loads of other people like him too.

"What the f*ck you smiling for?" they'd ask.

"My bad. I was feeling so good I forgot to frown," I'd respond. "You should try this feeling-good thing out for yourself," I'd encourage, sarcastically.

I got my sense of humor from my dad. Pop Duke had a reputation for never giving a serious answer. No matter what you said, he'd reply with some witty response followed by his "Unawsayin?!" chuckle. It sounded like he was trying to say "you know what I'm saying," but started laughing hysterically in the middle of it. Inheriting Dad's sense of humor and Mom's sarcasm made me the perfect "smart ass." You could see traits of both parents in me—the good, the bad, and the ugly.

Like Mom, Dad did his fair share of things that made him a neglectful parent. Reading between the lines of what my parents put me through, much of it dealt with: A) them attempting to prepare me for what was to come, or B) them trusting me…a bit too much at times. One experience when I was 12-years-old encompassed both of these reasons. My dad's preferred hustle at the time was selling weed. To his dismay, he discovered that I was smoking weed from one of my cousins. He entered my room, sat next to me on my bed, and tossed a nickel bag of some of the stickiest icky I'd ever seen just inches away from me.

"Roll it up," he said casually.

After the most awkward silence, I looked at him feigning to appear perplexed and naive. The ganja was close enough to smell. It was the distinctive Chocolate Thai.

"What's this?" I innocently responded.

"See now, you done gave yourself up!" he said. "This boy's going to act like he never saw a bag of weed before! Unawumsayn?!"

Pop Duke always referred to you in the third-person after he caught you in a lie. He always looked you in the eye when he did it, and this added more pressure. Check and mate. I didn't know what to say. He aimed a pack of rolling papers and flicked them, hitting me square in my forehead.

"I only know how to roll blunts," I said.

Pop Duke picked the papers off the ground and took one out.

"Watch and learn," he said. "I'm only going to show you once."

We lit the joint together, and for the next hour, had the most honest and insightful father-son conversation. Inevitably, we talked about Mom and him being addicted to that poison.

"I bed'not ever hear about you touching crack," he said, while exhaling the ganja smoke. "We came up in the 80s when it was the new thing to do. We had no idea it would hit us this hard."

Pop Duke was reinforcing something I had embraced at a very young age. Never touch that beige-white stuff your parents were tripping on.

"Being young and dumb was our excuse," he said, while looking me dead in the eye. "You ain't got no excuse though. You've seen this struggle your whole life. Ain't no excuse, Moose."

My parents called me "Moose" since I was a baby. They said it was because I looked like the "cutest lil' Moose," as if I should take it as a compliment. Dad never let go of the name. Occasionally he'd take the embarrassing name a step further and call me "Moosifer"...a moose-Lucifer. This name was used when I was doing something devious, mostly.

He passed me the barely-blazed joint without blinking or shifting his eyes from mine. Him being this serious was rare.

"I swear to God, Amir. If I ever hear about you smoking crack," he threatened, "you won't have to worry about struggling with the addiction for years like me. I'll beat you to death myself to save you from the misery. Word is bond."

I've read stories about slaves killing their children because they didn't want their kids to experience the horrors of slavery. After carrying another life in their womb for nine months, some mothers slit the throats of their newborns or drowned them in rivers. I always wondered how a mother could murder her own child. I guess they felt a quick inglorious death upon taking your first breaths was better than a long miserable life as a slave. My dad felt the same way. He was a slave to that poison and he would kill me before I experienced the misery of addiction myself.

Indeed, the War on Drugs and slavery have a lot in common. Based off what I've seen, learned and experienced, both deprive you of freedom. Both destroy the black family structure. Slave masters often sold children of the slaves they owned and separated families forever. Similarly, drugs and the resulting imprisonment/incarceration are the reasons why my father and countless other blacks are in prison right now and separated from their families. Slavery and drugs both leave you at the mercy of something white. In slavery, it was a white slave-master. On the streets, many of the most lethal drugs are white substances. In New Jersey, over 85% of the judges holding the fates of addicts in their hand are white. A prejudiced power structure and government perpetuated both systems. In America's most important document—the Constitution—the government declared my ancestors were only considered 3/5ths human. Today, books like Dark Alliance by Gary Webb reveal the government's role in increasing the flow of drugs into communities like mine. One of today's most destructive policies deals with the way we treat addicts and drug dealers. We e toss them in cages instead of providing proper rehabilitation or opportunities for improvement. I've watched my parents emerge from confinement with even more problems and a desire to chase the poison even harder.

When people say, "God Bless America," I wonder whose God they are talking about. Prejudiced laws are still in place today. Laws give people caught with one gram of crack the same prison sentence as someone caught with 500 grams of cocaine. Why? Well, crack impacts minorities more, and whites prefer powdered cocaine. I sell both crack and cocaine, and they are the same poison with identical side effects. Actually, more people overdose from cocaine than crack because it's sniffed or shot-up directly into the blood stream. You have to smoke crack. But, as long as black people do crack and white people do powder cocaine, much more prison time will continuously be given out for crack.

My dad's death threats from that conversation still echo in my head. Ironically, he never laid a hand on me and was not the violent type. Honesty is one of his most important values, and he prides himself on constantly "keeping it real." I could always ask him anything about sex, drugs, life or any other topic and he'd be honest in his answers. Dad has been locked up for just about a year now. Not sure what he was doing before he turned himself in, but he had a good run. We were always told "mind ya business," when we asked a question about what the adults were doing. So my siblings and I played dumb when Dad took us on shopping sprees in a brand-new sports car. We knew it wouldn't last long, but we were happy in the moment.

The physical resemblance between my dad and I is uncanny. It's even stronger between him and my brother. Same egg-shaped heads, same forehead that wrinkles up like the face of a pug when we're angry. I even have his laugh. I have my mom's nose, smile, and cheekbones. Older hustlers and fiends even call me "Lil J.T." or "Lil Tasha."

***

Speaking of parents, since neither of mine is providing for me right now, finna' hit the block again. I know it's starving on this Monday morning. Luckily, I have quite the appetite myself. Sheek should get here any moment. We'll grab breakfast when he comes. But for now, I must satisfy that other hunger.

As I touch down on the block, I'm greeted by one of its most familiar faces. From a distance, I see the slender figure of Crackhead Carol. She was one of the few fiends who maintained a nice body despite that poison. When she's not dope-sick and off "empty," she actually looks decent.

"I'd smash on a late-night creep," Sheek would often say.

Carol was one of our most consistent customers. But lately, she'd been making it a habit of being short a few dollars. She even begged for a crill on credit a couple of times. But Sheek and I had a strict no-credit policy. This ain't a furniture store or Wal-Mart layaway. Pure poison, straight cash. No exceptions.

Carol approached with a smirk, implying she wanted a favor again. I wasn't in the mood. No credit and nothing more than $2 short, I thought to myself.

"Hey Lil Tasha, can you do me a fav'?" she asked.

"Nope," I swiftly responded.

"Just let me get one today for $7," she pleaded.

I didn't respond. I just sat and looked at her. I could feel the angry wrinkles inherited from Pop Duke beginning to form on my forehead.

"If I had $8 would you let me get it?" she asked.

"Maybe this time," I said in my arrogant tone.

"Well, then I'm only a dollar short of that," she said. "Just let me slide!"

"Actually, you're a dollar short...from being two dollars short," I responded. "It's too early in the morning to be going through this. Matta-fact, we've let you slide too many times. Gave you a few breaks, and now you never come with more than $8. From now on, I ain't taking nothing less than $9 from you. Everybody on these streets knows this poison is $10."

I pause and delivered a silent stare to let her know that I may be young, but I'm ain't dumb.

"You wouldn't go to McDonald's and expect a double cheeseburger for 75 cents. The menu says they are a dollar. We are trying to run a business here too."

I was hungry and beginning to get grumpy. Selling poison has definitely made me a colder person. Attitude adjustments are inevitable if you want to survive here. I just wanted one sale, so breakfast could pay for itself. Now I was arguing with a crack-fiend over two dollars. I couldn't let them take advantage of me, though. My tender age and kind spirit caused them to take me lightly. She wouldn't dare go to an older hustler with a measly seven dollars. They'd laugh at her. To be honest, I wasn't concerned about the two dollars. It was just a matter of principle.

"Come on," Crackhead Carol said, "you know I'm the one who got you on this block in the first place."

She was relentless, and I was becoming angrier by the moment.

"You fiends always think somebody owes you a goddamn favor," I said. "You gotta work for yours just like I gotta work for mine. If you wanna earn your two dollars, then come by after I get breakfast. Matter of fact, you can earn $20!"

"Oh helllll no!" she exploded. "Don't you ever think you can talk to me like that, little boy! Crackbabies like you come and go on this block. Ya'll treat us like we the only fiends out here. Ya'll need to look at your damn selves. Need to learn some damn respect!" she screamed.

I stared back at her confused, wondering what she was talking about. First of all, I wasn't a crackbaby. Secondly, I barely smoked weed so how could I be the fiend?

"All that money you got, and you wanna argue over two dollars?" she continued. "You're the one who's really addicted. A greedy money-fiend with an appetite that will never be satisfied!"

Her words not only infuriated me, but left me utterly speechless. I wasn't perfect, but I never viewed myself as being addicted to anything. Death threats from Pop Duke and the disgust I had for people like Crackhead Carol made me think I was above addiction. But why didn't I stop hustling after reaching my original goal of making $250 for school clothes? I stopped thinking about that goal months ago, after attaining it in a week. Now I had ten times as much, with no plan of stopping anytime soon. Was I addicted? Before my thoughts could settle in, my growling stomach interrupted me. That second hunger is going to have to take the back seat for now.

I ended the argument with Crackhead Carol and headed to the store. On my way, I ran into Kurt, an O.G. hustler who had been on the block for years. Unlike the other established hustlers, Kurt would occasionally give us words of wisdom. He never looked down on us either.

"Lil J.T., let me holla at you for a minute," he said. "Heard you out there making a scene with Carol. You can't be like that. It makes the block hot when people call 5-0 to complain about the noise."

"My bad," I said. "I just had to set something straight for a second."

"Well, next time be wiser about it," he said. "You have to treat the block with respect, and it will respect you back. Don't be one of those dummies thinking they deserve special treatment."

He paused to give someone walking past a head nod. Kurt had a unique head nod that went off to the side. He always said it was him giving people permission to pass.

"Nobody's invincible," he continued. "Nobody escapes unscathed, but play it wise and you will last longer. Just don't think you can come to the block, eat, and leave without the block taking something from you in return. Nothing is forever, youngin'. You should be in school any ways. Looking just like your egg-headed father!"

***

Kurt was the first person to tell me to go to school in a long while. But in some ways, I was already in school and Kurt, even Crackhead Carol, were teachers. They were teaching me priceless principles that increased my chances of street survival. Nothing in real school seemed useful or applicable to my life anyway. I didn't need to know square roots to know how to get this paper.

Sheek appeared in the distance approaching on a bright pink and purple mountain bike—must belong to his girl cousins or something. His raw disregard for appearance, colors, and opinions made him oblivious to the fact that he looks like a gutter princess coasting down the block on his unicorn. I backtracked to my house to meet him.

"What's good?" he said.

"Nothing much, princess. Just out here arguing with Crackhead Carol. Your boy is starving though so let's go eat," I informed him.

"Word is bond," Sheek said. "And let me tell you 'bout your boy Nyce. He's willllding now son! Now he pulling armed robberies with them East End dudes. Before they were just beating people up, but now it's gun play."

Damn. Gunplay. A few dudes our age had been doing it for years.

"They are going to burn him if he gets caught. Armed robbery is felony level," I said.

"Crazy how everybody around here getting it in some way or another," said Sheek. "Some just want more than what they got, others have no choice. Even Puerto Rican Sammy next-door is hustlin'! His father is the one always calling the cops on us. Now, his very own son sellin' that poison."

Sammy was a few years older than us and usually had a job. He was laid off a few days ago and turned to the block as an alternative. It's too hard finding a job, and too easy to hustle. You can do it in our hood by simply walking to the corner store or walking to school.

"Yo, I heard Reggie and Lil Juju smoking crack now too," he said.

"What?! Juju Vasquez who went to elementary with us?" I asked.

We knew Juju since our second-grade class. Reggie was already in his twenties, but just the thought of somebody who was 15 years old like us messing with that poison sent chills through my spine. Was our generation stupid enough to fall victim to the same mistakes as our parents?

As I nodded my head in shame, Streetz, the stray cat mascot of the block, sprinted full-speed across my yard. What was he running from? Both Sheek's and my head followed his four legs. Upon turning our heads back to the front of the yard, we discovered what had caused Streetz to run. It was an army of over a dozen of Plainfield's finest jumpers—the Narcotics Task Force ("Narcs" for short). They rushed towards us, rumbling the ground like a stampede of elephants. We both stood there paralyzed and afraid. Our moments of paralysis ended after being slammed onto the cold concrete.

"Don't move!" one Narc screamed, pointing his gun inches away from my head.

"Ouch! Nobody was moving in the first place!" Sheek screamed. "You ain't have to slam us on the ground!"

Sheek never let cops treat him any old way they wanted to. He'd constantly argue with them.

"Keep talking, and I'll break ya face," one Narc said, as he delivered a kick to Sheek's rib cage.

The blow sounded like a sack of potatoes falling from a window, and Sheek groaned in pain. I naturally jumped after hearing my comrade's call. My effort was met with a nightstick's blow to the back that sent me back to the ground.

"Sit yo' a*s down," said the vigilant Narc. I got comfortable, face-flat on the concrete.

"We have a warrant to search the house. Tell us where the drugs are, and we won't tear the place up," he continued.

"Maaaaan…Suck my di*%!" Sheek said.

The Narc gave an evil Mr. Grinch smirk before delivering a round of kicks to Sheek's ribs that knocked the wind out of him. The jumpers always itched for reasons to beat dudes down. They were the playground bullies of Painfield who got away with whatever they wanted. They swore by god that they were Wild West cowboys rounding up the bad guys around here. Their eternal presence and agitation made them feel more like a military occupation force. In their minds, they were fighting a war anyways: the War on Drugs.

While one jumper was kicking Sheek, another group of them rammed through the door of my house. As they obliterated the door hinges, I heard my mom let out a scream from the kitchen.

"Noooo!" she yelled. "Get off me!"

After a few seconds of commotion, everything was silent.

Mom was apprehended too. They cuffed us all and sat us together in the ransacked living room. Mom's boyfriend, Bootsy, was there too. I greeted him with a look of disgust. He was probably the reason behind this drug raid in the first place. He hustled too, but with a lot less respect and compassion for the block. He made it hot by bringing too many white people round. Older hustlers constantly warned him. White people are taboo in our hood. The jumpers know you could go blocks without finding a white household. When they see adult-age white people in our hood, they assume they are looking for drugs. Ironically, it was a cop who told me this after randomly searching me when I was 13-years-old. He said that because he had just seen a white person around, he knew for sure someone must have sold him drugs. He said white people have no other reason to be here, even though he was white himself. It's sort of like seeing a zebra casually walking through the habitat of lions.

The team of Narcs began to tear apart our house. As my mother watched, her tears flowed.

"Watch that vase!" she screamed.

"Tell us where it is, and we won't have to break stuff looking for it," a Narc bargained.

No one responded.

"Bingo!" one Narc said, in the distance.

I knew he had found the drugs in my room. I stashed them in the case of my Dragon Ball Z videotapes. I wasn't about to fess up to it, though. Maybe they'd think they were my mom's boyfriend's. They had no proof that it was my room.

The short, stocky jumper entered the living room holding a videotape case and a piece of paper. He looked at the paper and asked,

"So... who is Mr. Amir Whitaker?"

"Him!" my mom's boyfriend proudly snitched.

Sheek lunged at him in handcuffs and delivered a swift head-butt to the mouth before the Narcs restrained him. My mom's boyfriend's lip busted open and started bleeding. Although the narcs would have found out eventually, snitches got stitches. Code of the streets.

"Well since your report card was hanging on the wall of the room with the drugs," the Narc said, "I think it's safe to say these are yours."

He tossed a few sandwich bags of poison inches away from me. Dammit. I forgot I hung my latest report card on the wall. I was proud that I had all A's and B's—except for the F in Spanish, of course. I was trying to get my mom to notice it and maybe be proud of my better grades. I would have put it on the refrigerator, but since there was never any food in there, she may have never noticed it. I knew my mom was always in my room searching for my stash of drugs. She never saw the report card or bothered to say anything about it if she did.

"Decent report card, Mr. Whitaker," the Narc said. "Doesn't really matter now though. Doubt you'll graduate after the smoke clears from this one. Everyone in this house is getting locked up!"

Knowing their mission was complete, the Narcs' mood became celebratory.

"Great job, folks," one Narc said. "Think I saw some malt liquor in the fridge. Time to toast and celebrate."

I told the cops that everything was mine in hopes that they would let my mother and Sheek go. They said Sheek could eventually go free, but my mom had to be charged because it was her house. The police van was packed with Sheek, myself, my mom, her boyfriend, and a few straggler fiends who were in the house. On the ride to the station, everyone had something to say but me. I just sat there in silence and pondered. What would become of me? Of the situation? Guess the block wasn't so loyal to me after all. Kurt's words echoed in my head. I'm going to miss those lavender sunrises, I thought, as I visualized them to keep myself calm. If not for my imagination, I would have lost my mind.

Chapter 3: Trap

Trap (n) /trap/- A system or device created to restrict, contain, or otherwise cease movement.

Traps are rarely visible or apparent. They frequently include bait or lures to entice entry and engagement. By design, few who enter a trap will be able to escape.

After the paddy wagon unloaded us at the police station, everyone was separated. Sheek was released shortly after. After getting "booked," I was transported to the Union County Juvenile Detention Center in the city of Elizabeth. I was finally going to be in the infamous, inevitable "juvie." I had heard many stories about juvie: the fights you might get into to prove yourself hard, the terrible food that causes more fights, the elementary-level education they provide you with. I was previously the only one out of the five Whitaker Boys who had not been there. Now, the Whitaker Boys were five for five. It's as if we were all destined to the same fate as our parents.

Ironically, because I was in juvie, I was in the closest proximity to both parents that I'd been in years. Both the Union County Men's Correctional Facility and Union County Women's Correctional Facility were directly across the street from me. Between our three buildings, me, my mom, and my dad made a triangle. A triangle that had been broken for years, thanks to that poison. Now it was the cause of our twisted reunification.

I had always heard that mothers could distinguish between many cries and know exactly which one belonged to their child. I wondered if I cried loud enough, would my mom know it was me across the street? Would my father know Moosifer was here? What are the odds of a son, mother, and father all being incarcerated on the same block, at the same time? Rare, I hope.

***

I wasn't feeling too proud. At juvie I was stripped, searched, fingerprinted, and given a number. They said that's all you are here—a number. Luckily, this number wouldn't be alone. My cousin, Pookie, was still in here. His brother Ray Ray just left here a few months ago. My brother also just came home a few weeks ago. There were always at least two out of the five Whitaker Boys in here at any given moment. We were somewhat notorious.

By the time they finished my paperwork, it was lunchtime. I completely forgot how hungry I was. I showered, put on the one-piece gunmetal-gray bodysuit the guard gave me, and was escorted to my room. On the way, the guard stopped at a storage closet and picked up a thin twin-sized mattress. I saw many familiar faces walking through the cafeteria. Some of the people I hadn't seen in so long, I thought they had moved. We were excited at the sight of each other.

"Aiiiight! Plainfield is running deep in this mutha! What's good Mir-Mir?" one voice exclaimed.

I turned to see who said it, before being met with a sharp smack on the back of my head.

POP!

"Keep looking straight," the guard said, after smacking me. You could hear the other youth laugh. Great. First day in juvie and I'm already the laughing stock.

"Mir!" another raspy voice said.

It was a voice that I had heard for 15 years, but I hadn't heard it in weeks.

"Pookie! Wut up!" I said, while continuing to look straight ahead to avoid another pop.

I got enough abuse today to last me a lifetime. Nonetheless, it was comforting to know that I wasn't alone.

"This is you," said the guard, as he showed me my room.

He tossed the mattress on the ground and pointed at it as if I was a dog trained by a master. Everything in the room was the same shade of brownish silver. A small amount of light crept through an opening in the wall a few inches wide. It wasn't big enough to be considered a window.

"We are packed-tight right now, so you gotta sleep on the floor," he said. "Your two roommates will be in here in a few hours after school finishes."

Three of us in this tiny room? And I had to sleep on the ground on something slightly thicker than a few cardboard boxes? They really do think we are animals, I thought.

"You're not allowed to leave your cell for the first 24 hours," the guard said. "Starting tomorrow, you will eat breakfast with the other hooligans and then go in front of the judge. In the meantime, get comfortable 'cuz you ain't going nowhere."

The thunderous slamming of the door signaled that I was all alone. In my solitude, I had ample time to reflect. That's all I did for hours. I couldn't help but think about the poison that put me here. I remembered how I originally started selling drugs to get money for school clothes. I passed my goal of making $250 in two days. Why did I keep going? Each time that I doubled my money, I told myself it would be the last flip. When $200 made $400, I told myself I would stop at $800. When $800 made $1600, I told myself I would stop there. For whatever reason, I didn't. I didn't have enough self-control. Crackhead Carol's words echoed in my head:

"You're the one who's really addicted. You're just a fiend for money, that's all."

Perhaps she was right. I was addicted. I was consumed and destroyed by my greed. To make matters worse, the police found all the money, and now I had nothing left. Not even the $25 birthday money I started with. After spending countless hours on the block, I was left with less than what I started with. Now I was sleeping on the ground in juvie. Rock. Bottom.

To cool my anger, I tried to summon the calming images of the lavender sunrise. It didn't work this time. It only made me angrier. It only reminded of that poison. I grew weary and frustrated with each hour in isolation. I thought about how much selling drugs had become a part of my lifestyle. I used to hate the sight and smell of it. As a youth, seeing family members smoke crack and fiends shoot up was agonizing and traumatizing. Once I began selling drugs, all of that went out the window. I acquired a convenient immunity.

I went back-and-forth in my mind in search of where to place the blame. I started trapping to satisfy basic needs. When the going got good, I couldn't let it go. The fact that I received support from my mother didn't help me either. I wondered what she was thinking right now. I wondered what my dad was thinking too. I wondered what he would think when he discovered that poison got me locked up too. It had all three of us trapped now. Caged. Mother, father, and son alike. My eyes were beginning to tear up.

I was searching for excuses that would allow me to stop being angry with myself. All I could think about was how, at first, selling drugs seemed to be a natural reaction to the hunger and starvation I had experienced—and not just the physical hunger from empty and aunt-guarded refrigerators either. There was also an emotional hunger resulting from my relationship with family. I guess I tried to fill that void with my relationship with the block and the money. I can't forget the materialistic hunger that came in the form of a need for school clothes. In time, each hunger evolved and consumed me as my appetite increased. I couldn't let go of the block. I hugged it with the compassion one usually hugged a mother. I craved being clenched in its captivity during those sunrises. Mother Block embraced me like her newborn child clinging to her bosom. She breastfed me the most wholesome milk in the form of dirty, fast money. Unfortunately, this mother did not pat me on my back and burp me. As a consequence, I vomited every drop of milk-money I consumed. All that remained was the ever-sour aftertaste of self-blame. But I couldn't be too mad. A starving infant would suck on any breast it could get its hands on, even if it was poisonous.

***

There are no clocks in juvie. Time is unmoving, and uncertain. I feel like I've been alone with these four walls for ten hours. It's probably less than half of that. I've stopped counting the times I've gotten up to stretch my back to ease the ache caused by sleeping on the floor. The two empty beds belonging to my unknown cellmates mock me. I can't bring myself to lay in them though. The thought of our introduction happening while I lay cozy on the only thing they can call their own in here is unsettling. Beef with the people I have to sleep next to is the last thing I need.

They put all new entries on "blackout" for the first 24-hours, restricting us to our rooms. There's nothing for me to do now except lay on this floor and stare at the ceiling. In my isolation, I find my mind drifting through memories. One lucid flashback of a similar experience when I was ten years old makes me feel like I'm reliving every moment.

***

When is she gonna get here? It seems like I've been sitting in the principal's office for a million years. I'm getting sent home from school for fighting, but I can't leave until Mom picks me up. They should just let me walk home by myself since I'm in the 4th grade now. My parents let me walk to school alone most of the time anyways.

I was fighting because they was making fun of my clothes and my hair. Well, it wasn't really a fight. I just punched Juju in the face, then kicked him in the stomach. I was gonna do a Macho Man Randy Savage wrestling move on him, but Mrs. D came and grabbed me. He escaped this time. But next time…ohhh yeaaa!!!

I told my Mom that I didn't want my hair done like this. I told her they would make fun of me. I begged her not to give me this stupid Jerry Curl, but she ain't listen.

They started laughing at me as soon as I walked in the class. I tried to keep a hat on for cover, but as soon as I walked into school, the Principal, Mrs. Jackson-Thomas, made me take it off. The hat only made the Jerry Curl worse, because it dried the Jerry Curl juice. Stupid Jerry Curls gotta stay wet all the time. When it's dry, it looks even worse. Our class made fun of people with them all the time.

"You can fry some chicken with all that grease!" said one student.

"You need a new pillow every time you take a nap!" said another.

"Follow the drip! Follow the drip!" the class chants.

I always thought it was funny when we made fun of other people. Damn sure ain't funny when they're laughing at you. And I did everything I could to stop Mom from putting it in my hair. She had to beat me until I was half-dead to put this slimy, slippery Jerry Curl kit in. It was the worst whooping I ever got. Worse than when Pop beat me with his work belt. Nana can beat you good too even though she's a girl. All three of them like to make you get a "switch" or little branch off the tree in the backyard. I get goose bumps every time I pass it. It's the tree right next to the tomatoes and collard greens Nana and Pop grow. Sometimes I refuse to eat the vegetables because it makes me think of that switch tree.

But a beating with a switch would've been like beating me with a feather, when you compare it to what Mom hit me with yesterday.

"Stop moving or I'm gonna beat your black a*s," she warned me, as she rinsed the Jerry Curl chemicals out of my hair.

I was already crying from my hair and eyes burning. Snot dripped from my nose into my mouth as I screamed. My hair was burning under the sink, but all I could think about was the Jerry Curl jokes everybody would say about me when I got to school.

"Your hair is gonna catch on fire like Michael Jackson! Hee heee!" they'd say.

Why was I going through all this physical pain to only go through more emotional pain at school? Whose idea was it to wear Jerry Curls anyway? Mom just wants me to do it so I won't have to get a haircut for another month. But they make your hair smell like a wet dog bathed in alcohol. They look like sheep's wool dipped in tar. I'm not even gonna call them Jerry Curls anymore. From now on, it's just "Jerry" …my worst enemy.

I let out a final scream and tried to move my head from under the sink. I felt a stinging smack from my mom pop the back of my neck. The water made the smack sting even more.

"This the last time I'm telling you! Stop moving!" she screamed.

As soon as mom loosened her grip, I leaped out of the chair and ran for the door. She tried to grab me by the head, but my hair was too slippery. I guess the Jerry kit was already starting to work.

Water was all over the kitchen, and I slipped and fell chin-first on the ground. My mouth was open from me screaming, and it made my teeth chomp down on the ground like Pac-Man eating a ghost.

Since the switch tree was too far away, Mom grabbed the closest thing to her. It was a thin brown extension cord.

WHIP! POP!

I let out a scream so loud, my aunt could hear it from the third floor.

WHIP! POP!

It was starting to sound like a song composed of three sounds:

1) The whipping sound the extension cord made cutting through the air.

2) The popping sound it made when it hit my soaked back.

3) The loud scream I made after getting hit.

After hearing it twice, I was getting tired of the song. I jumped up and darted out the house. My hair was on fire and my back stung. Half-naked and barefoot, Mom chased after me until I got out of the yard. Then she yelled at the neighbors to chase me and bring me back before the Jerry kit burned out all my hair. I knew you couldn't leave the chemicals in for too long, but I'd rather have no hair at all than a Jerry Curl anyways.

As I started running in the opposite direction, our neighbors jumped off their porches to chase me. Jerry's chemicals began to drip into my eye, burning and blurring my vision. Now, my hair, back, and eyes were all on fire. I didn't care. I'd rather be burned alive than have Jerry on my head.

I ran full-speed down the street and, before I knew it, I was four blocks away. Even the neighbor who was the star of the football team couldn't catch me. The only thing that made me stop was the busy street I came to. After eventually catching up to me, the star football player lifted me off the ground and carried me back to the house. Jerry was victorious.

By the time I got back home, Mom had a new friend with her. It was a thin switch from the tree. She didn't say a word. She just washed the Jerry chemicals out of my hair, then made another song. This one was longer and louder than the first one.

I was so nervous about going to school today, I forgot about the music we made. I took a deep breath before I walked into class because I knew what was coming. Then I counted….1….2….3.

When I walked into class, it was like they raised the red curtain to reveal a live comedy show. It started off with two or three people laughing. Then Juju pointed at me and screamed the famous line from the movie "Coming to America."

"SOOOOOULLL GLOOOO!"

That's when the whole class started laughing. I got so angry, I bit down on my teeth like there was Laffy Taffy between them. My eyebrows went low enough to touch my eyeballs. That's when I transformed into Macho Man Randy Savage on Juju. Before the laugh even came out his mouth, it was silenced by my fist.

Now I'm in Mrs. Jackson-Thomas' office waiting for Mom to come pick me up and take me home. It's not my first time in her office. Don't think it will be my last either.

"Don't give me that look like you're innocent," said Mrs. Jackson-Thomas. "I swear, it seems like every week I have a Whitaker Boy in this office. Your grandparents raised ya'll better than this."

Knock, knock, knock, knock.

I already knew from the type of knock that it was my mom.

She walked in looking happier than usual. Her smile was wide enough to connect her ears together. She didn't even look mad at me. That's weird, I thought. Maybe she feels sorry for that whooping she gave me yesterday. Lord knows my back still feels it. Last night I slept on my stomach because my back felt like a tiger had scratched it with its razor claws dipped in salt. I also slept on my stomach because I didn't want Jerry all over my pillow either.

Mrs. Jackson-Thomas starts telling my Mom the story, while I'm still wondering why she looks so happy. A moist drip of Jerry's juice slowly fell down my forehead to remind me of his victory yesterday. Another drop went down to the collar of the Power Ranger shirt I was wearing. Jerry is taunting me, and simultaneously destroying my favorite shirt.

"Listen, child," says Mrs. Jackson-Thomas, "I don't care what someone says. You can't put your hands on people like that. Come tell me next time and I'll get him for you," she joked.
"Mrs. D says you're not doing your homework either."

Not knowing what else to do, I looked at the ground. While staring, I saw one of Jerry's drips fall on Mrs. Johnson's carpet.

I was told to apologize to Juju and was sent home to cool off for the rest of the day. As my mom and I walked out of school, I suddenly saw why she was so happy. Our school is across the street from the Check Cashing Spot. The long line wrapped around the building meant that it was the 1st of the month. The line was so long, it could wrap around my whole school...twice. My school is the closest school to the two housing projects in Plainfield, so there are plenty of welfare checks to cash on this day. The smile on my mom's face lets me know she already cashed hers combined with her check from her job at the restaurant.

After grabbing my hand, my mother and I cross the street.

"Mir-Mir, you know better than to be fighting like that," she said.

"I know," I said. "But the whole class was laughing at me because of Jerry."

"Whose Jerry?" she asked.

"This stupid Jerry Curl!" I responded.

She let out a brief chuckle. Even my mom was laughing at me.

"Don't let it happen again," she said. "If somebody hits you, always fight back. But you don't need to start swinging every time someone teases you. This is the second time this year!"

I had completely forgotten about the first time.

"You want something from the store?" Mom asked.

"Not really," I said.

I knew we were going to spend food stamps because she just cashed the welfare check. I hate spending those embarrassing food stamps, especially if someone from my school is in the store. My class makes fun of people for spending food stamps too. Everybody's mama gets them, though. But everyone likes to pretend that they are somehow better than the rest.

At least my mom usually has a job, so food stamps ain't the only money we spend. But the money she makes working isn't enough to feed all of us. Damn sure ain't enough to buy her those drugs either. Dad makes extra money working at Grandpa's shop fixing cars, but I know he spends a lot of that on drugs too.

"How was school?" she asks.

"Ok, I guess. I had the fight before class even started. I was waiting in the office for you for like ten hours," I complained.

"Why ain't you doing your homework?" she asked.

"Cuz we keep moving and switching schools! This teacher be teaching different things than the last teacher. I don't get it. Why we gotta keep changing schools anyway? It's getting on my nerves," I whined.

"You're too young to have nerves," she responds, as she pulled my arm to cross the street. "I'm dropping you off at your Grandpa's shop so you can be with your dad. Dealing with you yesterday was enough."

I don't know if I'm too young to have nerves, but I do know I'm tired of moving around and having to go to different schools. I'm only in the 4th grade, and I've already been to four different schools. Each time we move to a new school, I have to make new friends and catch up on work. It's hard to make new friends at a new school in the middle or end of the school year. Everybody already chose their friends, and everybody already knows each other. Usually, they've been going to school together for years. I don't think I've ever even been at a school for a whole year.

I don't bother getting comfortable in a bedroom since we move so much, either. We started off at Nana's house, then Grandma's house, then back to Nana's, then to 2nd street, then 4th street, then Belvedere Blvd, then back to Nana's house, and now we're on 5th street. As soon as I get comfortable, we either get kicked out or got to move to something "better," but where we can use our Section 8. And there was that one time our apartment building caught on fire, so we were forced to move. Still, I'm 10 years old and I can already remember moving six or seven times. Last time we moved, I didn't even make any friends. I hate getting really close to people and having to move away. That's what happened with my friend TJ. We used to play together every day after school. Now I haven't seen him in months. That chump still has my Power Ranger toy too.

I'm kinda happy to be back at Stillman Elementary School though. This was the first school I ever went to, and it's my favorite. It's the closest school to Nana's house, where all my cousins live. I have lots of family and friends living on Nana's street and in the two project buildings nearby. Sometimes, we have block parties, where they close down the street and have a big BBQ with music and fun. Sometimes we close off the street ourselves to play football. I'm happy to be living a block away on 5th Street and Plainfield Ave now.

After walking two blocks, I try to take advantage of my mom's good mood.

"Mom when you gonna get me a new Power Ranger toy?" I ask.

"When you start doing your damn homework," she quickly responds, killing the conversation.

We walk holding hands, as Jerry continues to drip down my neck. I fantasize about the Power Ranger toy so much that it almost makes me want to do my homework. You should see it. It's a blaster gun that can magically change into a ninja sword. I see myself slicing my little sister, Shante, with it. I see myself shooting the blaster gun so much, the battery for the light and laser sound will die in three hours.

I want the black one because it's for the Black Ranger. He's my favorite. He's the only black person on the show. Almost all other superheroes and cartoons are white. Batman, X-Men, Superman, He-Man. All the ninja turtles sound white. I think that one Thundercat is black—at least his voice sounds black. I wonder why they don't let us black people save the day sometimes.

I like the Black Ranger so much that I'm gonna be him for Halloween this year. Mom said she's going to make the costume for me. She said I could wear a pair of her tights and high boots. We'll cut a white diamond from another shirt and sew it on the chest. Making Halloween costumes is always fun, almost as fun as stealing them. For some Halloweens, my brother, sister, and I get to walk into the store and choose whatever costume we want. After we point out our costumes, they appear like magic in the car a few minutes later. Mom and Dad always find some way to get them.

Halfway to Grandpa's shop, Mom decided to stop at the Liberty Street corner store. I told her I didn't feel like spending those damn food stamps, but she wanted to go anyway.

"I'll wait outside," I tell her, once we get to the storefront. "Can you get me a grape soda and some Cheez Doodles though?"

While I'm waiting outside, some stranger walks into the store. He's wearing the new Jordan's that just came out. Black shiny leather with firetruck red shoestrings. They look so clean, you could probably lick the bottom of them and not taste any dirt. His designer jeans were sagging so low, it made him walk like a penguin. He had a fresh high-top fade with a part down the middle. You could still smell the white powder from the barbershop on him. A thick gold rope chain hung around his neck, sparkling when the sun hit it. I probably would have to use both arms to lift it.

Jerry and I just stood in front of the store wishing we were half as fly.

Once he walked in the store, he started talking to my mom. I've never seen him before, but he and my mom are talking like they've known each other for years. She is smiling even more now. My mom gave him a twenty-dollar bill, and he gave her two tiny packages in return. She looks at me for a second, then turns away. I look at the ground again like I did when Mrs. Jackson-Thomas asked me about my homework. I know exactly what's going on, but as always, I'll pretend like I have no clue.

She's buying that crack stuff, and Mr. Fresh with the Jordan's must be the crack dealer. I don't know much about crack, but I do know selling it makes you a lot of money. People talk about how some of the students at my school are crackbabies. This happens when a kid's mother smokes crack while she is pregnant with them. That's what they say happened to the kids in the special classes who need extra help.

Sometimes I'm taken out of class to work with the "special teacher." They say I'm a good student, but my behavior gets in the way of me doing my classwork. They said it just means I need extra attention sometimes. I ain't no crackbaby like the rest of them, though. My mama ain't smoked no crack when she was pregnant with me. She ain't as bad as these other crackheads either. She just does it a little bit. She and Dad will close their door and tell us to not bother them. They'll come out five or ten minutes later. Calm attitudes with eyes that look like glass marbles. I always thought it made them look like squirrels. Next time they come out their room calm with those squirrel eyes, I'm gonna ask them to get me another Power Ranger toy. That's the best time to ask them for things. I can already see myself slicing Nana's switch tree with my ninja sword. HIIIIIYA!

"What's up, lil Power Ranger!" said Mr. Fresh, as he walked outside the store.

"What's up," I responded. I was just happy he was talking about my Power Ranger shirt and not Jerry.

We walked through the projects on Plainfield Avenue, then up another block to my grandpa's auto shop. I could smell the shop from down the street. It's a scent that's become really familiar from the many days my brother and I spend here. It's a mixture of car grease, stale cigarettes, coffee, and gasoline. I love the smell. If my dad had his own cologne, it would be that fragrance. Sometimes Dad has the whole house smelling like it.

The closer we get to the shop, the stronger the smell becomes. The unmistakable sound of Parliament-Funkadelic blasts through the radio, getting louder and louder as we approach.

"Is that's my Mi-Mi?" a loud voice says, as soon as I walk in.

"Grandpa!" I scream.

I rush to hug him and rest my head on his big belly.

"Mi-Mi" is the name everyone on Dad's side of the family calls me. Big-Ma, Grandma, and Aunt Linda call me it too. I'm the only one with a nickname, and it makes my siblings jealous.

"What you doing home from school, boy?" he asks.

I look down at the ground for the third time of the day.

"He was fighting like he ain't got no damn sense," my mom interrupts.

Grandpa starts laughing and shaking his head as my dad rolls himself out from under a car.

"Did you beat his a*s?" asks my dad, as he lifts himself off the ground.

"Damn right!" I responded.

As my dad hugs me, grease gets all over the Power Rangers on my shirt.

"Turn your shirt inside-out," Dad says. "You're gonna be our little helper today."

I take my shirt off, and notice the juice Jerry left around my neck. When my shirt brushes my back as I put it back on, I feel the burn from yesterday's battle scars.

"Why you hitting my Mi-Mi like that for, Tasha?" Grandpa asks.

"That boy was running down the street with a perm in his hair. Had the whole block chasing him," she says. "He lucky his hair didn't fall out. Why couldn't he be like his brother and just let me finish it?"

"Because I didn't want no stupid Jerry Curl like him," I respond.

With Grandpa there to protect me, I feel like I could say anything to my mom. Grandpa always takes up for me because I'm his favorite. My brother Jamal was always Dad's favorite because he's the oldest and knows the most about cars. When we're in the shop together, they let him do more than me. My little sister Shante is my mom's favorite because she is the youngest and the only girl.

The phone rings, and Grandpa answers it after two rings.

"Frank's Auto," he mumbles, before sipping his coffee.

Mom hands Dad something. Dad looks back at me for a second until I give him the "I didn't see anything" face. I look at the ground for the fourth time today.

"Come here, boy," my mom says, as she embraces me in a hug. She squeezed me so tight, my back burns again from the battle we had yesterday.

"You know I'm sorry," she said.

I break loose from her hug with the bravery my grandpa's presence provides. I walk away to the back of the shop without saying goodbye to her. Sorry don't cut it. Not when Grandpa's around.

Once in the back, I see the gruesome guard dog of the shop chained to a pipe. His name is Dirty Red. He's an 85-pound, pure-muscle, red-nose pitbull that scares most people without even barking. He tilts his head and looks at me confused, before letting out a loud bark that could shake the juice off of Jerry. I pause wondering why he's barking at me instead of wagging his short stubby tail. Damn you, Jerry. Changed my scent and appearance so much, my own dog don't recognize me!

Chapter 4: Gluttony

<u>Age</u>: 19 years old

<u>Gluttony</u> (noun)- Consuming far beyond one's appetite. An unreasonable and excessive greed that leads to undisciplined and savage indulgence. Gluttony evokes disregard for others, eliminates self-control, and brings out the worst in individuals.

This ain't a job for the weary. I'm getting a widow's wedding ring appraised at a jewelry store. It's the only remaining gift from her recently deceased husband, and I'm at a jewelry store seeing how much money I can get for it.

The jeweler takes the ring out of the cleaning machine and looks at it with his one-eyed monocle.

"Hmm..." he says before a long pause. "I could sell a ring like this for $7,000. The most I could give you is three grand for it. $1,500 now, and another $1,500 once I sell it," says the jeweler.

He takes off the eye piece he was using to inspect the diamond. His mustache and receding hairline still make him resemble the monopoly guy, though.

He must think I'm some stupid 19-year-old nigger who stole a ring. The last appraiser said it was worth $8,500 and the person who gave me the ring said at least $10,000.

"Not bad," I say. "Give me a few days to think about it and see some other places. Thanks."

I reach out to shake his hand, and he notices the thousands of dollars' worth of jewelry on my pinky and wrist.

"Nice ring and watch combination," he compliments.

"Thanks. This ain't for sale though," I respond.

Not MY bling. A two-carat diamond pinky ring and a brand new limited-edition Movado watch. My hand and wrist are worth more than $5,000.

You should see my hustling partner Sheek. I'll never forget the flabbergasted faces of the jewelry store staff when two black teenagers walked in and spent more than $10,000.

"Aiight. Later man," I say to the jeweler.

He responds with a look telling me he knows I won't be back.

"Listen, chief, the most I can do is four grand. Two now, two later," he says.

The monopoly guy means business. I kindly thank him again before walking out of the store. Something made me want to see if the ring was really worth over $10,000 like the widow said it was. The unfortunate widow's name is Stacy. She gave me her wedding ring as collateral for $5,000 worth of that poison. She buys more crack than most of our other customers combined. The days of grinding on street corners are over. It's stupid, risky, and crumbs for the birds. The block is too savage now, and the jumpers run rampant. Now big-time clients, like Stacy, come to us and make appointments to get their supply. We have young soldiers out in the streets doing the dirty work for us. They're learning the ropes just as we did back in the day.

Everybody's gotta pay dues when they're young by putting in work on the block. Many of my boys love the block and the glory that comes from standing on street corners like light posts. It took years, but I've grown wiser and focus mainly on a few heavy-spending customers a day. Crackheads spending $20 are TV dinners. Fiends like Stacy are lobster and shrimp.

The widow's ring is collateral for this crack, but I pray to the gods she doesn't pay me back. I told her she has until 7:00 p.m. Friday to bring the remaining cash, and not a second after. She almost didn't make this deal, but the poison has her clenched in a headlock—willing to give up her most treasured possessions. The ring is one of her few remaining possessions. If I were her husband, my ghost would haunt the hell out of her right now. Hell, I'd be haunting me, the dealer selling her that poison. That thought would haunt me, but my soul is too cold to be troubled. The game has made me numb.

The days of innocence are long gone. Sheek and I are two freshmen at Union County College, knee-deep in the drug game again. I held a few real jobs over the past couple of years. Once my college schedule demanded day AND night classes, my supermarket job no longer wanted to accommodate my schedule. It would have been easier if they just told me that. Instead, my supervisor started stealing money from my register and blaming it on me. I knew damn well my register wasn't short. Between my fast food and supermarket jobs, I had 3 years of cashier experience. Not to mention the thousands of dollars I accurately counted at lightning speed while selling drugs. My register and trapping money were never short. Nevertheless, the week I told my supervisor about my complicated new college schedule, my register was short three times. I got suspended and instead of fighting back, I simply went back to what I knew: trappin'. Two months later, my supervisor was caught stealing money and got fired. By that time, trapping had me trapped again.

Working for someone else is not my thing anyway. It was difficult for me to go from making over $200 an hour selling drugs when I was 15, to making $5.25 an hour flipping burgers at 16. I remember looking at checks after two weeks' worth of work and thinking, "I used to make this in a few hours, not weeks." By the time I was 18, I could no longer resist the temptation of fast money. My supermarket job no longer wanting me was just the straw that broke the camel's back. Seeing all my friends with the latest fashions, jewelry, and video games made it nearly impossible to resist. Every single friend I grew up with on 6th street is grinding hard in the drug game right now. It's almost like it's our destiny. Sheek and I are the only two in college. Only 3 out of nearly 20 of us graduated high school: Me, Sheek, and Nyce. I'm the only one out of the five Whitaker Boys to finish high school.

As I continue to walk out of Mr. Monopoly's jewelry store, an old friend greets me. It's Juju Garcia, the dude that caused me to transform into Macho Man Randy Savage in the 4th grade. Nowadays, he's doing whatever it takes for him to get his fix of that poison. He's one of the smaller, annoying customers: the TV dinners.

His hair is neatly slicked back and reminds me of why we used to call him "Chico Rico" in middle school. His short, stocky frame looks comfortable in the silky purple shirt he's been wearing faithfully for as long as I've known him.

"What's good, son!" he says, as he exhales cigarette smoke.

Before I get a chance to talk, he bombards me with his customer service concerns.

"Yo, that last batch ya'll had wasn't too good," he says. "My peoples ain't like it too much."

Because we grew up together, Juju prefers to pretend that he resells the crack we sell him. Sheek and I knew he was smoking it from the very beginning. At first, he spent $100 at a time. That was back when he was working and doing other things. As the habit began to dominate his life, he came with less and less money to spend— down to $50, then to $25. One time, he only had $10. We had to let him know we weren't lifting a finger for that kinda money. Nowadays, we only move for $100 or more. We sell it to him for the low as a "favor" because he's an old friend. But we actually don't like selling poison to Black and Latino drug addicts anymore—only to unfortunate white widows like Stacy. Watching our people die slow was becoming too much to bear. For some reason, I don't feel the same guilt when the person is white.

After you sell that poison to someone for a while, you're forced to watch their deterioration. Many are able to be "functioning addicts" and keep jobs while they use. They take care of their kids and half-heartedly handle basic responsibilities. Mom and Dad were like this half the time. Nonetheless, functioning addicts are rare.

"That stuff is just about gone," I say to Juju. "We getting some new stuff tomorrow. Holla at us then."

"Aiight," he responds. "I'm about to go handle some business right now. I should have a few hundred tomorrow."

"Aiight," I say, like I almost believe him. Nearly every conversation with Juju ends with the promise of a big come-up that will happen tomorrow.

Sheek and I are sitting on over $17,000 now. We've risen to become princes of the block—thousands of dollars in jewelry, shopping sprees, and magnums of champagne that I don't even like to drink. We'd easily have $30,000 if we didn't spoil ourselves. Sometimes we spend it just as fast as we make it. The days of hunger as a 15-year-old are long over. The $5,000 worth of jewelry I'm wearing is proof of that. Although we have more than enough to eat right now, something makes us want more. A healthy appetite still exists. We are urban entrepreneurs who have expanded our operation to include other drugs. Just two weeks ago, we bought ten bricks of heroin and 250 kilograms of cocaine. It's almost gone already. Each brick has 50 bags of dope, which brings us $500 in street sales. As for the coke, 250 grams is 1/4 a kilo. At this rate, we could move a kilo of cocaine in less than two months, but not raw coke though. A culinary ceremony is required to convert cocaine into the preferred poison: crack.

Sheek and I are gourmet chefs when it comes to cooking up crack. We used to have fiends cook it for us, but learned to do it ourselves after too many rocks started disappearing. It's quite simple, actually. You only need five things: baking soda, cocaine, water, a cooking pot, and a jar. We use a beaker Sheek swiped from our science lab at school. Using a scale for measuring allows you to cook up a more perfect batch of crack.

There are only five steps to making the poison:

1. Bring a pot of water to a boil.
2. Mix baking soda, cocaine, and water in a separate jar.
3. Drop the jar in the boiling water. Gently swirl it around.
4. Chill with an ice cube, or place the jar in cold water.
5. Drain and dry out the poison.

Crack is basically a cocaine cake that you can sell to people in $10 rocks. Despite it being the same chemical, crack gets you a lot more prison time. We can make upwards of $12,000 in crack from the 250 grams of coco. Combined with our heroin, we can move over $10,000 in a week in drug sales. We each take about 20% of that in profit. Not too bad for urban teenage entrepreneurs. Pick your poison: crack, heroin, coke. We even hustle weed and fresh white tees on the side to add a couple hundred a week and further satisfy our growing appetites.

The money and power are an addiction we call *Hustlitis*. It's nearly impossible to kick the habit. We are coming up in a world where the wicked are rewarded. Better yet, the wicked are worshiped. The rich and the hustlers are put on pedestals. The decadent lifestyle traps you. As Jay-Z said, "[t]hrough this life, we become addicted…sorta like the fiends we accustomed to serving." Fast, effortless, and consistent money is hard to resist.

Everybody wants to be the friend of the PushaMan. Sure, you're invited to the parties, just bring a few sacks of that magic earth leaf or some prescription pills to keep the party going. The benefits are great, but at any given moment, you could lose it all. It's an eternal tightrope walk, with fire on one side, and jagged spikes on another. A cage is waiting for you the moment you fall or get knocked off. Grimy goons with guns know you're holding money and weight. I had to learn the hard way to never carry much on you, not even for a second. When they run up on you with the heat, give them whatever you got. A stickup kid got me a few weeks ago. The older hustlers suggest you get used to this happening every once-in-a-while. It's never worth putting up a fight when it does happen. Count it as a loss, at least until you're reckless enough to shoot one to send a message. In the meantime, watch your front, back, and side.

People think this is easy work. Like we just hand people substances in exchange for money. But we manage inventory, quality control, security, employee/human resources, sales, customer service, and pretty much everything else you do when running a legit business. There is an art to it, too. You need a sixth sense for danger, an instinct to detect who can be trusted, a cool head to minimize the enemies and drama, and skin thicker than leather to cope with the trauma.

Since a youth, The Notorious B.I.G. warned us of the baggage that came with the territory. He dedicated his debut album and single to "…all the people that lived above the buildings that I was hustlin' in front of that called the police on me when I was just tryin' to make some money to feed my daughter." You feel the stigma stinging from all the non-trappers in the neighborhood. Thank God I don't have kids to support, but I've rationalized the choices I have had to make to "provide" for myself. There is little-to-no economic opportunity in Plainfield. We've created our own drug economy to alleviate the pain and humiliation of abandoned factories, underfunded schools, boarded-up houses, and other monuments of hopelessness in our barren landscape. Some of my friends have already picked up adult charges, so they are ineligible by law for the limited opportunities that do exist. Less than 20-years-old and already hopeless of obtaining any other life aside from trappin'. As Tupac said, "...no fairytale for this young black male. Some see me stranded in this land of hell, jail, and crack sales."

I've even employed my dad selling drugs for me now down in South Jersey. He came to me after he was laid off. He was clean at the moment and promised he wouldn't use it again, but he's already showing the symptoms. I may very well have provided Pop Duke with the poison that relapsed him. But he kept begging for it, and claimed he had no other way to get money. He wouldn't leave until I gave him a pack.

Dad hasn't been out of jail too long. We make one hell of a son-father drug dealing team. He's down in South Jersey and comes up every couple of days to get some more of that poison. This ain't your typical father-son relationship, but most people don't smoke weed with their father when they're 12 years old either. Mom Dukes started getting me alcohol around the same age too. Because of the environment, exposure to alcohol and drugs was inevitable. My parents never tried to hide the inescapable from me. Exposure to such things was usually accompanied by long talks about self-control and responsibility. Only time will tell if their parenting tactics were effective.

Both of my parents had to get furloughs, or special privileges, to leave their incarceration temporarily and come to my graduation. Nothing would stop them from seeing their son break the cycle. To show my appreciation, I took my graduation money from Grandma and split it between their commissary accounts.

Hard to believe Mom is still serving time from that raid we got caught in a few years ago. When they locked us up, they kept her longest because our apartment was in her name. She was released, but was taken back into custody for parole violations. Dirty urine from that poison. I still carry guilt over the fact that she missed most of my high school years because of the drug operation we ran back when I was 15-years-old.

***

As I say goodbye to Juju, I'm overwhelmed with feelings of guilt for recycling the pain of addiction and perpetuating the cycle of the trap. I've seen many lives go down the drain. Juju is far from the first. Tomorrow might be the last time I ever sell him drugs. After that, I'll only have to justify my destructive profession with white addicts, I tell myself.

I slap on my book bag and head to Byron's house for a haircut. Nyce is over there getting a tattoo, too. Byron's a peculiar addict, by far one of the grimiest cats you'll ever meet. The things he does to his parents lets you know he would not think twice about betraying you or anyone else. After what he did to me, I'll never trust him again.

As I bike down Front Street, I turn down several offers to buy poison.

"You straight?" they ask.

I simply nod my head no and keep moving. I'm not concerned with this little money or poisoning my own people anymore.

It's a picturesque spring day in Plainfield. The sun peeks through the clouds and a light wind cools my face. I can feel a brisk back sweat building under my book bag as I bike along. The further I go, the more trash I see sprinkled alongside the streets. The rubbish is accompanied by an increasing amount of graffiti, liquor stores, and dilapidated, abandoned houses. I'm almost there.

I arrive at Byron's house and notice it's in rare form—no one is standing in front or on the porch. Usually, you would think his yard was the only area in Hell with air conditioning, the way people crowd it. Clusters of pushers, crackheads, dope fiends, and other jungle junkies who didn't mind annoying Byron's parents congregate daily.

"Yuuurp!" I scream, as a signal.

I walk to the back of the house. By the time I get there, I see Byron standing behind the screen door in oversized jeans, stained to the point that you could not determine their original color. You can tell he got them before that poison made him drop 40 pounds. His top was a New York Jets jersey, small enough to indicate it wasn't his originally. His unkempt hair laid out behind a slightly receding hairline. As always, his face looks like it's seen better days. You would have never guessed he's just 28-years-old. You would have never guessed he was one of Plainfield's finest barbers and tattoo artists, either. But physical appearance is not his priority at this stage. He would never take the time to cut own his hair. He only cuts the hair of others to feed his poison habit.

"Who you be?" he jokes.

I shove past him and head to his basement, or as he likes to call it, The Sharpest Needle Tattoo Parlor and Barber Shop.

"What's good, Byron?" I respond.

Byron never went to tattoo or beauty school. Instead, he did six years in state prison and learned a few trades to support his habit. In three minutes, he could take a $20 pair of clippers and modify them to be so sharp, you'll grow scabs around your hairline a day after the haircut. He can also turn those $20 clippers into a tattoo gun by taking it apart and attaching a needle to the motor. This jail tattoo gun is slightly more painful than a regular tattoo gun, though. I got my first tatt from him when I was 15-years-old for $25. When he is desperately feening, he does tattoos for $10. I remember my brother, Jamal, crying when he got his tatt done. It's almost like a tradition in our hood. My boy, Nyce, is getting a tattoo today. I drew it for him earlier. A deteriorating scroll with the words "Only God can Judge Me" in the fanciest letters I could draw.

I walk through a cloud of menthol cigarette smoke as I enter the room. I'm bombarded with several scents in a battle with the lingering smell of recently burned incense, as I step through the smoke. The stench of stale malt liquor absorbed into the rug, grown-man musk, rubbing alcohol, and cigarettes easily defeats the incense. Black and brown spots from beer spills and cigarette ashes stain the blue carpet into a polka-dotted frenzy. Just like Byron, the room has seen better days.

Nyce sits reclining in a seat in the corner. His right arm is stretched out like someone begging for change. The other arm helps to elevate his thumb inside his mouth.

"Grown-ass Navy sailor getting a tattoo, but still sucking his thumb!" I joke. "Yo, Byron, tattoo 'Deez Nutz' on his thumb and see if he sucks it then!"

He cracks a smile, and his drool drips from his thumb.

"Wuck wu wigga!" he attempts to say with his thumb still in his mouth.

A sudden thumping on the steps gets our attention. It was someone racing down the steps as if a pit bull was chasing them. Having been in multiple drug raids already, it triggered a post-traumatic episode of a dozen jumpers jumping. I look at Byron and see he's calm as a butterfly resting on a flower. My street wisdom tells me he knows the person who is coming, and is probably expecting them. A tall, slender, light-skinned dude hustles into the room, panting for breath. He removes the ski mask he's wearing as a disguise. His gloved hands remove a silver handgun from his waist.

"I did it!" he says, with a loud exhale of breath.

He continues to gasp for air desperately. Nyce and I look on confused, as Byron cracks a sinister smile.

"Yea, my dude!" Byron says. "Told you that it would be a piece of cake. I set his a*s up easily for you. Did you lock the door behind you?"

The guy struggles to nod, while he continues to catch his breath. He runs to the closest seat and collapses into it. His long, lanky arms touch the ground, and his head tilts back looking at the ceiling. His facial expression changes from joyful to solemn. I looked at the corroded ceiling to see if he was looking at something besides the peeling paint.

"Let me get mine," Byron impatiently says.

"Yea. True. Good looking out for the setup," said the friend. "Couldn't have done it without you."

He hands Byron a few bags of that poison. Byron's eyes nearly pop out of his head in excitement. He runs to a small black bag sitting on a stained wood coffee table converted to a desk for him to sketch his tattoos. The black marks from cigarette burns make it look like leopard print. I briefly wonder who Byron set up, as he grabs a syringe out of the small black bag and rushes towards the door.

"Dammit! He's leaving again!" Nyce sobs. "Dude never gonna finish this tattoo! Bad enough his breath is smelling like rusty possum nuts!"

The stranger takes a long, deep breath, as if he's about to dive into the ocean. He slowly exhales.

"Stay away from this poison, young bloods, for real," he says. "I just robbed somebody I've been friends with for over 30 years. Damn."

He shakes his head in shame, before pulling out a crack pipe that's delicately stashed in his sock. He kisses the pipe like it's his long, lost soulmate. He inhales an even larger breath. As he slowly exhales the grayish-blue smoke, Nyce turns his face away and finally removes his thumb from his mouth.

"Come on bruh!" Nyce screams. "I'm in the military, and the last thing I need is that stuff coming up in my urine."

"My bad, young blood," the guy responds.

Byron reenters the room more mellow and lethargic. He's putting his belt back on indicating he's either just used it to tighten his arm to get a juicy vein to inject heroin into, or pulled down his pants to shoot-up in a vein in his penis. I've heard he does both. Either way, he's kissing the sky right now. Whatever part of Nyce's tattoo Byron didn't finish will likely remain undone now.

Byron pauses in the middle of the room and begins scratching his arm in a trance-like manner. His eyes roll to the back of his head, as his chin sinks to his chest.

"Aiight. A lil mo' to goooooo," he says.

With time, he collects himself and flops into the chair next to Nyce. He wipes the blood starting to drip out of Nyce's arm, before turning on his makeshift tattoo gun. Nyce grinds his teeth as Byron starts penetrating his skin.

At that moment, I ask Nyce a vital question.

"You brought your own needle, right?"

"Hell yea!" he responds, before squinting his eyes in pain.

"Ahhhh!" Nyce screams. "The more you stop, the more it hurts."

I gaze at the stranger only to see him staring at the ceiling again. Whatever he did is weighing heavy on his mind. Byron, on the other hand, seems to have already forgotten about it. The stranger kisses his crackpipe once again, blowing the smoke away from Nyce this time.

The sound of the tattoo gun ceases and I turn to see Byron starting to doze off into a dope nod. His eyes close and his head tilts to the side until his ear touches his shoulder.

"Mir... you got...ta finish...this for me," he slowly says, before lifting his head up. "Almost done."

Nyce and I just look at each other.

"Are you serious?" Nyce says.

"I charge three times as much, chump," I respond. "You're lucky. I'm the one who drew the damn thing anyway."

Nyce shakes his head in dissatisfaction.

"This is the last time I get a tattoo from a dope fiend," Nyce says as Byron stumbles out of the seat. He drags his leg like a zombie, as he walks out of the room scratching his arm.

I cautiously grab the tattoo gun with two fingers before putting it back down quickly.

"Where his gloves at?" I ask. "Dude probably just shot-up in his peter."

Nyce laughs before tossing me two latex gloves. There was a wet spot on the gloves from his thumb-sucking.

After putting the gloves on, I begin to finish the tattoo. I move the gun up and down to complete the letter "D" in "Judge."

My cell phone starts to vibrate on the leopard print coffee table. "Stacy $$" appears on the screen. When the widow calls, it reminds me that I'm in the middle of the hood with a $10,000 diamond ring in my pocket. I need to get out of here and soon. Luckily, Bryon and this dude who just robbed his longtime friend are neutralized.

I start a conversation with Nyce and ignore the ringing.

"Yo, Spring Break in Virginia Beach was crazy, son!" I say. "I can't wait to go back.

"Word is bond," he says. "Straight ballin'! I don't want to see another bottle of Moët or Hennessey for the rest of the year. We shut the club down, Jersey-style!"

Nyce recently relocated to a naval base in Virginia. Last month, Sheek and I took a trip down there for our first college spring break. It was our first time seeing Nyce since he left for basic training last year. We got a crackhead to rent us a brand-new car in her name and made the six-hour drive from Jersey. We had everything we needed: fake IDs, an endless supply of alcohol, too much money to spend, and a balla beachfront hotel suite on the 15th floor. For Sheek and me, it was the first time we'd gone on a trip without our parents. It was an unforgettable journey, and the subtle differences in Virginia compared to Jersey sparked a curiosity within me. It made me want to see more of the country. Hell, maybe even more of the world.

My phone vibrated again, interrupting my thoughts. It's "Stacy $$" again.

"Let me get this real quick," I say.

"Come on, man!" Nyce whimpers. "You got one more letter!"

I pick up the phone anyway.

"Mega, I need to see you right now," a scratchy female voice says. "I can be at our meeting spot in ten minutes."

All fiends know me "Mega" instead of "Amir." I learned a few months ago to stay anonymous to as many as possible. Mega stands for "Mega Mir." I borrowed it from one of my favorite video games, "Mega Man." Sheek's name is "Zero," Mega Man's best friend and reliable partner. To stay incognito, we never meet customers at our real houses either.

"You got what you owe us?" I ask.

"Not only that," she says, "but bring two of the usual! I have all the cash right now. I finally got my husband's life insurance money!"

I pause with a slight gasp. Stacy's "usual" comes to about $1,500. She only buys once a week, but when she does, she spends big. She spends a lot so she can get a "deal," but in actuality, she's just paying what we used to charge non-white people.

I do the math in my head. She already owes us $5,000. Two of her "usuals" equals $3,000. That makes eight grand total. Her buying 25 grams damn near depletes our crack inventory. Giving her two bricks of dope also empties our heroin inventory. We've been reluctant to re-up and buy more because we've been considering getting out of the drug game. Well, not "we," more like I have been considering getting out of the game. My partner Sheek would prefer if I stayed in the operation with him, but he knows that my heart isn't in it anymore. We've already got $17,000 stacked in the stash. This eight grand from Stacy could put us at $25,000.

"Aiight. See you in a few," I say to Stacy, before flipping the phone to hang up.

I finish Nyce's last letter and leave faster than I can say "peace out." The stranger is still staring at the wall with squirrel eyes, and Nyce has reverted to thumb-sucking. On the way out, I climb over Byron slumped over on his steps, asleep. As worried as his friend was, Byron was completely at peace. He'll probably wake up and forget what he did to induce his medicated state-of-mind. Tomorrow, he'll likely set up someone else.

Through my misfortune, I was once one of Byron's victims. I contemplated murdering him in retaliation after he set us up to get robbed. To his benefit, my love and respect for his mother stopped me. But I purchased the rat poison to lace his heroin and everything. He still doesn't know that I know he was the one behind the heist.

Stepping outside to fresh air helps me understand how funky Byron's Tattoo Parlor/Barbershop really was. I unlock my bike and head to my house for a pit stop. I need to re-up and empty out our inventory for Stacy.

My thoughts play back images of Byron's friend staring at the ceiling. I wonder how his friend of 30 years felt after being betrayed by someone so close. I think of other experiences I've had at Byron's house. Two days ago, I watched the ambulance pick up someone who overdosed on drugs I had sold them a few moments earlier.

A few days, I gave another dude a package of poison to sell for me. The next day, he died from a heart attack. We've given packages to countless people to sell. You never know who will go on a binge and use all the drugs themselves. I trusted this dude because he was my father's old friend. Now the guilt of his death looms over me like an eternal dark cloud. I should have at least attended his funeral, but my guilt wouldn't let me see him again in any capacity—even in a coffin. I couldn't look his children and family in the eye.

***

As I get on my bike, an eerie dream I had last night starts to play back in my head.

Two black caskets are in an empty white room. The lids on the caskets rise slowly and two corpses step out, resurrected. They struggle to get out and then slowly walk towards me.

"Why....Why...WHY!" they dreadfully ask.

The creatures resemble the two people whose deaths I helped bring about this past week. Only their skin is now mucus green, and as they walk, their flesh melts and leaves behind a trail of hundred-dollar bills. I turn around to run, but they magically appear in front of me. As they push me to the ground and pin me down, one grabs my arm and rips it out of its socket. Blood spreads, turning the entire room red.

The other decaying corpse snatches the two-karat diamond ring off the finger of my ripped arm. He elevates it in the air as it slowly turns to a white powder on the scarlet floor. He drops to his knees to snort the powder as the other zombie grabs my bloody, detached arm. In a similar action, he rips off my Movado watch and raises it to the sky. It transforms into a crack rock the size of a fist. His entire hand catches on fire and ignites the rock. He places it into the palm of my torn off hand. Setting the bloody end at his mouth, he takes a hit from my arm like it's a crackpipe. The other zombie raises his head off the ground and licks the white powder off his face with a long, reptilian tongue.

"Why!?" they scream in unison.

"Was it worth it!" echoes throughout the room.

One zombie pins my shoulders down to the ground as the other appears directly above me. He digs his hand into my chest, as I scream in agony. A bleeding, still-beating heart is removed from my chest. It quickly turns into white powder, covering my entire body. Both zombies lunge towards my torso and begin snorting the white substance off of me. Once it's nearly gone, they start eating my flesh.

***

I snap out of the replaying dream and notice my shirt collar is moist from sweat. Who am I to judge Byron for setting people up when my actions have killed people? Throughout my hustling career, I've literally taken the food out of kids' mouths, depriving them in the same manner that I was deprived as a child. I was pushing the same substance that had my parents, aunts, and uncles addicted. I remember growing up hating drugs because they were the most destructive force in my life. Now, my greed and gluttony are destroying lives in the same manner. And all for materialistic things that ultimately don't matter. I'm no longer that innocent 15-year-old who was just selling drugs to feed and clothe himself.

I uncomfortably removed my ring and watch, as the two main justifications for me selling drugs pop up in my head...

"If they want it, they gon' get it. It's going to happen regardless."

"This is the fastest and easiest money you will ever make."

I hop on my bike and tuck away this conscience confrontation for now.

Once home, I run to the stash. I grab a chair and remove a square piece from my room's ceiling. I feel around the dusty insides until I feel a short stack of money.

"Why is that there?" I say.

Every hustler knows not to keep money and drugs in the same place. I learned this the hard way after losing everything after that drug raid that got me arrested at age 15.

A close-up image of Stacy's rapidly deteriorating face appears in my head. She slowly transforms from the blue-eyed, blond-haired, moderately attractive person she was when we first met, to the saggy face fiend she is now. The image of her close-up face forces me to view the human side of her. Although she's white, her suffering is starting to bother me. The human struggle is beginning to seem more universal. Am I responsible for her deterioration? When she came to us, her husband had just died, and she was experimenting with that poison to cope. She went from spending $200 a week, to $500 a week, to over $1,000 a week. Now she is about to splurge $3,000. She's gonna smoke her husband's insurance money up one rock at a time. It might even put her under the ground with her late husband. Perhaps that's what she wants anyways.

After grabbing the drugs, I bike to meet Stacy. She's parked at our meeting spot with her car still running. From the distance, I see someone is in the back seat. Who? We have a strict policy forbidding fiends from having strangers in the car when we meet. You never know who could it be. Sometimes, we've refused sales because of it.

As I get closer to the car, I notice it's a toddler sitting in a car seat. I exhale in disappointment. I HATE it when kids are in the car during drug transactions. Ever since this one time a customer had her children in the car, and they kept begging her for ice cream.

"Sorry babe, we ain't got money for ice cream," said the mom, as she handed me three crisp twenty-dollar bills.

They've always said selling drugs is easier than "taking candy from a baby." Well, sometimes we take away their ice cream instead of candy.

I pull up to Stacy's passenger's side window on my bike. On the outside, she looks like an average person, at least from afar. Like the moon, the closer you get, the more imperfections you see. Instead of space rocks causing craters in the moon, crack rocks have been aging this young widow far too fast.

"Heyyyyy there, Mega." she says in a raspy voice, attempting to be sultry.

"Umm…hey," I say as I look uncomfortably at the two-year-old stranger in the back seat.

"I know I don't usually bring her, but I just picked her up from daycare," she explains. "This is Britney."

"Hello!" little Britney says, waving.

I wave back with one hand and reach into my pocket with the other. How am I going to pull this one off?

"You have my candy?" Stacy asks.

It triggers a memory of the time I asked what crack was as a youth, and they told me it was "grown-folk candy."

"I sure do," I respond. "Do you have my green candy? All eight stacks of them?"

"Yes sir," she says.

I hand Stacy her "candy," while Britney watches. I say a silent prayer for her never to remember this experience. Stacy takes off her shades to inspect the product. Her blue eyes squint like they are allergic to the sun. Her wrinkling skin and cheekbones remind me of how much she's deteriorated recently. A thick mask of makeup attempts to cover the madness and restore her original beauty. It's a mask that she wears in vain. I briefly remember the way she looked when I first saw her. Sheek and I both agreed that she could "get it." But then again, Sheek and I both usually agreed that most could "get it."

Stacy hands me an envelope of green candy. It's so heavy, I question whether all of it is cash. A quick inspection reveals that it is, indeed.

"8 grand, baby," she says.

Crisp bills sit comfortably inside the envelope. Stacy usually brings money straight from the bank, untouched by even her own hands.

"8 grand, baby!" Britney repeats. Stacy chuckles. I didn't find it funny.

"I knew you would come through, Stacy." I say, as I reach into my pocket.

I pull out a balled-up fist and open it before her. She stares at her wedding ring and becomes teary-eyed.

"You got it cleaned!" she sobs. "I don't know why I went so long without getting it cleaned. It looks as beautiful as it did on our wedding day."

I come up with the answer as to why she hasn't gotten it clean; it was because of that poison.

A tear slowly drips down her cheek. I try to tell myself that she's white and an outsider, so her suffering doesn't matter. It doesn't work this time.

She pats her pocket in search of something. She pulls out a crackpipe as she continues to cry, shaking her head furiously. A teardrop flies off her cheek and lands on her lap. I wonder if she's crying because she misses him, or because her habit was sucking the soul out of her life.

"Was it worth it?" I ponder. It echoed like it did in my nightmare when the zombies said it.

My blood goes cold. I swear I feel my blood cells freeze into sharp icicles and penetrate my skin.

Stacy breaks off a small rock of crack. She places it into the crackpipe before tongue kissing it like it's her recently deceased husband.

I look back at the toddler who is watching her mother smoke crack, and I feel sick to my stomach. She's wearing a pink Power Ranger shirt to match her OshKosh shoes. Even Scarface had a soft spot for children.

A childhood memory begins to play in my head. It was the one of my mom buying drugs at the corner store when I had on my Power Ranger shirt. Mr. Fresh with the Jordans and gold chain words echo in my head.

"What's up, little Power Ranger?"

I begin to see my struggle in the baby's blue eyes. Christmases without toys, the physical abuse. Worst of all, the pain of seeing your parents fight with something you are helpless to protect them against. Not only was Britney going to experience the same pain I did, but my gluttony and greed were going to contribute to it. I'm not that 15-year-old kid hustling to simply take care of himself anymore. I'm a 19-year-old adult whose greed is contributing to the deterioration of the world.

I grab the envelope and shove it into my pocket. As I ride away on my bike, I hear Stacy's sobbing fading into the distance.

***

By the time I get to my block, Sheek is in front of my house. A pair of boxing gloves hangs over his shoulder. His gold pinky ring and watch combination shine on the hand holding his gym bag. He must have just gotten home from boxing practice. The New Jersey Golden Glove Championship is coming up, and he's fighting in the finals. Now he trains and practices over 20 hours a week. Combined with school, it leaves little time for anything besides meeting a few big customers, like Stacy, a couple of times a day.

"Yurp!" he calls.

I stop my bike inches in front of him. We both extend our hands to complete our unique handshake. It's a complex combination of moves that end with us touching pinky rings to produce a clinking sound. My missing ring makes the handshake seem empty and hollow.

"Where's your ring at, kid?" he asks.

"Long story," I reply.

"You're not going to believe who just died son!" he says.

My eyes open widely in anticipation.

"Juju!" he exclaims. "He was trying to rob somebody, but the person killed him."

He pauses and waits for my response. I try to think of an appropriate one.

"But I just saw him earlier!" I say. "He said he was coming to see us tomorrow."

"Word is bond," Sheek says. "He was dead by the time the ambulance arrived on the scene."

We both pause. I think about Juju's kids now having to grow up without a father. The guilt of him robbing someone to buy drugs from me penetrates my soul. That makes three deaths within a week. Three people who might still be on earth with their families had I not done what I did.

"Let's go in the crib," I say. "I have eight stacks on me."

I ride my bike towards the back of the house. Using his Muhammad Ali quickness, Sheek comes from behind and jets in front of my bike.

He grabs my handlebars.

"Whoa, whoa, whoa!" he says. "You said you have eight grand on you!"

"Yup," I briefly reply, before climbing off my bike.

"How? When? We only had like $3,200 of work left," he says.

I lift the bike up and carry it up the steps.

"Stacy bought $3,000 of it and paid us the $5,000 she owed," I explained.

"We only have a little bit left," he states, realizing we're running low on goods.

I pause, nodding my head with eyes focused on Sheek.

"And I don't want to buy any more either," I finish. "I can't ruin lives the way our lives were destroyed. Some mothers would still have their sons if I wasn't out here trapping."

Sheek looks back at me, and slowly nods his head.

"I told you I support you no matter what, my dude," he says. "Don't feel guilty for nobody's choices though."

He pauses, and we stare at each other in silence.

"They are gonna get that poison regardless," he says before we pause again. "The world's a f*#% up place. It makes no difference if we do what we do."

Sheek always has an effortless way of putting things in perspective. It wasn't going to change my mind this time, though. I thought about how my gluttony has gotten me everything I wanted and more. Most of it, I didn't need. The mountains of DVDs, dozens of PlayStation games, clothes I rarely wear. I had become content with my overindulgent lifestyle, all obtained at the expense of other peoples' suffering. The hunger I had when I was 15 years old transformed into greed...or even worse... gluttony. Greed is when you desire much more than you need, and keep it all for yourself. I had much more than what I needed now. I had become the money addict that Crackhead Carol said I would become years ago. Gluttony was the reason why I couldn't stop when I was 15 years old. It's the reason why I had made it this far. It ends right now, though. Today.

"I'm tired of going to bed at night knowing I could be the reason why some kids are going to be hungry," I say.

"It's not you, bruh. It's the parents," he says. "Whether you sell the drugs to them or not, they will still get it."

During the next pause, I think about Juju. I never actually got to apologize to him for my Macho Man Randy Savage assault in elementary school.

"Of course it ain't fair!" Sheek continued, "but it's a cold world, nah-mean? I'm still feeling the chills from the days when the world was cold to us. We used to be those kids going to bed hungry. If anybody deserves to eat off this poison now, it's us!"

I sat in deep thought, speechless.

"I understand where you're coming from, though," he says. "It won't be the same without you, King. We build untouchable dynasties every time we come together for this. I can't sleep at night knowing that you can't sleep at night, though. You gotta do whatever brings you peace, kid."

"Are we selling to fiends, or are we the fiends ourselves?" I ask.

Sheek was not ready to let go yet. He had a look in his eyes. Not because of the gluttony or anything. It was because it was the only thing he knew. The streets caught him before any real job would hire him, and they haven't let go since day one. No one has ever just walked away from it. That is, until now.

Sheek was my brother in arms. We were like soldiers struggling in a war together. By some miracle, we were even in college together. Nobody ever told us to go. No one even told us to go to high school. We both have busy schedules now. We only meet a few people a few times a week to sell poison—giving us the ultimate flexibility and the highest return for the time we invest. With all the people we have hustling our packages for us, we literally make money in our sleep. Am I ready to leave this life alone?

"As a matter of fact," I say "you can keep the rest of that poison, or let me use it to get that guitar that dope fiend was trying to sell."

"I don't want it," Sheek says. "Get the guitar. You'll be the only nigga in the hood walking away from the game, and the only nigga in the hood with a guitar."

We sit in a brief silence.

I dig into my pocket and retrieve my pinky ring. Sheek delivers a sinister smirk as I put it on my pinky. We perform our ritualistic handshake, and our pink rings clamor louder than ever before.

"I guess the trap done made you tap out," he says. "This may be a defeat, but it's a defeat better than most victories."

This concludes 1/3rd of Origins. The full book is forthcoming.

BOOK TWO — MILLION: MONEY ON MY MIND

Miraculously completing high school after being expelled, Amir reluctantly enrolls in community college. After his thirst for knowledge is awakened, he doubles his high school GPA and plunges into a 12-year educational voyage across the country. In the process, Amir graduates from the top public university in New Jersey, receives his law degree from Florida's leading university in Miami, and obtains a doctorate in Los Angeles from one of the nation's top 25 universities. By the time he completes his fifth college degree, Amir discovers education's power to take him anywhere and allow him to do anything. But his lifelong passion to understand the world comes with a hefty consequence: a student debt bill close to a million dollars over his lifetime.

Chapter 1: Reckoning Day

In September 2014, I sent Amir a letter I'd been anxious to deliver for quite some time. He initially tossed it in a drawer and avoided opening it for weeks. Eventually, it became a ghost eerily taunting him. A few days before turning 30-years-old, he opened the letter in hopes that it would not kill his birthday vibe.

The letter contained a series of charts, numbers, legal jargon, and financial gibberish. The portion that had the greatest impact on Amir was a number: $918,031. He stared at it without blinking, thinking of what he could buy with that type of money. How he could live off of it for 25 years, at least. After pondering how long it would take to pay it off, he looked to the left of the letter and saw that I had already done precise calculations for him. It would take at least 28 years of payments, averaging $2,723 a month, to pay the debt.

"That's damn near my entire paycheck!" he said, "And they want me to pay it for just as long as I've been on this earth?!"

The name's Sammy. I'm Amir's estranged uncle. You can call me Uncle Sam, or "U.S." for short. I am the spirit of the richest and most influential country in the world, the United States of America. Samuel L. Jackson swiped my attitude and demeanor. Anthony Bourdain jacked my sarcasm and cynicism. The worst bits of my arrogance and greed inspired the Donald Trump's of the world. Amir owes me so much money, I figured I'd write this chronicle in his anthology to speed up the payment process. I've come to loom over his post-graduation life like a mini-raincloud, following his every step.

In his efforts to become one of the most educated people in the world, Amir racked up nearly $350,000 in student loans. He claims to have a plan to pay it off soon in order to avoid paying the tripled amount after interest is applied. Still, the letter sent a jolt through his system and caused him to question whether 12 years of college was the right investment. It didn't take him much consideration to conclude that it was worth every penny. The tangible qualifications from five college degrees were grand; but the intangible memories, moments, and people he encountered in the process were priceless. It critically shaped the person he became, and he couldn't imagine who he'd be if he had not experienced the 12 years.

It was a miracle that Amir completed high school in the first place. Throughout the process he got arrested, kicked out of school, and briefly dropped out. He lived in four different houses during these years bouncing between parents, grandmothers, and aunts. Unsure about what to do after getting his diploma, Amir signed up for a for-profit technical college. The school planned on charging Amir $20,000 for a "Computers and Technology Certificate" he would complete in a year. None of the course credits were eligible to transfer to a college where he could get an actual degree. He became uneasy about the school over the summer, while working at a supermarket (making $7.25 an hour) with a recent graduate of theirs.

Most people were shocked that Amir finished high school, and no one bothered to talk to him about college. He waited for the counselors like he'd seen on the TV shows, but they never came to his class. Everybody and their mama told him he was not "college material." Both of his parents were locked up for most of his high school years, and neither of them had gone to college themselves. Luckily, during the summer after graduation, his cousin —Deborah

Joyce Hinds (Rest in Peace)—was doing career development work and encouraged him to enroll in the local community college instead of the technical college. She saved him from making a $20,000 mistake just two weeks before classes started there.

Amir wasn't just the first person in his family to go to college. If you traced his genealogy of the direct line of males he descended from, he was the first male in his family to graduate high school. His father dropped out in the 1980's when drugs, mass incarceration, and de-industrialization decimated cities, hope, and opportunities. His maternal grandfather migrated from South Carolina to take a New York factory job in the 1950's, and this didn't require a diploma. His great-grandfather grew up in the rural south, and was a teenager during The Great Depression of the 1930's. The generation before that were sharecroppers in the early 1900's, with limited educational opportunities offered to Negroes. And the generations before that, which may be traceable to the 1700's, were forbidden from learning to read by law. In South Carolina, the Slave Code of 1740 prohibited slaves from learning to read and write, gathering without a white person present, or growing their own food. By the 1800s, some states expanded these laws to exclude free blacks from learning how to read as well.

"If any slave, Negro, or free person of color, or any white person, shall teach any other slave, Negro, or free person of color, to read or write … [he/she] shall be punished by fine and whipping, or fine or whipping"

-Slave Codes of the State of Georgia, 1848

You know, while we are on the topic, let's just address the elephant in the room. I'm friggin' sorry for slavery, okay! I know that's not enough, but my bad, from the bottom of my soul. Amir out rightly refuses to accept his Uncle Sam's apology. He views the hundreds of thousands of dollars paid out for his education as a form of reparations.

"Forty acres and a mule?" he said. "More like fo' hunnit thousand and some school!"

The mental chains forced on black people for most of American history were often Amir's motivation for taking his education to its zenith. Ironically, it came at a price high enough to make me damn-near own the mutha #$!%@. So this book—which is partially mine—is a narration of Amir's 12 years of college across America. We will relive the events, traditions, and courses that both answered his questions, and caused more confusion. We will reflect on some of his formative interactions: living with 16 different roommates, making dozens of friends, and taking classes with more than a hundred professors. Writings from his actual journals will tell most of the story. Throughout the journey, we'll share the wisdom and tips Amir learned the hard way—many of which could only happen in America.

God Bless me.

God Bless America.

Chapter 2: Union County College

The most difficult level of college for Amir was his first, and lowest. Like most community or county colleges, Union County College (UCC) in New Jersey only offered courses that went into the 200 level. The number assigned to a college course represents its level, year, or degree of difficulty. For example, English 101 is the universal freshman—or first-year course in English that all college students must take. Graduate school courses for masters and doctorate degrees go up to the 700 level.

Amir wasn't even at the 101 level his freshman year. He wishes he "started from the bottom" at UCC. Instead, he had to take several semesters of remedial courses to become college-ready. So his first year and a half of college was comprised of prerequisite English, Reading, and Mathematics courses to help him reach the level expected of all first-year American university students. Unfortunately, students do not receive college credit for these remedial courses. Starting with so many non-credit courses caused Amir to spend an extra year at UCC. These courses and inadequate preparation also contribute to the fact that less than 7% of UCC's students graduate within three years. Amir used leftover drug money to pay for extra summer courses in order to graduate within this timeframe. It was the first time he regretted cutting class, not turning in his homework, and rarely studying throughout high school.

The inner-city high school Amir graduated from was also not equipped to prepare him for college. Just look at this actual writing assignment he handed in freshman year at UCC! It's filled with misspellings and grammatical errors in every sentence.

I am a student out of Plainfield High School, one of the academiclly lowest school in the state of New Jersey. I have only been at UCC for about a week and I can see entirely signifacant difference in the amount of expectations amoung the teachers. In order to survive here and at a university, I will be needing many things to keep me motavated so I can stay focus along the way.

I think my strongest source of motavation is my fear of failure. I have this fear because I come from a family with little succes. In my intermediate family, my mom didnt make it past the 10th grade and my father didn't make it past the 11th. On both sides of my family, the grandchildren have already began to repeat the cycle of failure. Knowing how much my grandmothers want to see me succed also keep me strong.

I think my biggest problem will be with finances. With my college scedule and schoolwork , it will be hard to work enough hours to buy everything that I want and pay my bills. Another threat to my education is girls. In UCC it seems asif every 3.2 seconds a cute girls walks past that I have to look at. And if that isnt a big enough problem, I finnd myself thinking about girls for a consitarable amount of my day.

-Amir, Fall 2002

This career research assignment from later that year wasn't much better.

My major at UCC is Computer Science. After the completion of the Associate's degree program here, my plans are to transfer to Hawaii Pacific University. My career objectives begin with me starting with an internship, three months after that starting at Microsoft with my career as Computer Support Specialist, then maybe a couple of years later become a Technical Support Manager. My ultimate goal is to open a buisness with my brother entitled "Chips & Whips" where we specialize in computers and cars.

Aside from the slightly humiliating, but necessary, remedial courses at UCC, many external factors made Amir's first college experience the most difficult. He had to commute across campuses in three cities, day and night. This inconsistent schedule caused him to lose his job and resort to trappin'...again. Getting to UCC was also a hassle since his driver's license was suspended most of his freshman year. Because of the drug charges Amir was found guilty of at age 15, his license was suspended long before he even sat behind the wheel of a car. Driving and trappin' are not that related, but that's American justice for you. To make matters worse, teenage Amir was also fined nearly $2,000 for trappin'. Yup. We punish crimes of poverty with penalties the further engulf citizens in poverty.

After getting his license reinstated, three consecutive used cars broke down on Amir in his second year at UCC. Once again, he had to devote nearly 20 hours a week utilizing a most inconvenient network of buses and trains, along with his bicycle, to get to the campuses.

The emotional baggage and struggles that complicated his adolescence did not cease in young adulthood either. Financial struggles were abundant. He bailed five family members and friends out of jail for minor violations and arrest warrants. He sent money to incarcerated friends and family members. At times, he paid his grandparents' mortgage and bills. He damn-near lost his financial aid, until he collected a compilation of documents requested by the federal government. The U.S. Department of Education inquired about him listing his grandparents as his guardians when he applied for financial aid. The Department wanted proof that his grandparents were his legal guardians. In a humiliating letter, Amir explained that his parents were incarcerated, and as a result, he had unofficially fallen back into the custody of his grandparents.

Amir almost lost his financial aid a twice at UCC. In his second near-broke encounter, Amir was placed on financial aid probation for lack of "Satisfactory Academic Progress." Because he had to take so many non-credit remedial courses, Amir barely had a full year's credit at the end of his second year of college. His funding was frozen until he filed an appeal.

Mother Nature herself became a barrier during the historical and record-breaking snowstorm—The Blizzard of 2003. The storm struck the East Coast hard, covering cities in up to 30 inches of snow. For whatever reason, UCC was allergic to snow days. One day when Amir arrived on campus in the morning, there was "only" four or five inches of snow on the ground. Snowflakes fell relentless throughout the rest of the day, as the college slowly emptied out towards the evening. By the time his last class ended, nearly ten inches of snow had piled up. He waited several hours for canceled buses, before reluctantly asking his grandfather to come pick him up.

Nature, financial issues, transportation struggles, family problems, and an underdeveloped high school education collectively made Amir's community college experience more difficult than the three universities that followed. UCC broke him down to the closest he ever came to dropping out of college. Nevertheless, it also provided an essential academic foundation necessary to thrive at a university. The social-emotional struggle provided preparation for future challenges.

Chapter 3: The UCC Journals

Ages: 19-20 Years Old

February 24, 2004

Wut up Journal?

Today, I decided that many things happen every day that must be documented. Therefore, I will be writing something here every day, or at least trying.

Today was a typical day. Went to school, went to New York City for a bit to buy clothes to sell on the internet, then ran a few errands. But I learned something, more like noticed something that had always been. The generation before us has failed substantially. I started thinking about it when I gave my grandmother a check for $1,000. She said she had checks bouncing left and right and wasn't going to be able to pay anything until March. I offered to loan her some money. She said sure, and when I asked if $1,000 was enough, her eyes lit up with excitement. She didn't know what to say. I didn't mind doing it of course, but I'm her 19-year-old grandson. She has six children ages 38 through 45, and they should be taking care of their mother. But the past generation has failed. I also sent my cousin Ray Ray some money today in prison. His mother can't because she is incarcerated as well.

But there is some good news. I put the plates on my third car this year today. A cherry red 1998 Pontiac Sunfire.

February 25, 2004

<u>Discrimination</u>

The day started out normal. Got to campus, then went to Accounting II. I missed the last class but easily got up to pace. I also found out I had the highest score on the last test. The professor congratulated me as I walked in the class, late as usual. I haven't been on time yet, and I have also missed like 5 out of the 12 classes. Also, I share my book with my boys Sheek and Harry, and because of that, I wasn't able to study properly for the test. Regardless of the circumstances, I still aced it!! Not only that, but most of the class got at least 20 points below my score. I'm not sure why I'm so good at accounting. Could be the result of managing our books while we were trappin'. I have to take two levels of accounting for my major (Business/Information Systems).

At the end of the lecture, the Professor handed out an extra credit worksheet because the class had done so poorly on the test. When I attempted to get one, she wouldn't let me. She said that you had to have lower than a 70 on the test to qualify for extra credit. It seemed as if the entire class got one.

"That's discrimination!" I yelled, as I walked out of class.

"Real cute, Amir," she replied, as the class erupted in laughter.

Not only was I one of the few people to pass the test, but I was also one of three black people in the class.

After class, I went down to the common area and found my comrades politicking. Javon started telling a story about getting some girl's number. I pretended to listen. I handed Harry my accounting book so he could use it in his class tomorrow. After a few minutes, a cute girl walked past. Harry said "F*** it!" and got up to follow her. He returned a few moments later, saying he was successful in kicking it to her. I asked if he got her number.

"She took mine," he said. "She wanted to make sure that she heard from me."

Bullsh*t, I thought, before envisioning her throwing his number away after he left.

***

February 27th, 2004

<u>3rd Crushless Year</u>

Today was exhausting. It started with my boy Nyce waking me up at 6 a.m. to ask a question that really could have waited a few hours. He was all jizzed up on some no-doze pills that kept him from falling asleep while he drove from Jersey to Virginia. We were on the phone most of the night too. I didn't get much sleep. I woke up, then went to campus for the trip to Kean University. I didn't wanna go. I was going to be on campus every day this week except Sunday. I went, though, and was glad I did. It was my first time on a university campus. I can't wait to transfer and make new friends. I will be a master of the guitar by the time I transfer. I might go to Rutgers University on Tuesday. I was supposed to go help out at the church at 3:00 p.m., but I couldn't because me and the fellas went to New York for a bit. Good times, though.

When I finally got home, I was exhausted. I tried to take a nap, but couldn't. I promised my little brother Tyson that I would let him borrow some games. He's getting into trouble all of the time. He's under house arrest for 30 days. He has the same probation officer that me, our older brother Jamal, and Pookie had.

I stopped by my grandmother's house and chilled for a bit. There were four generations in the room: Nana, my mom, me, and my niece Tookie, who is a few months old. She is a piece-of-work. She got excited when she saw me. When I tried to leave, she started yelling and reaching out for me. They think she is mistaking me for her father, but she knows her Uncle Mir!

Today marked the third year that my grandfather left his physical form. February 27, 2001, he left me. Janice, his widow, printed a RIP anniversary picture in the paper. I have to stop by and see her. I miss Grandpa. I often wonder what it would be like if he were here today. I will never forget his last Christmas. I was 16 years old, and he was in the hospital very sick. I entered the room to see him, and his face lit up with joy. I was always his favorite grandson, "Mi-Mi." All of his hair had fallen out, and he couldn't even talk. He just kept murmuring. I understood him though. He said Janice was the only one who had come by to see him. Both my brother and father were in jail. They would have come if they could. But no one else came to see him, not even the people who looked like superstars in the limos during his funeral a few months later.

I was so alone at his funeral service without my brother and father. No one else understood the connection the four of us had. I still have the Get-Well card that I got Grandpa, but never had a chance to give him. Inside the card, I wrote, "Hurry up and get well so we can go fishing!" I couldn't get a ride to the hospital to see him for a while. By the time I could, he was in a coma. I remember my uncle saying, "I don't know why you brought that card. It ain't no good." I felt stupid.

I will never forget you, Grandpa.

***

March 9th, 2004

<u>Letter to Drug Court</u>

To Judge Dupri, Officer Marque, and the entire Union County Drug Court Staff:

My name is Amir Whitaker and I am the second oldest son of a participant in your program, named Tasha Whitaker. I would like to give you my greatest thanks for the improvement that you've made with my mom. In all my years of living, I have never seen her in better condition and happier. Now we say goodnight to each other and say that we love each other every day for the first time ever. As long as I can remember, my mom has had a problem with drugs and has never been able to provide for me like a mother should. But now she is there for me, and it makes me the happiest that I have been in my entire life. I can remember being in elementary school and always thinking that my mom never loved me because of how I was neglected. Now I'm a mature college student, and I understand that it was never her that didn't love me, it was the drugs. I can see now that drugs love no one, and they do nothing but cause problems. That's why I refuse to put them inside of my body. If my mom were not drug-free, it would make college even harder for me, but since I see a drug-free mother every day, it helps me get up in the morning and go to school. Almost every day I tell her if she was ever to touch drugs I would not have the least amount of respect for her, and she always screams back "I WON'T!!" It gives me the strength to give everything my best.

Again, thanks.
Sincerely,
Amir Whitaker

***

May 14, 2004

<u>Happy Mother's Day</u>

Not a week after Mother's Day, just informed.
Not a week after Mother's Day, and my soul's been scorned.
As I speak, my mom is in a cage.

Just a week after Mother's Day, and she couldn't maintain.
I guess her feelings of dissatisfaction will always remain.
Yesterday I was informed for the umpteenth time,
That my mother had been apprehended for a mysterious crime.

And it's not even a week after Mother's Day.

A Louis Vuitton bag with five pairs of matching designer Shades.
A card signed by three children that Hallmark made.
It's what she says she always wanted. She has been telling me for a while,
But when we showed it to her, she didn't even smile.
Symptoms that could have been seen by the blind.
It was so obvious she was in the danger zone.
As a recovering addict who just lost her job, and was forced to move into a drug-infested home.
And it wasn't even a week after Mother's Day.

* * *

July 2, 2004

<u>My Car, My System, My Problems</u>

Wut up.

     I know it's been awhile. I don't even know why. A lot has occurred. I had almost $7,500 three weeks ago. Now that is reduced to $1,500. Most days that I spent over $500 were not even premeditated. It sucks when you wake up consecutive days not thinking about spending money, but end up spending several hundred. $3,000 went to paying off my car, which was a wise choice. The balance was $3,888, but the cokehead car dealer was thirsty and said he would let it go for $3,000 more. So I paid about $6000 for the car total. Every penny of it earned by my hard work. I don't know another 19-year-old who has done that…legally.

     True financial issues came when I was raped for $641 from Discover. They said someone made a purchase from the clothing website I run with a stolen credit card. So I'm liable for the $641, as well as the $300+ in merchandise to fulfill the order. I also helped Nana out with more than $2,000 to pay her mortgage. When I woke up yesterday, I didn't plan to spend $500. I planned to get my brakes checked out because I heard a grinding noise. Come to find out, my rotors were f*****d up badly. It's an issue that should have been taken care of at the car dealership. I only had the car for four months.

     Justice does not exist. According to my calculations, I spent over $10,000 on cars within the past year. Being grown sucks. I remember as a child, we used to say "my car, my system" whenever we saw a decent car. Now I'm grown and have my own, along with all its problems.

     Mo cars, mo problems.

***

September 28, 2004

<u>At Least</u>

No more booties in my face until 3 o'clock. Well, I can make no promises. I'm still young you know. At least for another two weeks. We went to the strip club Charlie's Angels. I used a fake ID to get in and it was aiight. I don't think I will be going to many strip clubs though. It kind of hurts seeing my sistas degrade themselves. Didn't stop me from tipping them though.

A lot has changed, again. The amount of people here with me at Grandma's place has doubled from three to six. Now there is Uncle Reggie, Uncle Chuck, and my brother Jamal. Uncle Reggie is OK and shaking off the 12-year prison sentence he just came home from. He is already turning back to the street, not knowing what else to do.

School is back in session. So far, so good. These are some of the easiest professors ever. I'll try to get all A's this semester. I'm pretty sure I want to transfer to Rutgers now. I'm starting the application now. I should be good because of my 3.0 GPA, Dean's list, Phi Theta Kappa, and Black Heritage Club. Also, I have A's in three out of my five classes now.

Things are well otherwise. I'm much better on guitar, and so is Jamal. I don't have much money now, but it's not the first, and won't be the last time. Mom just came home from prison, but was medically discharged. They discovered that she had cancer and cut her prison time short so she could be home with family. I know hundreds of people who have been incarcerated, but only one to receive a medical discharged. He died shortly afterward from the illness they released him for. At this point, I've spent too much time contemplating if my mother is going to die soon. I'm through crying. I've cried headaches. All I can do now is enjoy every moment with her. I can't even pray anymore. I can't beg the Creator to do something different than what is already planned. I can't beg for the obvious. Surely the Creator knows that a son wants his mother to live, right? I hope she can at least see her grandchildren, my graduation from Rutgers, and my marriage.

At least.

***

January 27, 2005

Home Stretch

Wut up.

Thangs changing. Got a new gig as a tutor for the EOF program. This is the Education Opportunity Fund, a program that gives financial support to students from "educationally and economically disadvantaged backgrounds," like myself. In my three years at UCC, they have provided me with structure, forced me to study, and made sure I was on track to graduate. I wouldn't be graduating soon without the help of Brian, my EOF counselor.

I've been required to meet with him periodically since my first day here in 2002. He made sure I took my proper classes and stayed focus.

My typical day involves working as a tutor from 11 to 5 PM, then going to class from 5 to 10 PM. Yesterday was the first full day, and it wasn't too bad. I'm free at least 4 out of the 6 hours that I work. I do a lot of studying, writing, and reading…you know, just keeping my mind chiseled. I'm paid through this federal program called "work study," and that's kind of the point.

I have been writing some of my best rhymes. Pure fire, if I do say so myself. I'm also taking music more seriously. I started recording with a few local rappers, and we already have three songs done. My licks on the guitar are blazing. My rhymes make me want to consider being a rapper, but I can't. I have a far better chance getting a record deal with a band. Maybe I'll just write a hit for someone. One thing's for sure, music is keeping me out of trouble. There were a few times where I declined invitations to hang out with the fellas, and something went down (arrests, shooting, drama, etc.). Self-expression is literally saving my life. Getting that guitar a few years ago for $200 worth a crack was a great investment. Writing in this journal for hours over the past year also saved me from a bit of drama. Music and writing collectively allow me to pause and process the world while exploring my soul.

    I can't believe I'm in my last semester here at UCC. Home stretch, baby! I can't wait 'til that day in May. I'll feel so much better with that degree!

***

May 23, 2005

<u>Who's Who? I'm Me! With Honors!</u>

    Haven't felt this good in a while. Haven't had one of these graduation caps on in three years. I couldn't resist, even though there's still got 44 hours until graduation. My adrenaline rushed the moment I received it. I put it on and boogied around my room to some Funkadelic.

    I can't believe it's finally here! After three years of night classes, Saturday classes, summer classes, 2-mile walks to campus, four cars breaking down. Three years of hard grind. Sitting back reflecting, I went through a lot, but I'm only halfway there. Shhiiiiieeeeeed I feel like I can do this another ten years! If I don't have to pay, that is.

I'm just coming home from an awards ceremony. I got two prestigious award plaques. I gave one to Nana and one to Grandma. I was one of 20 UCC students (out of the 11,200) to receive the "Who's Who Among UCC Students" Honor. Professors select winners based on academic achievement, community service, and leadership. I'm also graduating with gold on, too. Honors cords! I remember in my high school graduation looking at the handful of people with gold, feeling jealous. Thinking how their parents forced them to get good grades, while my parents didn't even force me to go to school. They wouldn't have been able to do much anyways from behind prison walls. Now I wonder how the hundreds of graduates will feel looking at my gold on graduation. Bling Bling, n*gga!

I remember I was ashamed of attending a community college at first. I had family and friends say it wasn't a "real college," but that couldn't be further from the truth. It's like saying the bottom three steps are not part of a staircase. They may be the bottom three steps, but they're still higher than the ground, and still get you closer to the sky. I'm moving on up in 44 hours.

***

June 10, 2005

<u>Progress</u>

Same panoramic view as last summer when I came here to visit my mom. Only this time, I'm not coming to pay visits to anyone. We drove here three-deep, but it will most likely only be two of us on the way back. Today is my little brother Tyson's court date.

"Are you coming in?" asked my dad.

"No," I replied. "I don't want to see that sh*t."

So, I'm by myself here, parked in the same spot as that Sunday morning when I was visiting my mom at the county jail last year. I had to be here at 7 o'clock in the morning to put my name on the list for the 11 o'clock visits. Instead of driving back home for an hour, I brought my guitar and practiced in the car. Today is a bit different, though, because I brought my notebook instead. This time, I also have a fancy piece of paper. One that no one in my family or anyone from my neighborhood has. It's a college degree. Just because I got one, I don't rub it in either.

"You're real humble about it," Nyce said.

My graduation cookout was incredible! I can't believe all those people were there to celebrate ME—people from the church, from the hood, family, friends, and others. I got over $500 in the cards.

"At least someone in the f*cking family did it!" said my cousin, Ray Ray.

"You are the only one to do it, Mir!" said the homies.

Many people came through that I hadn't seen in a while. The celebration reminded me of where I came from, and what I overcame. All in all, it was probably the best day of my life. It was also my first performance, too. Me, Jamal, and Uncle Kev just jammed out for the crowd. It was aiight for a group that didn't rehearse.

Chapter 4: Rutgers University

By the time Amir made it to Rutgers University, he was beginning to fall into the rhythm of college. He began "feelin' himself," as his confidence grew, both academically and socially. It was a way for him to cope with his insecurities about transitioning from a college to a university. The insecurity was elevated by doubts about his ability to succeed as a first-generation college student, who was underprepared at his public schools.

Of the 4,000+ colleges across the United States, Rutgers University was one of the first to exist. It was one of the nine "Colonial Colleges" formed before the American Revolution was fought and America officially became a country. From the 1630's to the 1760's, these colleges laid the foundation for American education. Seven of the nine colleges went on to become the Ivy League schools we know today. You know: Harvard, Yale, Princeton, Cornell, University of Pennsylvania, Brown, and Dartmouth. Rutgers is not a part of the "Ivy Club," because it chose to remain more accessible by continuing as a public university and rejecting the social elitism of the other institutions. Rutgers is still considered a "Public Ivy" though, which puts it in a class with schools like UCLA, University of North Carolina, Penn State, and Berkeley. Amir was sold on Rutgers after his favorite book, The Autobiography of Malcolm X (1965), referred to Rutgers as an Ivy League institution.

"I had spoken at well over fifty colleges and universities, like Brown, Harvard, Yale, Columbia, and Rutgers, in the Ivy League, and others throughout the country." -Malcolm X

Rutgers University, or "RU," started in 1766, but not for people like Amir. For most of its history, it was only open to white males. If this is surprising to you, you might wanna brush up on my history. As was the case with many elite American universities, admission was not open to women and Negroes until the 20th century. (Pardon my use of the word "Negro." It's a habit I have when discussing Neg-... black history before the 1960's.) In 1915, Paul Robeson became the third African American student to attend Rutgers. He was the first Negro student to try out for the Rutgers Scarlet Knights football team. During tryouts, unnecessary roughness fueled by the racism of the other players, lead to a broken nose and dislocated shoulder. When the Scarlet Knights played some southern teams, the opponents refused to play unless Robeson remained off the field. Now that's some serious hateration. They felt they were too good to step on the same graaaaaaaass as the n*gga! (Ok...sorry for the use of the "N" word. My angry Samuel L. Jackson attitude comes out when narrating dark moments in history.)

Paul Robeson went on to become the only RU athlete in his class to make the All-American team. He played several sports, dominated on the debate team, and graduated as the valedictorian of his class. While playing in the National Football League (NFL), he received his degree from Columbia Law School. After graduating, his acting and singing helped catapult the Harlem Renaissance—the Cultural Revolution that is the grandfather of hip-hop and other American arts. Robeson was a major force in the Civil Rights Movement, and was so radical that the government took his passport and restricted his travel. That's how the land of the free rolls sometimes, ya know. Robeson was Amir's hero because, in the face of adversity, he took his Rutgers education and went on to become one of the greatest Americans who ever lived. He paved the way for Amir to go to RU in blood, sweat, tears, and broken body parts.

By the time Amir got to Rutgers in 2005, it had become one of the most diverse universities in the country. Today it's 42% white, 26% Asian, 13% Hispanic, 8% Black, with 7% international students on top of that. Rutgers has remained the highest-ranking public university in the New Jersey and New York area for quite some time. It attracted Amir because of the combination of low price and high quality. The private universities he attended later on in his educational career cost four times as much per credit. The annual federal grants that covered Amir's three years at UCC also covered all of his Rutgers' tuition. These grants are part of the billions of dollars that I, Uncle Sam—I mean, the United States government—provides to help students from low-income families pay for college. Amir scored two free college degrees from me, but that's aiight, though. As they say in The Trap, "The first one is always free."

The few thousand dollars in student loans Amir had to take out while at Rutgers paid for his dorm and other college costs. The increased opportunity to focus, and the lifelong friends he made by staying on campus made this well worth the investment. During his first year, he lived in the Livingston Campus' Quad 3 with his roommate, Jay. He was an economics major and sneakerhead from Madagascar, by way of Maryland. Half of their 14 x 15 foot dorm stayed covered in rare Nikes, many still in their original orange boxes.

During his final year at Rutgers, Amir moved into a house a few blocks from the New Brunswick campus with four guys he met in Quad 3. Each one had a distinctive personality that, I swear to God on my country, mirrored the four Teenage Mutant Ninja Turtles. These four white boys were critical in healing Amir's previous I-want-to-destroy-the-white-race-one-crack-rock-at-a-time attitude. Combined, they were the perfect blend of chill that led to legendary memories, moments, and parties.

Well, I take that back. That roommate Rob was a young man with "no chill." Absolutely none, whatsoever. He had the character traits of the Ninja Turtle named Raphael: occasionally hot-tempered and loud-mouthed, but a lot more wise-cracking. He was the most die-hard Yankees fan in the universe, and could not resist talking trash to anyone wearing a Mets, Red Sox, or Phillies hat. While living in Quad 3, Rob and Jay tormented random students with Howard Stern-style prank calls. They were so severe, students called the campus police on them...several times. Rob got a real kick out of reading about it the day after on the police blotter. Amir and the squad often came close to brawls with fellow students because of Rob's slick mouth.

"Take a look at this sh*t-stain!" Rob said, as he pointed at a guy, previously minding his own damn business.

It was directed at a short white boy with a Red Sox hat turned to the back, wearing hip-hop style clothing. For whatever reason, Rob hated white people who wore backwards hats. A heated argument ensued, but luckily the crew was near their campus bus stop. There were only two things that slowed Rob down: his girlfriend Emilia, and mandatory bed rest after twisting his ankle due to sloppy drunken tumbles. Hailing from South Jersey, Rob studied economics at Rutgers.

Another roommate lacking in chill was Michael T. Ross. Because there were so many guys named Mike or Michael, everyone eternally referred to this roommate as "Mike-Ross," even when talking directly to him.

"Yo Mike-Ross," said Rob, "You know the rules man. No Ikes in the house after 10 p.m. on weeknights."

Out of the five roommates, Mike-Ross raged the hardest, by far. He favored the outgoing, party animal Ninja Turtle with the same name: Mike aka Michelangelo. "The Ikes" were his compadres who paralleled Mike-Ross' ragefest tendencies. The term originated in 2006 during a conversation amongst the four new roommates faced with a dilemma. The roommates were vexed with the reality that their fifth roommate, Mike-Ross, rolled with a crew of suburban hooligans with a wicked tendency to drunkenly rage their faces off. They were as loud as hurricanes, and equally destructive to everything in their path. Something had to be done to ensure the house remained in one piece so that the roommates received their security deposits back. The four roommates strategized ways to control Mike-Ross' friends during parties and gatherings.

"They need to wear bright orange vests and friggin 'Warning' labels."- Roommate 1, Rob

"And hard hats. And Mike-Ross has to pack up all sharp and breakable objects before they come over."- Roommate 2, Nate

"We must restrict them from 80% of the house. We can limit them to the front porch when they are really raging."- Roommate 3, Chris

"We'll call them 'Mike & Ikes' like the candy. We'll scream 'Ike-Alert,' when they start getting reckless."- Roommate 4, Amir

Countless Ike-Alerts ensued, along with the unstoppable annihilation of their college house. Attempts to halt the destruction were futile. The walls became holier than Swiss cheese— penetrated by fists, chairs, and the occasional head-butt. The Ikes were responsible for all three "Disturbing the Peace" ticket violations, which cost hundreds of dollars and frequently brought the police to the house. The house came equipped with a fire extinguisher for emergencies, but the Ikes used it to cover the kitchen and each other in its yellow powder. If you fell asleep around an Ike, you might wake up with your toenails painted black, or something worse resulting from their homoerotic torment tactics (i.e. "tea bagging"). Bar fights were a common occurrence with the Ikes, who usually forgot what the scrap was for a few hours later.

Luckily, most of the Ikes went to out-of-state colleges like the University of North Carolina (UNC), New York University (NYU), and Princeton, so the ninja turtle roommates only had to worry about them on occasional weekends when they came home. But the Ikes who attended Rutgers were permanent fixtures—

magically appearing every Thursday evening with a case of beer so cheap, it damn-near tasted like water. Often times, Mike-Ross himself would blackout twice in one weekend...before Saturday. Amir was accustomed to Mike-Ross knocking on his door in the morning, disheveled and confused, seeking assistance in recollecting the night's escapades.

"We pre-gamed here until things got too rowdy," said Amir. "On the way to Knight Club, you stole someone's lawn furniture. You put it on our front porch, but decided we should at least have the decency to hide it in the backyard. After two rounds of drinks, we got kicked out of Knight Club because Ike #2 wouldn't stop screaming 'Bon Jovi!' to the DJ every minute or so. We then went to a frat party, which was an epic sausagefest. Ike #3 stole the tap right off their keg. Next, we stopped for some Fat Sandwiches, only to throw them up later. Ike #4 almost got into a fight while we were waiting for the food. We came home and passed out...sorta. Ike # 2 drew a large penis on the wall and autographed it. Last, but certainly not least, Ike #3 may or may not have teabagged your forehead."

One night, Amir tapped into his inner-Ike, doing a kegstand that resulted in him flipping over and landing on his neck. During this classic college party move, companions scream "Chug! Chug! Chug!," while the participant clings upside-down to the 50-gallon bucket of ice holding the keg of beer. Supporters hold the participant's legs up in the air while he/she guzzles beer straight from the keg's spigot. Because both arms are required to support your body during the handstand, every drop of the beer is forced into your mouth until your companions feel you've had enough. It's an intricate operation that usually takes four or five people to execute (or two to three Ikes). When Amir did this kegstand, the ice bucket slipped out from under him because of the melted ice water. With nothing to break his fall, Amir had no option but to land on his face. As he healed, he couldn't help but wonder if the Ikes had flipped him on purpose to deliver similar unnecessary roughness like Paul Robeson was subjected to decades earlier. Amir later learned that the experience was a secret society style initiation into the Ike Brotherhood.

The Ikes had their own language and vocabulary. They'd often remove the second part of a word to make it sound hipper. So instead of something being "decent," it was simply "deece." Instead of it being "definitely not," it was "deff not." Levels of drunkenness were also represented by combining the word "sh*t" with completely unrelated words. If you were stumbling or throwing up, you were considered a "sh*t-show." The spectrum also included words like shi*t-faced, sh*t-wrecked, sh*t-housed, sh*t-rocked, and plenty of others describing the magnitude of Ike recklessness.

By the time they moved out of the house, the roommates would not receive a single penny of their $2,200 security deposit because of the havoc and destruction of the Ikes. Instead of apologizing or paying the roommates back, the Ikes felt the roommates actually owed them money for providing "The Time of Your Frickin' Life!"

The last two roommates in Amir's Ninja Turtle House were chiller than polar bears' toenails when compared to Mike-Ross. You may remember Nate, the Renaissance Man who Amir rendezvoused with all around the world. Nate was often the unofficial leader of the house, the Leonardo of the Ninja Turtles. It was his idea to charge $3 for drinks at their house parties, host gambling tournaments, and engage in other quasi-illegal schemes for come-ups. Lastly, there was Chris from North Dakota. He was the Donatello of the Ninja Turtles, the brainiest of the roommates. Chris was a philosophy major and possessed a plethora of random knowledge. Rob called him "Chrisopedia." Rob also had endless jokes about Chris experiencing culture shock from the Jersey shrewdness and other varying regional social norms he never experienced in the Midwest.

The four roommates, the Ikes, and various other college interactions provided Amir with a much-needed education in "White People 101." In his high school graduating class of hundreds, there were only two white guys—John and Jeff. Aside from Arthur from the baseball team, Amir didn't recall any other white peers from his adolescence. Rutgers also introduced Amir to people of other diverse backgrounds and personality types. He met black people who were strikingly different from those he knew from his hometown of Plainfield. People like Lance, the fellow history major/music minor with dreadlocks. Amir started a college band with Lance. L-Trane used the word "nigga" more than your favorite pop rapper, but it did not carry the same endearment. He would never refer to Amir or anyone he respected as "my nigga." When Lance dropped the N-bomb, it was in sharp critique of behavior he thought was "niggerish." At a gig in an upscale Harlem restaurant, Lance was outraged at the watermelon martini drink special that was repeatedly announced between their performance sets.

"Fancy ass n*ggas," Lance mumbled, as he shook his head back and forth.

When Amir moved to California after graduating in 2007, Lance took over his lease and replaced him in the Ninja Turtles' house. The antics actually amplified without Amir around to mellow things out. Ike #2 also moved in on the couch, and argued with Lance daily. Lance is still salty at Amir for not warning him about the full force of the Ikes and Ninja Turtles.

The brotherhood Amir found with Lance and his Ninja Turtle roommates convinced him that he did not need to join a fraternity at Rutgers. He almost pledged one of the divine Negro fraternities, until he discovered they could cost over $1,000 a semester. He often regrets not doing it, and balances it against what he spent his money on otherwise: musical instruments and travel.

Fraternities and sororities—or Greek Life—play a critical role in the lives of millions of college students across the country. Their parties are legendary, their networks can open doors and provide opportunities for a lifetime after college, and they provide university students with community and companionship. They are an age-old tradition carried on by generations of students. Greek Life is also the most segregated aspect of college life. Most fraternities and sororities were never integrated, since they were designed for specific ethnic/cultural groups. A classic stereotypical view of Greek Life can be seen in the 1978 comedy *Animal House*. Toga! Toga! Toga!

Black Greek Life is on display in films like Spike Lee's 1988 classic *School Daze*. Step-show competitions, fashion shows, and inter-race racism weave together for an interesting college underdog story. The first black fraternity—Alpha Phi Alpha—was started at Cornell in 1906, amidst racial tensions on campus. Seven black men created a union for survival. The Brotherhood spread throughout the country, and eventually included people like Martin Luther King Jr., Thurgood Marshall, Cornell West, Duke Ellington, and Paul Robeson among its members. If Amir could have afforded to pledge a fraternity, it would have been Alpha Phi Alpha—the Benevolent Bruhs. Either that, or Broke Phi Broke—the satirical fraternity narrating Kanye West's *Graduation* album.

To survive as a starving student (and resist the temptation of selling drugs), Amir picked up a few jobs and hustles between classes at Rutgers: security guard, substitute teacher, low-budget music engineer and producer, counterfeit fashion wholesaler, banquet and fancy restaurant guitarist, and my favorite—Soul Mercenary. In this job, Amir played guitar for churches all over central Jersey for $35-$100 a service. His spirit underwent salvation, as he was forced to listen to hours of unwavering preachers' sermons. As a broke college student, he admittedly was not there for the Good Word. He actually despised one of the churches. This hustle became just as gritty as his days as a crack dealer. In a temporary church in Newark, he and Lance watched the shady pastor get handcuffed and escorted out by police for unknown reasons. All they knew was their last check from the pastor had bounced, and several of the women in the congregation were said to have had relations with him. Earlier in the sermon, the capricious preacher had described a fight he had gotten into during his younger days.

"I shouldn't have gotten into the brawl, but luckily GAAAWWWWD gave me the VICTORY!" he screamed.

"Well I guess he gave that other guy an a*s-whuppin," said Lance.

Two weeks earlier, the pastor had strong-armed shammed Amir into joining his church. After the Greater Greatness Swindling Missionary Church fiasco, the Soul Mercenary was born. A strictly-business relationship was developed between Amir and Baby Jesus. Amir would play for up to five churches on a single Sunday for nothing more than the money.

This spiritual quest was just one of many ways Amir developed during college. The soul chops he picked up playing in churches came in handy during jam sessions and gigs with dozens of musicians at Rutgers. Musicians like Damien, the quirky drummer who was addicted to 1990's R&B. Or T.C., the violinist with a Stevie Wonder old soul. Or Sugarfoot Sarah, the 5'1 white girl drummer who could groove like ?uestlove from the hip-hop band, The Roots. Performing on stages across the East Coast forced Amir out of his shell. Life as a college student-musician created connections and experiences that rivaled joining a fraternity. Practicing guitar and being creative kept him out of trouble too. So buying more guitars instead of pledging wasn't such a bad idea after all.

Chapter 5: The Scarlet Knight Chronicles

Ages: 20-22 Years Old

August 20, 2005

<u>Round 4</u>

Right now, I am at my new job as a security guard. Been working here a month-and-a-half and it's aiight. The only problem is my porn hungry co-workers. I only work weekends, but from 12 a.m. til 12 p.m. That's already starting to be a problem. While I'm working tonight, a concert will be starting that I would have died to see a few months ago. Bootsy Collins, Snoop Dogg, and the Red Hot Chili Peppers. But I don't even want to request off or call out. Partly cuz I need the money, and partly cuz I'm not feeling it right now. Can't even find anybody to go with. I gotta expand my circle of friends.

Well, in less than a week, I will be packing my bags to go away to school. I know Rutgers is only 20 minutes away, but I still feel like I will be on my own. I'm ready to party, open up, make new friends, and find a chick I can chill with. At times it seems like I have none of these. Sheek and Nyce are getting money in VA right now. I wasn't even invited to go...but I guess they would have known my response. The girl I'm dating is acting immature. Dad is running the streets so hard, he missed his only daughter's graduation last week. Mom is not far behind. I got her and my little sister cell phones on my account, but neither have paid anything on our bill in the last four months. Credit cards are maxed out. Bank accounts have a negative balance. Not sure how I will pay for school survival. And so we enter Round Four with a handicap!

FIGHT!

***

October 16, 2005

<u>Mannish-Boi</u>

Yeah, it's official. More than two decades under my belt now. Guess I'm a man in the eyes of the government because I'm 21. But I was always a man. Ever since I was 16-years-old. Paying my own bills, paying my parents' bills, or grandparents' bills, my siblings' bills, bailing family and friends out of jail, buying a few cars, paying insurance, and many other responsibilities. Now I stand before you, feeling no different. I just won't break the law as much I guess since I can drink legally. But then again, I've never been one to let something as simple as the "law" get in the way of what I do.

Anyways, school is going good. When compared to students in one of the world's greatest universities, I am slightly above-average, in the B+ area. Not bad for someone coming from where I'm from. I'm fairly certain classmates didn't climb from the bottom in a school where less than 11% of students pass the state tests.

Three years ago, I graduated from high school without a plan to go to college. If you would have told me then that I would be 21, have a degree, be at a public Ivy League school, have a decent car, and be on my way to becoming a teacher, I would have laughed.

Three years ago, I wasn't even thinking about today. To quote the great Rick James...

"One thing 'bout the ghetto, you don't have to worry. It will be there tomorrow, so brother don't you worry."

But here I am, luckily put on one of the ships that made it through winds and fierce currents that left others stranded...to sink in the Atlantic. All praises due to whoever is giving me the strength. Have mercy on me for not knowing who you are. Your presence is acknowledged.

So what is the plan for 24? I imagine myself still a full-time college student, with several platinum songs under my belt as a producer and musician, and on my way to becoming a history teacher at Hubbard! Maybe owning a one-bedroom condo and living the Bachelor Life!

***

November 27, 2005

<u>Step the Funk Up</u>

Yeah, I'm no longer a studio musician. Just did my first few gigs! Jammed with some musicians from the England named P-Theory. Met some musicians and poets in different Rutgers student organizations. They asked me to play with them and introduced me to even more musicians. Some Asian kid with a guitar style like Eric Clapton knocked on my dorm door with his guitar after finding me on Facebook. Met a violinist named T.C., who is also sick on the keys. She is a recent graduate of Rutgers, and teaches music at a middle school. I'm working with her as a studio engineer and musician for a Christmas album. I think we might start a band together! Time will tell. She invited me to sit in on a 4-hour set, and we tore the roof off the muthasucka! I wasn't as good as the other musicians, so I had to sit out a few songs. I don't understand music theory much yet, so I can't really communicate with them. I was musically illiterate, but I held it down. I got a few loud cheers during guitar solos. It was motivation to practice and learn more. I think I want to minor in music now, too. My boy, Chris, came out to support.

School is going great. Meeting a lot of cool people. My grades will be two A's and three B's, the highest I've ever gotten. Finances are hell. Little Sister somehow ran the phone bill up to $900. Couldn't resist buying a new guitar with my credit card. A custom 1972 Fender Telecaster, Thinline Edition. Natural tan wood finished with a shimmery pearl white pickguard. It was the guitar of my dreams.

***

Fall 2005

One inebriated evening, me and the fellas in the Quad 3 dorms decided to record a "Rutgers University Theme Song." I spit a few bars of hot fire on it, produced the beat, engineered the track, and took my signature (over-extended) guitar solo. The song had a brief buzz after spreading through the Rutgers' radio station, 88.7 FM WRSU, and student file-sharing network.

R.U. Drunk?

R…you forced to live in the quads?
U…killin' the battery on your iPod?
R…you on Facebook all day?
U…really listening to your R.A.?

R...ready for tomorrow's Calc exam?
U...running on f***** meal plans?
R...ready to break your roommate's radio?
U...hunting for that 5-to-1 ratio? (sup bro?)
R...ready to eat, but you lost your ID.
U...just want your f***** bachelor's degree.

***

January 2, 2006

<u>New Yea'z</u>

What a year! 2005 was the most progressive year in my life by far. As a guitarist, my skills more than doubled. A year ago, I wouldn't believe that I would be this good. As a scholar, my wisdom increased considerably. I did more reading, writing, learning, and studying in my first semester at Rutgers than previously in my entire life. I'm 100% sure that I want to be a history teacher at Hubbard, my old middle school. Can't imagine doing anything else. I started my career as a producer in 2005, too. A year ago, I couldn't imagine myself producing songs, but by the end of the year I produced too many to count with dozens of artists. Some successful albums too.

Socially this was the most productive year. I met people who seem like they will be cool peoples like Jay, Rob, Nate, Marcus, TC, RealEyez, all through Rutgers. This school is showing me so much in many aspects. One being love. Rutgers introduced me to a new breed of ladies very different from the traditional Plainfield hood boogers. Some for the better, some for the worse. Most relevant being this chick named Janet. This girl was so many things I thought I wanted...until she was too much. We ended up breaking it off over a misunderstanding, and I've never felt such pain over a chick. Long story short, I still don't know what I want, but I'm a lot closer, and I know how I'm going to get it, too: by being friends first. And no more wasting time with ones that won't go anywhere.

This year's resolutions are: jam with another ten Plainfield musicians, lose 30 lbs (245 now!), complete a solo album, form a band, develop a sound, do 30 gigs, read 20 books, maintain a 3.0. All very much possible.

***

March 2006

<u>Mr. Substitute</u>

Got a job as a substitute teacher in Plainfield making $85 a day. I've returned home to my favorite old school after eight years. Now I'm a teacher instead of a student. Memories play back like late-night reruns. Reflecting on the anarchy that I brought here at Hubbard Middle School.

The teacher didn't leave much work, so a small crowd of students are assembled around the computer playing the latest pop-rap. I'm the do-whatever-the-hell-you-want-just-keep-quiet type of substitute. I just lead by example by studying myself if they don't want my one-on-one assistance. A good student sits in his lonesome corner and does his homework. Curious kids give me eye contact and wonder what I'm doing sitting behind this desk. In 1998, I was a 13-year-old sitting in their seats. Profanity echoes from their lips. I sit at this teacher's desk and reminisce on the simple days. Before trappin', before bills, before responsibilities, before friends became enemies, before Bloods and Crips, before serious homework, before loneliness.

Yea, they don't take me seriously. Turn the tables, I wouldn't either. Vivid memories of how we use to torment the substitute teachers. The young white girl we sent home crying after a few books flew in her direction.

!!!%#*@+^#^!!!

My bad, had to break up a fight!

The class calms down and attention clusters around a student in the back corner. He has their undivided attention. Long gold necklace dangling back and forth, emitting the familiar clinking sound. Prying eyes stare, as he narrates a war story they wish they had the "privilege" of living. He was robbed at gunpoint over the weekend. It seems I am the only one disgusted by it. It excites the girls and pumps the adrenaline of the boys. As for me, it reminds me of The Notorious B.I.G.'s song *I Got a Story to Tell*, told from the victim's perspective. Now it is even glorious to be robbed. Any experience in the streets is a confirmation of our manhood. Puberty is reached within prison walls and on probation. I still remember one of the little soldiers Sheek and I had trappin' for us bragging after he got arrested with the pack-o-crack we gave him to sell.

"You heard I got knocked by the Po-Po, right?!" he said with a huge smirk.

He looked as if he had discovered his first strands of public hair. I guess losing your freedom is so common where we come from, it has come to signify a milestone.

We are the world, we are the children, we are the future, and we are doomed.

I can't run away from the fire just because I made it out. Flesh still boiling, skin melting, dripping like a leaky faucet, wounds too fresh to be considered scars. I'll charge back into the fire to perish as a sacrifice. That's in my imagination.

And now, reality bites, inflicting yet another scar. It camouflages with my many war-scars. Wounds that are too obvious to avoid the pity. I'm in the middle of a soul-search. Pitch-black room, blindfolded, barefoot, with broken glass ...everywhere. I wonder if these tween middle school students know what's about to hit them. When I was their age, I was clueless.

Ignorance was bliss, so I won't interrupt their fairy tale.

**

April 2006

I don't know how much longer I can take this. The only way I can stomach this job is by adopting an apathetic attitude. I never thought I would say something like this, but I care too much to work here. They don't know what they're doing to their future, the same way I didn't. They are kids, and they are doing what kids do. But they will be fully responsible for the consequences from their lollygagging. They are already falling behind, and they don't even know it. Some may never even realize it.

This job ain't for me. Teachers respect you even less than the students. Administrators don't care, so nobody else does. I would never work in a restaurant I didn't see fit to eat in. Yet much of the school staff won't let their kids attend the very same schools they teach in. But then again, I know first-hand the consequences of attending these Plainfield public schools.

Fu*k...my wallet was just stolen out of my coat pocket, and it was all my fault.

"There is no reason for you to bring your wallet in here anyway," said the highest authority of the school. "You should keep it in your car!"

I stopped and considered the odds of someone breaking into my car in comparison to a kid searching my coat pocket, while I grabbed a student with half of his body hanging out the window. Maybe I should have let him fall, I thought. I guess I was too trusting of the rascals to consider such a scheme. A significant code of the street echoed in my head: never underestimate anyone.

The $6 in my wallet was irrelevant. I am more concerned about the $24 to replace my license, $15 for my school ID, $8 for my debit card, and $5 for miscellaneous stuff. It added up to my total pay for the day after taxes, but that wasn't my initial concern either. I was more troubled about the hours of inconvenience it would take to replace everything—taking me away from studying. I've never gotten out of the DMV in less than three hours. I imagine a 12-year-old wouldn't know about that, though. At least I hope not. They are just thinking about the corner-store candy and cafeteria cookies they can buy with my $6.

***

May 17, 2006

Summa, Summa, Summa Tyme (Part 2)

Academically, I'm in an Ali-rhythm now. I got a 3.6 GPA this semester...and surprisingly did the most slacking of any semester. Some weeks I spent over 40 hours in the library to catch up, but I did it! I got 3 A's and 2 B's. First time getting more than two A's. Played 15 gigs total. Before this semester, I only played two or three my entire life. Sometimes, I would be out until 3 AM playing a show, then have a final exam at 8 AM. Boss! I'm about to complete my first full week of teaching too. During the semester, I could only do it on Mondays and Wednesdays, the two days when I only had night classes. Now I can teach every day until the end of the school year. The Plainfield Board of Education needs to stop f****** with my money though.

"Aww we got some young blood up here now, brotha!!" my old science teacher, Mr. Showers said, before trying to convince me to pursue a teaching career.

Hubbard was/is the shiznit!! But I love the adorable second graders that call me "Mr. Willikers." I can't substitute teach at the Plainfield high anymore, though. Almost got into a scuffle with a student. After asking him to take his seat for the third time, he called me out.

"N*gga, I remember you from my gym class freshman year! Nobody gotta listen to you!" he said.

In other news, my band is also taking off! The permanent line-up is Me, Lance, Damien, and TC. Everyone is ready to record an album too. We murdered our last gig! My skills on the guitar are amazing now, and I believe in myself. So do all my P-Funk teachers. I got an "A" in music theory, and TC and Lance are helping me apply everything on the guitar. When the P-Funk play-by-ear style mixes with music theory and practice, I WILL be the baddest!

All this good news, though…still no smile. In some ways, I have never been this lonely in my life. Velvet feels like splintered wood.

***

May 23, 2006

From: Tyson (Little Bro)
To: Mir
Time: 10:00 AM

What's good Mir? Me, just big backin.' Waiting to go down to Jamesburg Residential Detention Center. I saw classification last month. I got 18 points. I probably got like 20 now cuz I hit this boy from Camden with a lunch tray. I was in the box for 5 days. What's goin' on with you? Tell Grandma n Jamal I say Hi. What's good with Dad, same old? It's beat (boring) down here. We be in our room most of the time. But I work in the kitchen.
But I got to go.

Tyson

***

June 17, 2006

<u>Happy Father's Day</u>

Papa was a rolling stone, Grandpa ain't get to see me make it.
Regardless of the past, everything's appreciated.
Papa spent more time in jail than home, don't know how he could take it.
Still, the little things are very much appreciated.
The memorieeeeeees are eternally sacred (said like Tupac).

Sup Pops, Happy Father's Day,
Know you feel you owe me an eternal apology.
Truth be told, the past doesn't bother me,
But the future is on my mind constantly.
Don't feel like your day is in disregard,
Cuz your kids ain't get you mad gifts, and put chips in your cards.
Struggling right now...times is hard.

We had our fair share of mishaps in life,
You took me back to school when I was suspended,
I bailed you out of jail twice.
I left the door unlocked when the Cops came for child support,
You never returned my bail money after they gave it back in court.
U sold me sleazy used cars, damn this goes on,
But so does life, and that's why we move on.
U too old to be relapsing now, gotta stay strong.

Smoking that sh*t since before I touched this earth,
Think of all the sh*t u lost, and analyze your worth.
You brought DJing to Jerzy, you were the first,
But there has to be a blessing, somewhere in the curse.

1992 was like the only Christmas that you wasn't locked.
I'll never forget those summer days: Grandpa's shop,
Red Towers coffee and Ferraro's Pizza nonstop.
Grandpa telling me "MiMi turn the wheel right,"
You under the car, and Jamal under the hood with the light.

Rest in peace Grandpa. Goddamn, I miss him.
You passed right after promising we would go fishin'.
I still have the brim hat you gave me for 8th grade prom.

I pray to God I'm making you proud.
I swear I see your face in the clouds.
Can't understand why Lord ain't allow,
You to see your first great-grandchild,
Tookie, and her beautiful smile.
Wish I could have jammed with you on the drums.
'Preciate everything that you've done.

***

Summer, 2006

I'm Not a Thug

If knowledge is power...when will the scholar,
Over tower the gangsta.
If knowledge is power...when will the scholar,
Rise above the thug.

  not a thug. Perhaps I'm a coward instead.
Ever received a call saying your cousin's been shot in the head?
Trust me, this is not a good feeling. Not a feeling I want to be
responsible for.

You ever watched someone overdose off the poison you sold em'?
Have you ever had a meal taken from your mouth?
Have you ever been deprived of school clothing?

How do these rappers glorify killings?
I'm far too familiar with the feeling.
They ain't thugs either. Just ruthless-houses without ceiling.
The sound of ambulance sirens,
Accompanied by two black women crying.
Pray for the Mom and Grandma. We endangered, species dying.
Beyoncé telling these girls to want "Soldiers." Guess I can mess with them.
Already got more war-scars than muthaf***** veteran.

***

July 2006

<u>A'miracle: The Gratefully-Blessed, Non-Praying, Questioner</u>

They say I'm predestined. How can I be blessed when…?
I don't even pray.
Dear Lord,
Why should I beg you to do your will?
If it's part of your plan, it'll happen regardless…still.
That's like asking for rain under a dark cloud.
When my silent prayers go unanswered, should I pray aloud?
Can you read my mind since you designed it?
Am I a lost soul?
Is it even worth tryin' to find it?
Heard I didn't have the authority to ask you questions.
But too many things are unanswered, and I'm tired of guessing.
A true student cannot remain quiet the entire lesson.

I acknowledge your undeniable glory and blessings.
I still remember what it's like feeling cursed.

Remember Big Mama used to pray before drinking a glass of water?
As if you came down from the heavens and put in ice cubes for her?
I guess you kinda did since you gave her the strength.
You do 100% of the work, now the pastors want more than a tenth.
But my tithes don't go to heaven.
So, I usually put in 5, 6 dollars...at most, 7.

Certain events in my life confirm your existence,
Certain things in my life are more than a coincidence.
They are a miracle.
I am a miracle.
I am Amir'acle.

Can't deal with religion.
I am just spiritual.
(Skip the four-play and tell me)
What are we living fo'?

***

July 16, 2006

<u>What are the Odds? (WATO?)</u>

Can you get your soul saved and stolen on the same day? WATO? Life is changing at lightning speeds. Been playing in a few churches the past few weeks. Today I actually joined one— Rewarding Faith in Newark. The pastor called me a "devil" last week for not belonging to a (his) church. Whateva.

"What's the use of having all that talent if you're gonna play in hell?" he said with a demonic smirk.

I got a standing ovation from the church after my guitar solo, but Pastor Strong-Arm killed my joy. My soul's a constant battleground. I'm not gonna ask someone to do what they want (God's will), so I still can't pray. If someone asks me to go to college and succeed every day, it would be a waste of time. I plan to do it, regardless. So I guess I'm still neither Christian or Muslim.

Something was definitely in my space today, though. I swore I felt a higher power interfere when I was playing in the first church in Plainfield. I never felt like not playing so much in my life. Like there was a muzzle on my soul. Then at the second church, two very rare things happened. My effects pedal failed on me, and this only happened one or two times out of my 40+ performances at this point. Then, my guitar amp just stopped working. This never happened out of the hundreds of times I played with it. WATO? Is it God telling me to stay out of his sanctuary until I become a fully-devoted believer? Or is the devil trying to f**** with me? Either way, today sucked...even for a Sunday. The first church only paid me $35 for two weeks...less than the $60 they originally promised. The second church I played at didn't mention anything about their check bouncing, but I'm confident they know. I'm so broke right now. I gotta pay this $600 off for my laptop by the 21st. Then rent, credit card, phone, and thangs.

Something tells me I need to pray, but I can't. The muzzle on my soul and my refusal to beg for the obvious does not allow for such.

***

September 26, 2006

<u>Peanut Butter and Jelly</u>

"Jamal, show your lil brother the right way to make a peanut butter and jelly sandwich!" my dad said.

"See…you have to spread the jelly first, cuz the peanut butter will rip the bread," Jamal said.

I was about seven-years-old at the time. Fifteen years later, I'm still making the same mistake. Gotta smooth thangs out before you put the rough sh*t on. My brother taught me a lot of thangs 'bout life. I remember always asking him questions when I was little, thinking he had infinite knowledge because he was older. He got off track for a while…a long while…but now he seems to be back on. Dad and Mom are back on too. The P-Funk Board of Ed screwed me out of 11 days' pay, so I had to borrow rent money from Mom, Nana, and Grandma. I paid them all back, and let Nana borrow $1,000 for another van.

My roommates suck. I drank five out of the last seven days, and it's only Tuesday! We have parties every Thursday with two kegs (330 beers). It seems like I'm the only one who actually cleans this place. I'm the only single one…every Thursday night when my roommates go to their rooms, I'm the only one alone. Never been so lonely in my life. Relationships with old friends are disintegrating as well. Everybody is doing their own thing, so we're never around each other anymore.

***

October 2006

A Manifesto to Dismantle Du-rag Discrimination

Last week, I hopped around a few of the college bars throughout New Brunswick with the roommates and the Ikes. At our last bar, I was forbidden from entering. I was also the only Black student, but that was not the justification for the discrimination—at least not the stated one. The bouncer told me I couldn't enter the bar because of the dress code.

"There's no dress code here" said Mike-Ross.

"Yea there is," said the bouncer. "No du-rags."

He pointed at the navy blue headwrap on my head that kept my waves spinning. It's common among young Black males with short haircuts, or waves like mine. Rappers, like 50 Cent and Nelly, can be seen wearing them on their album covers. Ironically, a 50 Cent song was blasting from the bar as I was banished. I rarely wore du-rags, but I didn't have time or money for a haircut that week.

"That's bullsh*t," said Rob. "You're wearing that sh*tastic Mets hat, and my buddy can't come in with a du-rag?"

"Didn't make the rules," said the bouncer. "Just enforce 'em."

"Didn't make it to college either," Rob said. "So now you stand at a door all night enforcing stupid rules."

The bar was full of people with all types of headwear: baseball caps, fedoras, tennis brims, beanie skullcaps, etc. But the bouncer stood fast in his ability to forbid me from entering. With my hair looking like a hotmess under my du-rag, I wasn't willing to remove the headwrap. Most of the crew stood in solidarity with me, as we found another bar where I was welcomed inside.

My experience with the selectively arbitrary dress code plays back every night when I put on my du-rag before going to bed. We all knew who they're trying to exclude with their policy, and it didn't sit well with me. At one point, I even began drafting a plan to protest the policy. It never got off the ground. Still, it's nice to dream. Even more nice to be free.

Du-Rag Radicals' Manifesto

Protest Purpose: To change the subtle forms of discriminations that unnoticed, that continue to segregate society.

Repercussions: Never be able to go to bars again. May get tossed around by a bouncer. Can cops write tickets? The clubs could enforce a stricter dress code and the rest of Rutgers could hate us. (So what)

Benefits: Contribute to the progress of mankind.

Strategies: We will organize a group of students to go to the establishment. We will line the front of the bar and order our drinks, then we'd remove du-rags from our pocket and put them on our heads. We'd refuse to leave and create a ruckus around the discriminatory policy. We will declare a day "Du-Rag Day," and hand out du-rags to random college students. We demand that they kick everyone out with a hat on. If we won't leave, we can actually block the bar, there-by disrupting their revenue.

What we want: Bars to change the dress code.

Speech: A du-rag represents an aspect of the hip hop culture. So while our music is good enough to have a monopoly on your DJ's playlist, certain aspects of the culture are disenfranchised. America is changing, whether you like it or not. We are going to have to live together. We want $2 Long Island iced teas too, dammit!

***

December 06, 2006

Block Huggaz Bluez

Don't ever expect to go nowhere playing by the rules.
I can't be living wrong if there are no other options to choose.

Considering reviving old ways of getting money. I have $8.73 to my name. And boy, do I know how to get money. A victim of ghetto-demand.

Of course, everybody I came up with is still trappin'. The temptation is haunting when you're down to your last dime. Sadly, little remains left from my days of trappin' except for the jewelry I refuse to wear. That, and the memories of feeling infinite, invincible, and terrified. Buried beneath this confusion is deep regret for the pain, destruction, and death that I contributed to. The agony of having nothing to show for all the suffering you caused is indescribable. The experience has shown me two things:

1) Karma is a beeyotch
2) Skeletons do not remain quiet in your closet.

***

December 23, 2006

Day One of a New Life

Wrote over 100 pages this semester. Read over 1,000. Grew more in the past year than I did in the past decade. I'm living for a different purpose. I have different goals. Guess you can say I'm a different person. So a new life begins now at 83 Richardson Street.

I am the only one in our house today. My other roommates went back to their homes, to their beds. Since my only bed is here, this is my home. More pressure to succeed since I have nowhere to go back to. No other options besides getting my own. Jamal recently moved into my old room at Grandma's house, but I really don't want to go back anyways.

Recently I found the girl I thought I wanted from my hometown is at my fingertips. She has a one-year-old daughter too, along with the drama. Not working, on welfare, about to get her own spot in the projects...a few houses down from the unit she grew up in. Carrying on the tradition. Back against the wall now, acknowledging the fact that she went into the corner herself. It is indeed P-Funk's fault. It raised us to be that way. Nothing told us otherwise.

***

February 2, 2007

<u>83 Richardson Rap</u>

By: Rob, The Rowdy Roommate
In the Style of Nas's *Got Yourself a Gun*

Our first party had no famous guest appearances,
The outcome, the ladies cleared this sh*t.
That party ended up just like our dirty fridge,
Plenty of beer, and sausages.
We didn't care, had to do better,
We got another keg, for a little more cheddar.
That meant a longer party and more ladies,
Till the Ikes rolled up in the stretch Mercedes.
Hopped out and said here we are,
We bout to put some f****** holes in your walls,
Now our house got more holes than Swiss cheese.
And Amir's pissed keeps, sayin "N*gga, please."

Only at 83 Richardson...
You want a free drink, hope you Got Urself a Gun
Unless Mike-Ross is on cups, cause he don't give a f***
We got more beer than girls at 83 Richardson.

***

March 2007

Black Rage/Them Changes

    Something's going on. Something serious. I think it is maturity. If so, I'd rather not grow up. This sh*t is painful, man. What makes it even more painful is the inability to abandon those who may never escape or grow. So carefree. I wish I didn't have to care. Wish I ain't have to fight. Wish I didn't have to know. Serves me right for seeking all of the world's knowledge. Now as a consequence, I must suffer. The pain is inevitable, son.

    Then again, I'm blessed with a different intuition. Maybe that will help me discover a solution unseen. The search will drive me crazy, but I'm crazy any damn way. I can't be enlightened to this and not do anything about it. So much trouble in this world. It's just getting worse. Not on my clock.

    I almost want to die and get it over with. Just end it now. It feels like there's nothing I can do. Well...I guess I don't know enough. Learning this much has been so damn painful, though. I'm only 22. This sh*t is killing me! Driving me out of my mind. I'm becoming more aware of the system. The realization of the fact that I have to try harder scares me. Then again, am I even tryin' as hard as I can? How much longer can I take it? A lot more, because I refuse to do anything else. People are surviving with much more struggle than me. My day is actually not that bad. A bed to sleep in, running water, and opportunities of a college graduate, a vast amount of wisdom, decent health (can get better though!). Millions are starving, dying, in war, poor, with no opportunities. That makes me even less comfortable with mine.

"To be a Negro in this country and to be relatively conscious is to be in a rage almost all the time." -Author and Activist James Baldwin

***

April 17, 2007

Sorry, I've been dreaming for a while. Why not? Reality bites, like a well-trained German shepherd. I was thinking about going to South Africa for the summer and Cali for the fall. Still…dreaming. Matter fact, it's not a dream. It's a possibility. A possibility out of my hands. It's up to the past.

But isn't the future always dependent upon the past?

Stay chiseled. All I know is that I tried. Well… I'm trying.

California. South Africa. I guess I'm going to run away from what's here. You will RUN RUN RUN, like the ending of "Coolie High." I will. I did. I am leaving this town.

Drove past my old house in Plainfield yesterday, and it no longer felt like my home. I know I'm welcomed to stay with Grandma whenever I want, but I don't even have a bed there anymore. As soon as I moved to the Rutgers campus, my older brother Jamal promptly moved into my old room. During the first few visits home, I would yell at him for not keeping "my room" clean. I treated him like a tenant because of the mere fact that he was sleeping on MY sheets, watching MY TV, wearing MY clothes from MY closet, and enjoying a dark room because MY curtain blocked the sunlight. By the time I came home after the second semester, he barely allowed me in the room. Whenever we'd argue, I'd say, "I paid for the damn curtains on da wall." Never got me off the couch, though. Since this is our grandmother's house, I don't really have the right to complain, anyways. I just need to get my own. I don't have anything of my own. At this point, failure is not an option.

***

May 18, 2007

<u>Congrats Kid</u>

Yeah, who would've thought. Your mom even told you herself. Even your teachers. The day I graduated high school five years ago, I would not have believed my current status. I now have TWO college degrees. Most of my friends and family don't even have high school diplomas. I knew I would cry. At least nobody saw me. So, I guess I'm more of a man? F*** masculinity.

All I know…S***…I know all. At least I want to. I want to see all. This type of thinking will keep me dreaming. Ain't nothing wrong with that. For as long as you dream, you have something to strive for. If I get comfortable to the point that I no longer want to reach for anything else, then why live? Stagnation is a form of death.

Anyways, I'm overcome with joy, yet still sad. I had to leave many behind to get to where I'm at. I've always told myself I would keep my head to the sky. I guess that requires you to not look back.

Keep your head to the sky, kid. Despite your position, never look down on where you came from. Be grateful for the experiences that made you.

***

May 27, 2007

<u>Pressure, Doubt, Confidence</u>

No longer California Dreaming…it's a reality now. When signing off on the form for me to declare my history major,

Professor (Christopher Leslie) Brown suggested I look into schools in California. He's a Rhodes Scholar who went to Oxford and Yale, so I welcomed his academic advice. Still, I didn't think I'd get into the University of Southern California. Just found out that I got accepted, and there's no turning back.

Can you really make a difference? You seem to talk a good game, but are you really willing to deal with the sacrifices necessary to reform things? Is it even possible to change the centuries of oppression, in your lifetime? What makes you so special?

I'm so confident in myself, I answered most of these questions before I even finished writing them!

1. Yes, I can make a difference. I already have. I have said and done things that will alter peoples' lives for the better. I can and will do a lot more, though.

2. I not only talk a good game, but I walk it too, chief. I rarely pat myself on the back, but I have accomplished a lot. I am a "rose out of the concrete." I have dealt with many sacrifices. I know my objectives will require much more.

Mind: read more books, increase vocabulary, work on debating skills, improve oral skills, stay chiseled.

Body: treat it like I only got one, get into the best shape of your life, you will live longer.

Soul: express yourself through music and writing to determine what your soul sounds like, get sucka-free, know sex is not everything, connect with others and become a people-person.

3. It will take a lot to reform this system, but what else will you settle for? Indeed, all struggle regardless...naw, f*** that excuse. I don't even know. I guess I have to find out, huh? There are books out there...read them to find out. You've always been good at putting things together and seeing things others may not. Use that talent and get your fata** into shape. You will feel more confident that way.

July 25, 2007

<u>Laws of Man (Written in South Africa)</u>

God made perfect. Man made flaws.
Incarcerated for breaking man-made laws.
The injustice acts that Man may cause,
Remember, God made peace...and Man made war.

Why should I obey...anything you say?
As if your blood ain't red, or your flesh won't decay?
As if I can't end your life, right here today!
As if God only listens when YOU pray?

They say God made perfect, and Man made flaws.
Incarcerated for breaking man-made laws.
The injustice acts that Man may cause,
Remember, God made peace...and Man made war.

Law is simply words given power... depending on who wrote them.
Sometimes justice doesn't exist until these laws are broken.
They say change gon' come, but I'm tired of hoping.
Who wrote that law for my ancestors to cross that ocean?

Kidnapped and exploited to build this house on stolen land.
Then told for centuries that we could only wait outside.
All this was written into law. A well-orchestrated plan.
The legacies of Jim Crow and Apartheid.

Chapter 6: University of Southern California

The conversation between Amir and the Financial Aid staff at USC was priceless. He gave them a call the summer before his first semester in 2007 to ask about the "federal grants" he had hoped to receive. No one told him about the important distinction between graduate and undergraduate studies.

"Good morning," he said. "I'm looking at my financial aid summary, and I see a few things missing."

"What's your social security number, sir?" asked the young woman.

After Amir provided the number that I had given him at birth, she pulled up his records. He explained that he was beginning his master's degree in the fall, but only saw student loans as tuition payment options.

"You see, my tuition is usually paid for by the government because my family is poor," he said.

"Like reaaaally poor. Matter of fact, we just po'. Can't even afford the 'o-r!'"

The young women explained to him that he was a graduate student now, so he no longer qualified for federal grants. He didn't believe her though, so he asked to talk to her manager. This was a tactic his roommate, Chris, always used to get what he wanted. Keep asking to speak to someone's supervisor, and you'll eventually get what you want. When Amir talked to the person in charge of the financial aid office, it wasn't quite as simple.

"I'm sorry, sir," explained the manager. "You're in graduate school now, and government financial aid is only available in the form of subsidized loans. The most they will do now is pay the interest on the $50K you need to borrow to complete this degree." A long pause commenced.

"Hello?" she said.

"Um...yea," said Amir.

Amir was becoming the proverbial 22-year-old nephew expecting to sleep on the family couch, assuming he could mooch forever. The conversation helped him accept the fact that he was officially an adult with college degrees now. No more free rides or using poverty as an excuse. You've got your bootstraps, kid, now lift yourself up and get a damn job.

Since Amir's birth in the 1980's, the cost of college has multiplied fivefold. Over the same period, the average income has not even doubled. Older generations had the benefit of being able to work part-time and pay for college, or graduating debt-free. In the 1970's, states covered 75% of college costs. By 2012, for the first time in history, universities received more money from students than state governments. The Governor of California while Amir lived there explained where much of the money was going.

"30 years ago, 10% of the general fund went to higher education, and 3% went to prisons. Today, almost 11% goes to prisons, and only 7.5% goes to higher education."

-California Governor Arnold Schwarzenegger, 2010

Please allow me to introduce you to my friend, Issa Trappman. I know what you're thinking. Yes, that movie star dude was elected to run the most populated state in the country! Trust me, Americans have done—and will do—worse.

Anyways, Amir almost didn't take out the $50,000 required to start graduate school in LA. But he decided to take the gamble and invest in himself. He borrowed more money than he'd ever made. He was still in shock that he had gained admission into one of the top 25 universities in the country. In his mind, he had to take the risk. He day-dreamed about USC's beautiful Los Angeles campus; with forty-foot palm trees, manicured courtyards, infinite fountains, and delicate statues. He'd uncontrollably stare at the rows of shiny bronzed bodies tanning on the campus grass. He'd heard it never rained in Southern California, and that most days were full of sunshine. He was in.

* * *

During his first few months in Cali, Amir still kept up with his hometown by reading the local paper. This tradition stopped after reading an article about two teenagers getting shot on a corner just two blocks from his grandparents' house. A call soon confirmed his worries: one of the kids was his 16-year-old little brother, Tyson. The local paper also distracted him with countless run-ins with the law and arrests of his family and childhood friends.

Not knowing a single person for thousands of miles, Amir was forced out of his comfort zone to make friends at USC. The random and transient nature of the Los Angeles metropolis (and the constant use of Craigslist to advertise) caused Amir to cycle through six roommates in the two-bedroom duplex unit he rented. This included two Asians, a Lebanese girl, a negro, two white boys, and Morales—a Mexican dude from Southeast LA.

Morales was a die-hard USC fan—born and raised in the city. He was a 31-year-old special education teacher, and a classmate in Amir's doctoral program at USC. The roommates would often ask themselves "How the hell did we get here?!" Whenever he'd get to drankin', Morales wouldn't shut up about the "greatness" of USC.

"Friggin' SC, man!" he'd slur. "More NFL draft picks, Hall-of-Famers, and Heisman Trophy winners than any other school!"

"We got more Olympic athletes than any other school, kid! Bringin' home more gold than entire countries! Mmmm, mmm!"

"Friggin' SC. Graduates like John Wayne, George Lucas, Paul McCartney, and Neil Armstrong—the first man to walk on the friggin' moon! Friggin'…the friggin' Presidents of Egypt and Japan went to USC?! We are in the top 15 for producing Fortune 500 CEOs!"

There were two things Morales hated: 1) someone using the word "retarded" and 2) anyone affiliated with the crosstown rival, UCLA. He'd get into fights over both. His childhood buddy, Valez, received two degrees from UCLA—which made Morales hate him twice as much. Whenever they'd go out, Amir would wait to see who'd be the first to get pissed-off and take a taxi home.

Amir and Morales became co-founders of the Educational Doctoral Student Assembly (EDSA), an organization comprised of hundreds of doctoral students across So-Cal. Amir drafted the constitution and shared the first term as President. Morales was the Social Chair, who organized parties at their place—Casa de EDSA. During the "Endless Parties Tailgate Olympics" for student organizations, the duo helped capture medals in the beer-chugging and flip-cup contests.

Much of Amir's awakening came from exploring the science of the mind and education at USC. His four years there were spent studying behavior, learning, development, and motivation in school settings through the discipline of educational psychology. He had to memorize the components of memory, and learn everything about learning. He had to study theories of human motivation under a microscope, and this fascinated him the most. Deep inside, he wanted to uncover what motivated him to become one of a few to graduate high school—and the only person to graduate college—from his childhood. He sought to understand what made him want to quit school at one point, only to return and pursue numerous degrees later on. In the process, he discovered scientific proof that the metal detectors and high-tech security system that had greeted him at his high school created a discouraging climate and false sense of security. Educational psychology helped him realize that he was not actually a high school dropout, but was a "pushout" through the School-to-Prison-Pipeline. He'd later come to devote his legal career to dismantling the de facto system. At USC, he developed rage and resentment for this system and others he saw impacting his friends and family members.

Much of USC's cost were offset by the fellowship Amir received during his last two years. As part of the fellowship, Amir was required to teach undergraduate educational psychology courses. In exchange for lecturing during weekly lab sessions and grading freshman papers, the fellowship covered all of his tuition and provided a small stipend. He worked under a full-time professor who lectured on Mondays, and Amir taught and reviewed on Wednesdays. Students referred to Amir as "The B.A.-T.A," or "bad a**" teaching assistant, because of his frequent swearing, informal style, disregard for norms, and badass attitude. [See B.A.T.A. drawing from USC student in back of book]

"B.A.-T.A. I saw you twice last weekend!" one student said. "First, you were drunkenly screaming at the football game. Then I saw you the next day in red tights and a Rick James wig for Halloween!"

"You're the third student to say this," said Amir. "Apparently, I have an evil twin living near campus."

To pay for his living expenses and travel addiction while in graduate school, Amir usually held several jobs. His favorite was working in two South Central LA high schools, shortly after he arrived in 2007. When he started teaching at USC for his fellowship in 2009, he became part-time at one of the high schools. He taught an elective, started an after-school program, and helped hundreds of kids pursue higher education as a college counselor. In another part-time job, Amir worked one-on-one with struggling students in areas like Compton and Inglewood.

Although he retired as a Soul Mercenary, Amir still played a few random music gigs throughout the LA scene. Still, his most intriguing and lucrative side-hustle involved parking cars in the vacant lot next to his duplex.

Amir lived directly across the street from the Los Angeles Coliseum, a monstrous facility capable of packing 93,000 people inside. It has been the venue used for two Olympic Games, several Super Bowls (including the first ever in 1967), concerts by The Rolling Stones, masses by Pope John Paul II, a World Series, WrestleMania, and many other events, which make the site a national landmark. It's also been the home of teams like the Los Angeles Raiders and the Los Angeles Dodgers. It is the current home of the USC Trojans football team and the Los Angeles Rams NFL team.

From Amir's house, the massive crowd could be heard erupting after each touchdown scored in the Coliseum. The same year Amir moved to LA, the Coliseum became the original host of the Electronic Daisy Carnival—one of the largest musical festivals in the world. In 2010, over 185,000 ravers packed the area for the festival. It was a recipe for disaster, and a chaotic crowd stampede at the event sent more than 100 people to the hospital. This fiasco, combined with teenagers overdosing, caused the city of Los Angeles to end the tradition and send the festival to Las Vegas.

Amir's front porch on Figueroa Street had a view of the Coliseum accompanied by a purple and scarlet sunset every evening. The front yard could fit four cars, and event patrons would happily pay $20-$120 to park there. The Coliseum was by far the coolest neighbor Amir had ever had. It made his LA experience more "LA."

During the weekend Coliseum events, Amir's landlord would give him the keys to the vacant lot next door, and 54 tickets for patrons parking their cars. She knew exactly 50 cars could fit in the lot, and four could fit in the front yard. Amir was expected to fork over all of the $1,000-$5,000 he made, except the $14 an hour pay he could deduct for his labor. The only time the landlord actually came by the property was the day after some events to pick up the cash, packaged in an envelope.

This is how it worked for two weekends, until Amir met one of the most fascinating LA characters—a middle-aged, Italian guy from New York, he called "Joey Coliseum." He approached Amir, who was working the lot by himself during the USC vs. Norte Dame football game. This was a high-profile game, where patrons paid $80 each to park in the lot. While Amir was trying to understand how people could effortlessly afford what would take him nearly six hours to earn, Joey approached and broke the ice.

"Hey, man," said Joey, "Ya workin' this lot?" Amir reluctantly answered, thinking Joey was an undercover cop.

"Yes," Amir said. "I live next door, and my landlord owns it."

"What's she payin' ya? Fifteen an hour?" Joey asked. Joey had a remarkable talent for nearly precise predictions. He knew there were 50 parking spaces, what time cars would arrive and depart, and had lightning-fast mental math skills.

"Here's what I'll do for ya," he proposed. "Let me park the cars for the people instead of you letting them park themselves. I can squeeze in 80 at least. That's an extra two grand we can split. Much more than the hundred bucks she's gonna give ya for the day."

The proposal was so assertive and effortless, Amir couldn't refuse. Game recognized game, and Joey seemed familiar. Amir let Joey work his magic, while collecting the wads of money. Once Amir developed trust with Joey, he'd let him work the lot by himself, while Amir tailgated and watched the USC Trojans play. The funds helped pay for Amir's dream trips to places like Japan, France, Brazil, Costa Rica, and all over Central America (See Street Traveler).

In between parking cars, Joey was incapable of shutting up or standing still. He'd tell random stories about the varying hustles he created to survive.

"Neva paid a dollar in taxes!" he proudly boasted.

Don't worry Joey Coliseum, Uncle Sam will catch up with you eventually. I always do.

During his final year at USC, Amir no longer had to take any more classes. Instead, his life as a student revolved around conducting research and publishing a study—his dissertation. All doctoral students are required to publish a dissertation if they want those fancy letters before and after their name. It must have taken thousands of hours of research and writing for Amir to produce the 234-page paper. This would be the greatest academic challenge Amir ever encountered. To complete it, he applied several of the motivational theories that he had studied and was writing about in his dissertation study paper. He and Morales called each other "Doc" to boost their self-efficacy. To make the task less daunting, Amir set weekly short-term goals to accomplish larger monthly objectives. A multitude of positive reinforcements were provided in the form of time in nature and nightlife. Snowboarding trips, hikes across the California terrain, and Hollywood nights-out awaited if objectives were met. Peer support was critical in the homestretch. He and a few classmates started hosting writing retreats at the cabins at Big Bear Mountain. These retreats forced them to write for up to ten hours a day. They'd reward themselves in the evening with drinks in the jacuzzi. Still, the factor that had the biggest impact on Amir's motivation was his interest and passion for the subject of his dissertation.

The title of the dissertation was "Reducing the Risk Among the Most At-Risk." It focused on the group of students most likely to drop out of school and end up arrested: Black males with behavioral problems or in special education classes. For his study, Amir wanted to look at a group of students who fit this description in South Central LA. The statistics among them were familiarly abysmal. Roughly 75% of the young Black males would end up arrested and/or after failed to complete high school. In his study, Amir wanted to determine what the rare 25% of students who graduated and avoided incarceration had that the other 75% did not. It was a simplistic and naïve way of looking at the issues, as if he could bottle up the solutions and share it with KnuckleHeads across the country. Nevertheless, the research could help him discover the qualities and characteristics that had helped him escape the Trap.

Amir stayed motivated during the dissertation process knowing that he'd eventually put everything he was learning into a non-profit organization to help the "at-risk" youth overcome—just as he had. Despite the star-studded evenings, weekend road trips to Mexico and Las Vegas, and endless parties at Casa de EDSA, this was Amir's true reason for going to California. He arrived in 2007 as a 22-year-old curious boy, but left in 2011 as a 26-year-old awakened and empowered young man. No matter where he lives in his future, California will always be remembered as the place where he became a man.

Chapter 7: The Trojan Chronicles

Ages: 22-26 Years Old

August 16, 2007

<u>Tears of Uncertainty</u>

I must be one of the few people in the world to touch the Atlantic, Indian, and Pacific Oceans all within the past week. Just got back from Cape Town, South Africa last week. I was in Atlantic City, New Jersey yesterday. And now, I just touched down in Los Angeles, California. It's scary though. When I got off the airplane, the reality hit me like a James Brown break beat: everyone here is a stranger, and I don't know a single soul in this city.

I'm making the transition from a Rutgers Scarlet Knight to a USC Trojan. At least I can stay on my high horse. Still, I cried today after talking to a little girl. My niece Tookie's fourth birthday was a day after I left for Africa this summer, and I couldn't be there for it. To make things worse, I couldn't hug and kiss her goodbye before moving to Cali. I just kinda left without saying anything. She may grow older and forget about me. She was just the spark for this fire.

I'm 3,000 miles away from home, about to embark on a tough task, and I'm all alone. The tears are for uncertainty as well. Who knows what the future holds? Then again, I never did. Last year this time, if you told me I would be in LA just returning from Africa, I would have proclaimed that to be Cosmic Debris. Nonetheless, I am still dreaming…with the fear that it may just turn into a nightmare.

***

September 1, 2007

<u>Home Sick</u>

Of course I hate it. My lifestyle has changed dramatically. New friends, new mindset, etc. I left everything I knew in Jersey. So I guess I have to adapt. Either that or adapt things to me. I suppose I'm more of an adapter, huh? Things can be hard to change. The world, society, etc. So go ahead and compromise, young man.

But I can't sit and accept things as they are. Like Howard Zinn said, "You can't be neutral on a moving train." In many ways, society is not going in the right direction, and by doing nothing, you are part of the problem. So call me the martyr who is willing to get run over by the train to slow it down a lil' bit. But I have to do a lot more in this physical frame. Within me is the capacity to make a change. We all have the potential to create change, but not many of us see it. So how can I motivate people to see their potential? By telling them my story!

Anyway, LA is not the city for me. I'm sure it needs change and everything, but I gotta fix my own house first. So I will soon be returning home. I can tell that I'm homesick. I talked to all my family and friends in the past few days. When it's time to hang up, I'm upset. I always want to cry. Ironically, I rarely shed tears. But maybe things will get better. Always hope.

***

October 9, 2007

<u>23, Pardon Me</u>

A decade ago, ignorance was such bliss. You think you know, but you don't have a clue. All I know is Black people are disproportionately suffering... still.

So today I realized that I must be in hell. If there is a God responsible for the state of things and our condition, He/She is not worth worshipping. This vision occurred to me when I was at a stoplight, and a homeless Black man walked past pushing a cart containing every single one of his earthly possessions. Then, as I crossed the street, a homeless Black Vietnam vet in a wheelchair rolled past me. I had just got off a bus where it felt like everyone was looking at me, as if I was responsible for all the crime and poverty in the world.

Maybe I'm too self-conscious, but Blackness is starting to feel like a curse. Countless tried, until there was no longer any use trying. Now some of us don't even want to try anymore... others fail to see the opportunities our generation is the first to have. In my Human Motivation class this semester, I learned about this as the concept of "learned helplessness." This is "a condition in which a person suffers from a sense of powerlessness, arising from a traumatic event or persistent failure to succeed. It is thought to be one of the underlying causes of depression." We are studying it because it frequently occurs among students struggling in school. But I believe there is a generational "learned helplessness" among American negroes. It can be seen among those I came up with who disregard higher education.

In other news, these LA girls ain't worth a damn. Having hang-ups, let downs, bad breaks, and setbacks. Tomorrow is my 23rd birthday, but who cares when all your family and friends are 3,000 miles away.

Dear Future Amir,
Remember who you are. But please, redefine.
As for today, your sh*t's weak.
Without a paddle, up Sh*t's Creek.

So…what do you want in life?
Why are you always looking for solutions?
Because there are sooo many problems.
Next year, 10/10/08—Who knows where I will be.
Chicago? New Jersey? California?
If I could change anything…what would it be?
I would paint the White House Black.
I would educate many because education/awareness changes things.

***

October 2007

Why Blink in the Dark?

If you blink in the dark, when you're already blind,
Is that wasted energy, wasted time?
No. To blink is mere instinct.
Never be blinded by what mere men think.

For if you did not blink, your eyes would dry.

The same way body parts must naturally rest,
The soul can only go so far, before it needs to catch its breath.
Blink! Better yet, rest your eyes. Rest your soul.
Chew your food before you digest it.
Embrace the knowledge manifested.

Focus on one thing, and try to fix it.
Easier said than done.
Out of breath right now, from both the chase, *and* the run.
Chasing a dream, hoping they let me up in the gate.
Running from a lifestyle, that seems impossible to escape.
Double-time tired.

I'm eternally fearful of what will become of my friends, family, community, and the world. It creates a constant anxiety that I pray this California sunshine heals.

Learned today in my educational psychology class that Black males are the only students who do not connect their academic achievement and self-esteem. In other words, we are the only students who can get F's or fail a test, and still feel good about ourselves. It's what allows us to frequently have the lowest grades. I remember this reality as a high school student. Me and my comrades never felt our grades were an accurate reflection of our intelligence. We always felt we had a genius that would rarely get acknowledged. This became an excuse for ignorance and underperformance.

I hate ignorance!!

We used to be so hungry. Now, many of us would prefer to starve. It may be hard to solve other problems unless we address this one first. Before we address the problem, we must acknowledge it as a problem.

Soul's weary.
Better blink in this room with no light.
Double-time darkness.

***

November 2007

Things are much better, but I'm still in repair. Saving the world requires upgrades.

I'm movin' on up. I'm finally finding reasons to love California. Still, I'm a bit annoyed that a party with 25,000 people is going on across the street at the Coliseum. I guess God is telling me to put this book away and enjoy my youth. Oh, I hear thee. If you can't beat 'em, join 'em. You can't study all day. Treat yourself.

'Joy yo self.

***

December 7, 2007

Yea, so I'm a California veteran now...somewhat. I mean, I still haven't seen much beyond LA. Life is less painful away from fam and friends. I've concluded that I've met some cool people out here I can consider friends. All my ed psych classmates are pretty cool. Most of them are full-time teachers or counselors. All races: Black, White, Latino, Asian. We are all quite "colorful," as one classmate remarked. Finally got a job out here too. Working in two schools for the non-profit Mental Health America of Los Angeles. My co-workers are awesome too.

I'm most definitely loving the way I am growing out here. I think I'm finally figuring out who Amir Whitaker is. I see what I stand for and what my purpose is. I think I love educational psychology.

I'm excited to return home to Jersey in two weeks for the holidays. I wonder if they'll be able to see the difference. Can't wait for Grandma to see her California Raisin.

***

January 1, 2008

Handcuffed and powerless last night, the officer told me to leave behind most of what I knew. Happy New Year's to me and the jail cell I just left in my Jersey hometown.

I told the cops the truth, but that didn't matter. Me and the boys had just watched the ball drop for New Year's. We were at Sheek's baby-momma's apartment in the projects. On the way to the car, we ran into old comrades I hadn't seen in a while. We were on our way to the club, but stood there for small talk a bit too long. The police soon arrived in the parking lot to investigate a report of "shots fired." Some idiots in the area decided to bring in the New Year by letting off a few bullets in the air.

The cops searched all eight of us, but found nothing. They held us for as long as they could and asked meaningless questions. A group of teenagers across the street caught their attention, and they decided to search them too. This time, they were lucky. One of the kids had a gun on him. They used this to justify searching OUR cars. Naturally, they found Nyce's licensed and legal handgun. He is in the military and just returned from his second tour in the Middle East. Still, he was not supposed to be traveling from Virginia with his weapon. They arrested all of us without telling us the charge or reading us our rights. I eventually learned that I was charged with loitering or trespassing, or something.

Maybe I shoulda known better, like the officer said. Know better than what? Than to hang out with my best friends? The night was just bullsh*t. I'm free, just in time for my flight back to California. But both of my brothers are still locked up in cages. Old warrants and drama. I couldn't even tell them goodbye. All eight of us have hundreds of dollars in fines and future court dates now as a result of this nonsense. I officially have an adult arrest record. I tried so hard to break that cycle.

I've failed, but it's not my fault. I swear to God it's not my fault.

***

January 15, 2008

About four months away from another college degree. Oh, what to do?! Many options exist. Viewing the future as nothing more than a series of possibilities, based on the decisions I make today.

I wrote the word "bombdiggity" on my right hand today, to frequently remind me of what I may become. Trying to boost my confidence, as I apply to Ph.D. programs at schools like Columbia. Thinkin' bout taking this education thang a bit further. Feelin' like I ain't done yet.

In other news, I have loved, and I've lost. It happens to the best. Deeply upset with these L.A. broads. Lovin' this bitchin' new ride I just got. A used, but clean, powder-blue Audi A6 to cruise down Hollywood Boulevard. I could afford it no problem on my first salary.

The semester just started. Working full-time while taking four graduate-level courses again. Classes are a few days a week from 4:00p.m.-10:00 p.m. Weekdays without class are usually spent at the library for about the same time. So, most days are touching 15 hours. And most weekends, I go even harder...then cruise the strip in my bitchin' new ride.

***

February 21, 2008

Should I accept the fact that "it is what it is?"

Just watched a documentary highlighting a million different ways justice is jacked. While one out of every 100 Americans are in prison, one out of every nine Black males are in prison. And even though the United States has 5% of the world's population, we have 25% of the prison population. You get the same amount of prison time for five grams of crack-cocaine as you get for 500 grams of powdered cocaine. Studies show the drugs have the same side effects, and more people actually overdose off of powdered cocaine. But more Black people are arrested for crack, so the powers-that-be could care less. States with the death penalty still have higher crime rates. Government sanctioned murder—capital punishment—is not working, but they don't care. Justice is jacked.

I'm having a rough week...to say the least. The documentary didn't help. There are already enough issues for me to solve in education. But I will not be stopped. This is merely a comma...not a period.

It is what it is.
Well, at least it "ain't."
In the dark, where light is faint.
Somewhere torn between the gods and saints.

Accept it as it is, since you can do little to change it.
All you can do is act in ways that get you closer to the desired situation.
If those actions or decisions don't bring you the desirable results,
Deal with them. Learn from it.
If you learn from it, then it is not a complete waste of time.
However, if you stay angry over it, it is a complete waste of energy.
Instead, invest your time into overcoming the situation.
For that is the only way to bring about change...

If change is even possible.

So, look forward to tomorrow as a new day, in which you are wiser than yesterday.

At least the same mistake won't happen again.

Learn, live, and love.

Or ignore, be angry, and be troubled.

In other words, die.

Life is short. Move forward each day stronger.

Worship yesterday's teachings.

Look at what the ancestors and those before you have done.

Don't ignore history.

They've been fighting this problem for centuries.

Recognize that God loves you.

That's why you made it this far in the first place.

Take it as it comes.

After all, it is what it is.

***

March 22, 2008

Education is God

     Shhiiiiiiieeed, I'd worship anything that could take me to Africa and California. Well, money can. And some people are born with it. But education can take you places too. And so, ignorance is my worst enemy.

     I still remember my educational enlightenment starting when reading Malcolm X's autobiography my first year in college. His perspective of knowledge helped me view learning as necessary and enjoyable. He was so sharp, it motivated me to be sharp. I also began hating ignorance. I hated not knowing things. Even though there is no possible way for me to possess all of the world's knowledge, I made it my goal to learn as much as possible. I began writing this poem I made up on the inside cover of every book I own:

I thirst for knowledge for those unable to attain. I won't be satisfied until all the world's knowledge fills my brain. I have educational opportunities the ancestors could only dream of.

I won't waste it.

***

April 2008

Didn't even get to enjoy the holiday because of stupid homework. Just got the tickets for my third college graduation. The only thing standing in the way? A friggin' thesis.

Oh...just got accepted into a doctoral program at USC, too. Dr. Whitaker...yea, that sounds nice.

Thinking I'll stay here for a while.

***

May 20, 2008

MasterMind—Master's Mine

I made it. I just finished my third college degree, a Masters in Educational Psychology. To make things better, I'm in Los Angeles—a city I've only dreamed of visiting since I was a kid (although I'm still not the biggest fan of the city). I still remember people laughing at me when I used to tell them this very dream. Just six years ago I was a confused 17-year-old graduating high school with a GPA below 2.0. I had to take every basic reading, English and math class even to be considered college-level. Six years later I'm the only Black male in my entire class, and also the youngest and one of the highest achieving. Got a 3.9 GPA, which is twice the GPA I had in high school. I got all A's, except for that one B+ in my Memory and Cognition class. It only happened because a Supreme Ike visited me and we partied a little too hard. We got kicked out of every campus bar. Leave it to the white man to always bring you down. Haha.

This time, I actually cried at the graduation. Speaking of being the youngest, I'm also the youngest person to be admitted into this doctoral program at USC. But USC is not the only school I've been accepted to. I also got into NYU. These are two of the greatest schools in the country. Two schools that would have laughed at my high school transcripts. Now they are fighting for me to come to their school and become Dr. Whitaker. Only one out of every 100 people get their doctorate. The numbers are even less for black males, as usual. Well, find another 99, cuz I'm 'bout to get mine!

I will most likely continue my education at USC. Don't get me wrong, I would love to move back near my family—and New York's a hell of a lot better than LA, however, I see both opportunities and commitments in this city.

I almost didn't move here in the first place. When my acceptance letter arrived in 2007, my mom ripped it up. She didn't want her son moving across the country to a state where he didn't know a single person. I didn't find out that USC had accepted me until they called me to see if I was going to attend. I've been here for almost a year now, and although I didn't meet the girl of my dreams like I swore I would, I'm not ready to leave it all behind just yet. The weather, my school, and my job are just too magnificent.

If I stay at my job, I will have the privilege of helping the 11th graders I taught this year get into college as seniors. I consider them more like little brothers and sisters instead of students. I even

let them call me by my first name. They remind me of little brother Tyson who is their age. After he was shot in that drive-by after I moved to LA, it made me feel as if I failed as a big brother. Eventually, I accepted the fact that the streets take ahold of whomever they like. Working with the students at Huntington Park High helped get me through it. They were actually the first I told when I got accepted into the USC doctoral program. I didn't bother telling Mom yet, because I know it would make her have two heart attacks. One from the pain of her son deciding to stay in California, and another from the fact that her son will be Dr. Whitaker in a few years.

While I am becoming Dr. Whitaker, I can think of no better privilege than helping my students get into college. That's what's keeping me in this god-awful city...which I'm learning to love. Well, them, and the fact that it never rains here. And the chicks tanning on USC's campus in bikinis. It helps make every day a lovely day to study.

When you feel like you can't go any further, look back at how far you've already come. What you become will always be the result of what you do. Where you're from, and where you are now don't matter. Your current condition is irrelevant. Let your technique speak.

***

June 15, 2008

Curse those Los Angeles Lakers! I live on the same street as the Staples Center where they play. It's 20 blocks down Figueroa. They are about to win the NBA Championship. My class is canceled tomorrow...and it could be related. Either way, it's like a muthafu@!*# snow day in June! I have one week left of classes, both as a teacher and a student.

Thought I already hated BET as much as humanly possible, until the BET Awards happened three blocks away from my house. I swear I saw John Legend drive past me.

***

December 2, 2008

Preparing for finals in my 13th semester of college. That second-wind should kick in any moment now. Partied like an undergrad all semester, now I must pull all-nighters like one too. Was studying just fine until the Kanye West and Common concert started across the street at the Coliseum. I can hear every word muffled through the walls of my living room. Talk about distractions! Eventually relocated to the front door to study to the soundtrack of the concert.

***

December 17, 2008

On a flight back to Jersey. Just reflecting on the amount of growth I experience between each trip home. It became evident while packing this time. No Timberland boots or Nike Air Force Ones. Instead, only a $25 pair of Payless shoes. No anxiety over visiting everyone. I'm just going to wing it. Old flames are not a priority. At first, I thought this was a transition from boy to man...but I believe that it's much bigger.

I can almost say that I'm comfortable in LA. I have friends and a strong social network. Guess I have a decent hold on my doctoral program. Getting straight A's is no longer a priority. Balancing and enjoying my youth is. I'm coming back to Jersey much more comfortable and aware of who I am as a person. I must

admit that LA is at least partially responsible for this. It forced it out of me.

Now back to the Olde Country.

***

December 27, 2008

Just flew from NY to LA, and I'm happy to be home. Yes, LA is HOME now! Still in shock over everything I saw in the past three months. L.A, San Francisco, Mexico, New Jersey, New York, San Diego, Las Vegas.

When I'm out of town and people ask me where I'm from, I'll tell them "Los Angeles by way of Jersey."

***

February 3, 2009

<u>22 Random Things About Amir</u>

Dating in this city is weird. A girl I met on Hollywood Blvd two weeks asked me to send her 25 random things about myself. In a strange, fetish-like manner, she asked for me to write them in the third person. I want her bad enough to give it a shot. I could only make it to 22 though.

Who is Amir?

1. He has no middle name. It's just Amir Whitaker. Perhaps his parents were in a rush. Both his brother and sister have middle names, though.

2. He is also a middle child. Combined with his lack of a middle name, he felt really insignificant as a child.

3. He doesn't know if he *worships* education/knowledge, or just *despises* ignorance. Whatever it is, he wants to spend the rest of his life teaching and learning.

4. He owns thousands of dollars in jewelry that he refuses to wear because it reminds him of a lifestyle he doesn't want to be reminded of. He wants to give it to his son one day and say "I did that....so you don't have to go through that."

5. He has performed at concerts in Los Angeles, New York, Delaware, Philly, Pittsburgh, all over Jersey, and many other places.

6. He can count the childhood Christmases that his father was not locked-up on one hand.

7. He made a vow to travel to a different country every year in 2007.

8. His biggest pet peeve is people who wear Bluetooth headsets as fashionable accessories, or when they are not (or shouldn't be) having a conversation (in the club, in important meetings, in pictures, shopping, in class, etc.)

9. He has been told by five of his students "I want to be like you when I grow up" in the past year. His response is always "I ain't grown yet!"

10. He works for a non-profit organization and volunteers for two other non-profits.

11. He graduated five times in the span of ten years: 1998-2008 (Hubbard '98, PHS '02, UCC '05, Rutgers '07, USC '08). The ceremony is getting repetitive and boring.

13. He will be Dr. Whitaker in 27 months.

14. Has finished roughly 50 pages of a potential autobiography.

15. His most played songs on his iTunes are Nas- "Still Dreaming" (147 times), John Coltrane- "Naima" (114 times), Ben Harper- "The Woman" (103 times). His iTunes library is 52.7 gigs, 10,962 songs, and 64.5 days' worth of music.

16. He looks like he is breastfeeding Don King if he doesn't shave his nipples every two weeks. He has no other chest hair.

17. He has not had a real girlfriend since being dumped on Prom Night seven years ago. It's complicated.

18. He wants to learn salsa, breakdancing, and capoeira this year.

19. He has an alter ego that is an arrogant womanizer with a British accent. His name is Sebastian. He only exists in his head.

20. He was once a prejudice drug dealer hell-bent on destroying the white race one crack-rock at a time. Unfortunately, he experienced a bit of success.

21. He has to get braces and is NOT looking forward to it.

22. He was born with a heart murmur. He was told he would grow out of it by the time he was 13. His heart occasionally skips a beat.

***

May 20, 2009

Wrapped up another year of college, and completed my application for federal financial aid for the 8th year in a row. I almost heard the federal government laugh out loud, after I submitted the application.

Experienced two earthquakes in one week. Further proof that God hates LA. Still, offering myself the proposition: if the Lakers win the Championship again, I will finally embrace LA as my new home (after living here for 2 years), stop saying "I hate LA," and maybe even become a Lakers/Dodgers fan.

In other news, I'm never drinking Red Bull and vodka again. That stuff is the Devil's Piss, and is ironically the same color as urine.

***

June 20th, 2009

Gratitude

A lil bit of gratitude never hurt nobody. Decided to try this assignment where you reflect on areas of your life and focus on the things you are grateful for.

GRATITUDE #1: Work/professional growth is better than ever. More than any time before, I feel like my hours of labor have paid off. The 11th graders I taught at HP and later provided "guidance" to just graduated high school and will start college. Some of them say I inspire them…that I'm one of the only people they look up to…that I convinced them to go to college when they were not previously thinking about it.

I had no idea that I had this kind of impact on them. The yearbook of the HPHS Class of 2009 will serve as my motivation when I feel like I've had enough. It includes an intricate full-page work of art that a student did for me, describing some memorable moments—and cussin' me out for the days I was at my other school, Narbonne High.

To. Dr. Amir (cough cough)

Hello ... well its soon to be a goodbye..
I remember when we met you in that class ...
you probably hated us back then. It was
nice working with you eventhough you were
not there those days i needed to clear my
detention hours and you were absent thanks
alot...!! Thats why i had to leave those
disturbing letters in your mailbox haha... Well
I want to say thank you for all your help..
i appreciate everything you did for me.. and
i like the passion you have for your work...
I would like to be a "Amir" when i grow
up. haha really .. you are one of the few people
i look up to and i know that without
your help i would not of comed so far.. Thanks
for taking your time with me and offering your
help. Your an amazing person and sorry if i
was ever a pain...haha. I hope to see you later
on in life and yeah come for a visit at CSULA.
ill hope to see you then. Hope your studies
turn out good and you became an even
awsomer person than you really are. Take
care and stay away from sexual predators
and pimps! haha. You have changed the way
i see things and i like humanity Lol... I like
what you do :) Thank you so much... I like
your tatto and i will be a tatto person some
day and come over to my shop and ill tatto you
a dead dinasaur haha..
                                    GoodNIGHT
                                          -y

Lion King!!

That's all I want to do for the rest of my life…inspire. I like doing it on an individual level. That's the reason why I never want to leave the classroom or student interaction. I think I have decent interpersonal skills. At the same time, those skills could be used to lead a team to meet larger goals...perhaps...time will tell. I really like working with high school students, though. Seniors are the most awesome, or as one of them says, "supremely-awesome-to the max-over 9,000." It's been a pleasure watching them grow.

I've been thinking a lot about "what I want to be when I grow up." I have a couple options. Call it arrogant, but I honestly believe that I can do anything...go anywhere. It's really all on me. Still, I think I get the most satisfaction out of helping people on an individual level. The problem lies with me being restricted in how I help people. I really need to be my own boss. This is why I propose opening up juvenile facilities that are truly education and rehabilitation-driven. I would make an impact while not having to worry about finances. It would be nice to have them up and running by age 40. That gives me 15 years to get experience, do some planning, design curriculum, coordinate a team, etc. This is doubly gratifying because it decreases prison rates among people of color, while increasing educational attainment. They are interconnected, you know.

So, what do I have to do now? Well...first and foremost, I must LEARN. What are the most effective ways to "rehabilitate" urban, minority, "at-risk" youth? Sounds like a dissertation, or at least a literature review. But there is so much to learn: how to write grants, how to start and run a non-profit, what are the most effective educational strategies for "delinquent" youth, etc...

GRATITUDE #2: School is going great, I guess. Finished up seven years of college, and I'm not too tired. I definitely will survive...maybe even do a second doctorate, if there is still an unexplored area/knowledge gap. My GPA is 3.87 or so. I only have one year of classes remaining. I start a T.A. fellowship in a couple months at USC. I'm looking forward to this more than any other job ever. Me?! Lecturing college students?!

GRATITUDE #3: Family/Friends are good, as well. I no longer consider Jersey my home, but I know family is still important. I could probably make some more calls than I do, though. We lost a few this year. Uncle Twin passed in April. Aunt Mary Ann died too. Both deaths brought the family closer together. I feel like being apart can actually bring you closer.

I moved my big brother, Jamal, out here with me to go to school. He is good most of the time, but his actions/focus occasionally make me question the decision. He's been out here six months and still doesn't have a job. He's not helping out financially, either. Probably only gave me $150 total since he's been here. We are about to have a serious conversation. I will give him three months to shape up. He is the big brother, and I am not going to be taking care of him like a baby. Doing his laundry, feeding him, etc. His irresponsibility and inability to step up to the plate are interfering with things. I just want him to reach his potential. You think I like giving up some of my freedoms as a bachelor?!

Mom could move out here in another year, herself. I tell you right now...one of them mofos better get a driver's license. I ain't gonna be the chauffeur for grown people. No excuses at this point...well...except for fines they probably have related to charges having nothing to do with driving.

Father's Day is tomorrow. Haven't talked to my dad since Uncle Twin's funeral. The unconditional love is still there...that's just the kind of relationship that we have. I think the limited communication is the result of him being away serving time in prison so often in my formative years.

Pop is getting old and worrying me. He is getting more sluggish. Still Pop though. Nana is maintaining like she always does. That woman has the strength of the gods. Grandma does as well. She is doing good and moving to Delaware. I need to talk to all of them more though. Whatever happened to the Family/Friends' Sundays? I would spend hours talking to everyone on Sundays when I first moved here.

Sheek, Chris, and Nyce are maintaining as well. Sheek just had a son. Visiting Nyce in VA in a couple weeks. Chris is expanding his mind and reading books on ancient wisdom.

GRATITUDE #4: Finances: Mucho dinero, but maaaad student loans. They are a problem for another day. Just trying not to go over 100k. I have an official "budget" now for the first time. Trying to save $500 a month/$6,000 a year so I can get a house in 2011. It doesn't have to be in LA either. It's an investment.

GRATITUDE #5: Health-wise: I am in the best shape ever. Leaner, stronger, faster, healthier. This is both mentally and physically. Had a physical yesterday. I need to lose about ten more pounds and I will be in ideal shape. I'm about 210 lbs now. I have complex and individualized workout routines. Taking a weightlifting class in the summer with my students, too.

GRATITUDE #6: Spiritual/Soul: It is what it is. Too liberated for my own good. I'm satisfied though. As long as I try not to deliberately hurt people…as long as I intentionally want to help people…I'm ok by the judgment of any god I would want to worship. I'm still trying to reconcile the state of my people with an all-knowing, all-creating God. I know that She/He/it is there though. I'm embracing the fact that spiritual/soul satisfaction comes about through music and dance for me. Still making music and playing guitar. I'm part of the USC Salsa Club, and boy, do I have a serious two-step! I'm also part of USC 25-piece Saved by Grace gospel choir. Some LA redemption for the ol' Soul Mercenary. We even performed at the Staples Center where the LA Lakers play!

GRATITUDE #7: **Most Importantly** Satisfaction and Happiness: All in all, I am highly satisfied with what I have and where I'm at. Of course, I can go further and grow more, but that is exactly what I'm doing every day. I'm still in repair. Mental and physical repair…getting mind and body where I want to be.

***

June 21, 2009

Recently got a new tattoo. It says "African Roots, American Fruit" next to a tree that takes up nearly half of my upper arm. The roots of the tree form Africa, and the leaves and branches form America. I've descended from African royalty brought here in chains, exploited for the wealth and riches of others. Centuries of oppression made the roots deeper and stronger. We managed to grow, regardless. I am the fruit that finally has an opportunity to ripen, thanks to the struggle of those before me. So this tattoo is a tribute to them. It also symbolizes the Black diaspora being deeply embedded within America. I designed and drew it myself. The idea has been in my head for years. Wasn't bold enough before, because my pride as an American was limited due to its 400-year history of stiffing my people.

But now, my President is Black, my Audi A6 is blue. Knowing that someone who looks like me is running this country makes me so proud to be an American, a bald eagle soars by and screams every morning to wake me up 6:30 a.m.

***

July 12, 2009

You ever try to stay up as late as possible to delay tomorrow's hangover? Stupidest idea ever. Goodnight...or good morning, since it's 5:30 AM!

Anyways, FINALLY, I have a new roommate. It's my 10th roommate total, but the first female. God help her. I hope she lasts longer than these other LA transients and students. The last two have averaged five-month stays.

***

August 2009

<u>I Just Want to Be…</u>

I'm at the airport in Philly waiting for my connecting flight back to LA. Just got back from Europe. The trip had its ups and downs, but in the end, I can honestly say I'm glad I did it. One word to describe it? ENLIGHTENING. Nice to finally see the things I was forced to learn about in school. It makes you appreciate them at a higher level.

Of course, the most painful part of traveling abroad involves seeing the status of Black folk. Sometimes I feel like I'm traveling the world to discover a place where Black people are *not* suffering disproportionately. Needless to say, this was not the case in Europe (duh!). It was the most painful in Barcelona, Spain, where most Black women were rumored to be prostitutes and most Black men are merchants in the "informal sector." They were mostly recent immigrants from Africa.

Paris was great, but some people weren't the friendliest. It's like the entire country has resting b***** face or something. Sometimes, their stares penetrate your soul, making you feel like sh*t. London was cool. Blacks seem to be doing the best there.

People appear to be doing the best there overall. It was just really expensive.

As Keyshawn and I journeyed throughout Western Europe, we eternally reflected on the fact that we can travel almost anywhere in the world at our leisure. It's something that very few people in the world can do, and we are both young Black males in our 20s. I really can't think of any peers I came up with who be able to do such a thing. It brought up the question of "success." There is a new catchy song out called "Successful" by Drake, that emphasizes material possessions and women as the definition of success.

I want the money, (money)
Money and the cars, (cars)
Cars and the clothes, (clothes)
The hoes, (hoes) I suppose,
I just wanna be... I just wanna be, successful.

As catchy as the song is, I couldn't disagree more with Drizzy. I don't think any of that stuff translates into success. Throughout my life, I have tasted some of these things Drake defines as measures of success, often in abundance. They can only fulfill so much. Certainly, they can't sustain a happy and prosperous life. I actually learned that people derive more long-term happiness from experiences (like travel) more than material possessions. I guess because of the memories they gain. I agree. With my Audi A6 breaking down, this recent Europe trip will be cherished much more down the road.

"What is success?" Keyshawn asked me, in one of his many questions.

"Achieving what you want to accomplish," I said. "For some, it's a particular car or woman. Success for me is making the world a better place, and relinquishing the suffering of people."

So am I successful? Weeeelll... some would say so. My yearbook from HP proves the impact that I have made. I can travel anywhere I want. I have my own place, car, bank account, etc. But what does it all mean?

Tomorrow I go to a USC Rossier School of Education Conference to select my dissertation topic. I'm contemplating topics that will contribute to my success. Something that will make the world a better place. There are so many things to be improved in education. I'm having a hard time making up my mind. I'm really looking forward to getting back to LA and finishing this journey.

I just want to be...

I just want to BE.

That's all.

***

August 23, 2009

Preparing to begin my 8th year of college tomorrow. This time, I'll be on the other side of the class delivering the lecture. It's the first day of school so it will be the first time lecturing these USC freshmen. Kinda nervous...

***

September 15, 2009

Don't know what I want to be when I grow up, but it DAMN sure ain't a professor. Only halfway thru the 100+ pages that I need to grade for my USC students. THEN I can grade my high-schoolers' papers, THEN read my own 100+ pages of homework. Some days I'm on campus for 13 hours a day (grading, lecture, studying, gym, class).

Things at HPHS are good. We took the students on a field trip to the Museum of Tolerance. After an incredibly powerful experience, we ran into the late-night show host, Conan O'Brien, filming a skit. He was super chill, and couldn't say anything that wasn't a joke. Only in LA! Sometimes I wonder if I'm dreaming. Life is beautiful... until those goddamn 13-hour days come.

Happy we are entering the Libra zodiac soon. Still, I am the author of my own horoscope. This is an idea I'm learning to embrace as I approach age 25.

***

October 11, 2009

Flew home for a few reasons. I planned and paid for Nana and Pop's 50th Wedding Anniversary Banquet. It was a surprise and almost caused them to have heart attacks. Cost me over $2,000. The rest of the family was supposed to chip in. Nobody has given me a single dime, though. I knew my grandparents deserved it, so I didn't let anything get in the way. This parking-lot-pimping-side-gig is feeding me so fat, these two stacks were nothing.

While in Jersey, I got to rendezvous with the Ninja Turtles and Ikes for the Rutgers Homecoming, which was actually on my 25th birthday. Woke up on a cold, random college couch extremely hungover after having 25 drinks over the 24-hour period. The Ikes made me do it. Worst idea EVER. White man stays bringin' you down! Or getting you drunk as f#*%.

***

October 12, 2009

<u>6 Things I've Realized at 25-years-old</u>

I'm halfway through my 20's. My car insurance rate will significantly decrease now. I can even rent cars. Tupac died at this age, and Biggie didn't even live to see it—nor did countless others, many of whom I came up with. I've reached that quarter-century milestone, the final milestone of "youth." Here are six things that I've finally realized:

1) I (or anyone else) CAN DO ANYTHING. Of course, everyone's heard the phrase "you can do anything you set your mind to" since they were little, but our actions usually don't reflect this. The problem is DOUBT. We let hesitation and disbelief cripple us too often. Sometimes it comes from another individual, or "hater." They say things like "you can't do that" or "that's more than you can handle." Sometimes it comes from yourself saying things like, "I can't do that." However, if you truly realize your potential, there is nothing that anyone else can say or do to get in your way. Higher education was not a tradition where I came from. I remember teachers and people telling me I'd never amount to much. In spite of it all, I will be Dr. Whitaker in 17 months. I've been to six different countries, and no one in my family has ever even left the East Coast. I've lost 55 pounds over the past couple years. I've also just successfully planned and put on my grandparents' 50th Wedding Anniversary Banquet, requiring countless hours and thousands of dollars. Of course I've doubted myself at times, because I'm human. But at the end of the day, I never forgot that I can make anything happen.

2) MY PURPOSE IN LIFE is to help people realize their potential. Doubt will always be the Kryptonite, and it will always exist on some level. However, helping people believe in themselves is like awakening their super powers. I'm still not sure what I want to "be when I grow up," but it will involve inspiring people to see their potential for excellence. I think this comes through education in our public school system. I've already helped hundreds of students get to college as a counselor. I've inspired many more as a teacher. I LOVE

doing what I do. I love learning about ways to do a better job. I'm certain that this is my life's purpose.

3) MONEY ISN'T HAPPINESS. It took me a while to figure this out. Growing up poor made me see money as the root of many problems. However, just because not having something causes problems, attaining it does not automatically make you happy. I remember childhood Christmases and birthdays where I got next to nothing and I was still happy. I also remember being a teenage drug dealer with thousands of dollars who still thought life sucked.

4) The world is FAR from where it should be. I've traveled the world and still see that people of color and poor people struggle more than other groups EVERYWHERE. Part of this is because we don't recognize our potential (See #1 and #2 above). Centuries of oppression have created these deficit mindsets in some. Racism and systematic bias remain in less obvious ways. Our potential is not recognized (by ourselves or others) outside of entertainment, sports, etc. For Blacks, much of our mindset is the result of slavery and oppression, and it won't change by itself. I plan on spending my life on the frontlines trying to reverse this slave mentality, and the white supremacy that birthed it. Freedom of the mind.

5) Not all white people suck. Of course many of them do and yes, they've caused irreversible damage through imperialism, chattel slavery, neocolonialism, etc...but many white folks have also helped the world. I will openly admit that I had an intense dislike for white people growing up. This came from knowing history's atrocities, and seeing the many poor Black folk compared to the many rich white folk. But hate is wasted energy, folk. Indeed, coming from a sh*tty high school, unstable family situation, and struggling community made it harder for me to get to where I am in comparison to the average (white) person benefiting from generation of privilege.

Nonetheless, I am still here, and still pressing on. And now some of my best friends are white.

White privilege still exists, and has to be dismantled. As long as there is white privilege, then there is racial inequality and oppression. White people inheriting this privilege today (usually) haven't made the conscious decision to be racist like previous generations have throughout most of American history. Don't worry about trying to convince them that a privilege exists, or that racism is still alive. Focus on fighting this new sh*t that has evolved from the simplistic racism of the past. Much of today's oppression/discrimination may not be rooted in deliberate racist behavior, and this complicates things. Modern oppression exists because 400 years of foul history cannot be undone by a few laws over a few decades

You do know you are one of the first generation of Negroes to be "free" right? It took eight years of college, four rambunctious white roommates at Rutgers, a Black President, and a trip to Europe to help me realize not all White people. Many people never do, and the same is true for the reverse.

6)   Last but certainly not least, I'M A GROWN A*S MAN! I'm fully independent and self-sufficient. I realized this about two weeks ago when I got home from MY job, I parked MY car in MY yard, walked into MY apartment, slept in MY bed...butt-naked...because I'm a grown a$$ man. I moved 3,000 miles away from everyone I ever knew, because I'm grown. I will probably do it again. New Orleans, Miami, or Atlanta sound nice. Although I'm grown, I acknowledge that I am still GROWING. I'm progressing and changing every day. Life is a constant evolution.

Song of the Year: *G.O.D (Gaining One's Definition)* (1997)
Artist: Common

"In time brotha, you will discover the light...

A rich man is one with knowledge, happiness and his health"

***

October 2009

Just came back from my first Swap Meet. It's basically a glorified flea market. Never seen so much hair weave, gold, or rims in my life...Ghetto Superficial Paradise. But I needed a fresh, fly shirt. Prolly shouldn't go so hard this weekend. Grades are due for both my high school and college students on Monday. Mid-term exam of my own on Wednesday.

I'm studying/researching/grading for hours with my three study-buddies: John Coltrane, Charles Mingus, and Miles Davis. Feeling good that I've earned a trip to the gym after four semi-productive hours of grading and studying. Never thought I'd have to "earn" a trip to the friggin' gym. Discipline is a virtue. Reframing things as rewards motivates me to do them more.

Whatever it takes.

***

November 22, 2009

I'm studying in one of USC's libraries, despite the 70-foot Ferris wheel and live music in the courtyard outside the window. It's some commemorative concert. A firework show broke out a few minutes ago. It's God telling me to put the books down and go shake my stankin' a$$ at a club in Hollywood. Last weekend, I ran into Wesley Snipes in the bathroom at a hoity-toity lounge! Like most other celebrities you meet in person, he is shorter than you'd think.

***

November 26, 2009

I've got a lot to be thankful for this Thanksgiving. Missing my family too much to be around any other family, so I'm staying home alone. Nana's sweet potato pie and Grandma's turkey salad woulda been worth the 11 hours of flying to and from the Olde Country. Still thankful.

***

December 4, 2009

Just finished my last class of the semester. Fifteen college semesters down (22 if you include summers!), and three more to go. Dropkicked Career Day today. Bout to suplex some bluebook exams, before I powerbomb these presentations and papers. A few more days, and this week is down for the count. Guess that's not bad, when you look at it like that.

If I get through everything before next Saturday, I can celebrate by going snowboarding for a few hours. Tonight, I'll hit up the EDSA Party at Busby's, then indulge in some of the stickiest icky west of the Mississippi. Ewww weeee!!

***

December 2009

NOTE FROM ROOMMATE:

"I always leave a bunch of old crap in the little sink filter thing. I have this weird phobia of cleaning it. HAHA. I can't ever force myself to grab that thing and empty it into the trashcan. Guess that'll always be your job :) SORRY and THANKS! Man, how do you still eat after touching that thing? Haha!"

***

December 25, 2009

Finally in the Olde Country after 12 hours of flights, layovers, trains, and subways. Finally realizing that catching the flight straight from the club was a baaaad idea.

In other news, I have a dream...that one day, I will be able to wear USC or Rutgers gear without hearing things like "What sport do u play?" or "Ohh, are u a fan?" This happened four times this month, and many more throughout college. When I achieve my dream, people will see me for my academic and intellectual potential as a student or alumni.

Fu*k it. Tell people you play football and take it as a compliment to your imposing Negro stature. Worse-comes-to-worse, you tell a lie. If all goes well, you could get a free drink or get lucky. Bout to research the full name, jersey number, and stats of a player of a similar build. Betta yet, just use the name of one of the student athletes in the Ed Psych class you teach. They'll probably get a kick out of it. Give them extra credit to play along. Haha.

***

January 27, 2010

Who has two thumbs and just handed in Chapter One of his dissertation?!!! This guy! Can't wait to celebrate tonight with some of my favorite musicians and bands at the Grammy's Party in Downtown LA. Talib Kweli, Foreign Exchange, etc. It's hosted by Kiss-n-Grind and DJ Vikter Duplaix. One chapter down, six more to go. Keep choppin' wood.

Also got a season pass for Mt. High, a mountain resort 90 miles northeast of LA. Some Saturdays, I'm there for eight hours of "S & S" cycles where I study for an hour, then snowboard for an hour. Zooming down a mountain 25-miles per hour attached to five-feet of fiberglass clears your mind. The frosty mountains in the distance add to the relaxation. In some parts of the trail, all you hear is the wind whizzing past your ear or soft snow crunching beneath your board. I do this same one-for-one, study-and-play technique in other places too. Sometimes on Venice Beach. Sometimes at this mountain hiking trail behind Dodger Stadium. Southern California's weather and terrain are unreal. You can swim at a beach near dolphins, not too far away from frozen mountains.

***

March 2010

Can't sleep…my mind is focused too much on dreams. I can't wait to wake up tomorrow and continue the quest for my dreams. So anxious that I can't sleep at 3 a.m.!? Thinking about the things I want to do this year, the places I want to go. With this parking lot hustle, I'm gonna travel to both Japan and Brazil over the next few months. I'll probably backpack through all seven countries in Central

America during winter break, too. If I backpack and stay in hostels on the trip, I can visit all nine of these countries for less than six grand. I can easily save that working these three jobs. Watch me now.

***

April 6, 2010

Somewhere in Japan

Just had one of the greatest nights of my life partying 'til sunrise in the Land of the Rising Sun. Now I've been to seven countries and four continents. Can't wait for South America and Brazil this summer! Well-worth the grind multiple jobs.

Met some of the kindest spirits in Osaka and Kyoto. Tokyo was aiight, until they refused Keyshawn and I admission into Club Harlem—the most famous hip-hop club in Japan. They are not fans of foreigners. The image and irony of Japanese 20 somethings dressed in hip hop attire blasting Lil Jon, telling me I can't get into their club will stay with me forever. Haha. I wonder if they know that discrimination like that is what created Harlem in the first place. In the early 20th century, Blacks couldn't move to other parts of NYC because of segregation and discrimination, so we were concentrated in Harlem. Forgive them, for they know not what they perpetuate.

They just wanna boogie.

***

April 11, 2010

I think my new roommate saw me playing with my swords and screaming through the window. I was in my underwear at the time. Don't ask why. Sweet first impression, ninja boi! Also sliced my curtain in half with the swords by mistake. Not crazy, just loving my favorite souvenirs from Japan.

***

April 2010

NOTE FROM ROOMMATE:

"Jeez, can you STOP taking naked pictures of yourself?! At least let me come over with my SLR & we'll turn it into a real steamy, high-quality picture. Hah, you wish. You narcissist, you. Haha!
Anywayyyys, I still gots your lock! Puhaha, maybe I'll hold it hostage. You should really stop lending me stuff."

***

May 12, 2010

Just handed in the last paper of my 8th year of college. Eight years down, one to go...at least until I become Dr. Whitaker. I'm thinking about doing law school or applying for a Fulbright scholarship afterwards. Why not? I've been using education to learn, travel, work at jobs I love, make a difference, and party...and bullsh*t... and party...and bullsh*t...over the past eight years. What's another three or four?!

Was so busy grading my USC students' papers, I didn't get a chance to plan a lesson for my high school students. Netflix saves the day again with a documentary. I can no longer criticize teachers who just showed movies and graded our papers back in the day.

The only thing I dislike more than taking exams is grading them! Also hate the fact that this doctoral program only gives us a week off in between the spring and summer semesters. No true summer break. The time went by fast, now 250 pages have to be read before the first day of class on Thursday. Now back to academic-ninja-mode until the next time our program gives us a measly week off between the summer and fall semesters. Already planning on taking my black a*s to Brazil for that one.

***

June 17, 2010

Living between South Central LA and the Staples Center Arena allows for interesting sound interpretations. At times I wonder if the loud bangs are fireworks...or gunshots. Either way, I'm staying in the crib tonight!

Had a long, tiring day at work cuz she kept me up 'til 5 a.m. again. She was begging for more all night, so I only got three hours of sleep. Thinking about what I'm gonna do to her next is keeping me up all night. Tonight will be another all-nighter with her. Yup, she's my dissertation.

Sometimes, I head to the library with four boxes of Lunchables, a 62-song/8-hour John Coltrane and Miles Davis playlist, and 8 hours of battery life on my laptop. I'm not allowed to leave until one of them is finished. It's usually the Lunchables.

***

June 19, 2010

Happy Juneteenth! Take advantage of the freedom/opportunities you have. They cost your forbearers 400 years of blood, sweat, and tears. The ancestors could only dream of these things. 145 years ago, I woulda been killed for knowing how to read or leaving the plantation. Today, I'm 11 months away from my 4th college degree, and two months away from visiting my 8th country. Bout to hit up festivals in Compton, Inglewood, and other LA areas with beautiful Black folk.

***

June 21, 2010

I'm teaching summer classes at USC, so I just met my new class of college students today. Ironically, saying goodbye to my high school students tomorrow at graduation. Now I'm studying at the USC library while Kobe and the LAKER'S PARADE is literally happening two blocks away—just across the street from my house! True Ninja discipline? Or lack of concern for the Lakers?

***

August 21, 2010
Rio De Janiero, Brazil

It's 7 a.m. in Rio. Dissertation + Partying = Not sleeping for two days. Tomorrow's my last night here, and still soooo much to do. I land in Los Angeles at 10:00 a.m. Monday, just two hours before the first class I'm teaching at USC this semester. My latest group of students must understand: "Rockstar lifestyle, might don't make it."

— 185 —

One night, I was up until 2:45 a.m. in Rio, but not because of the infinite alluring clubs. It was because I had to hand in an 83-page draft of three dissertation chapters by 9 a.m. Spent the day at Copacabana Beach choppin' away at it. Voluptuously curved bodies pranced about the beach providing a beautiful distraction. I rewarded myself the next night by carving up the Rio nightlife scene in my dancing shoes. The perfect way to celebrate the fact that I got A's in 22 out of the 24 classes in my masters and doctorate. Not bad for a kid who failed nearly every class his freshman year of high school.

***

September 7, 2010

Who has two thumbs and just SMASHED his qualifying exam? THIS GUY! All that stands between me and graduation now is one more exam and two more chapters of my dissertation. Starting year nine of college. It is the year of no classes, just research. I'm more confident than ever.... I'm a veteran at this.

***

October 9, 2010

Next weekend, I'm taking an 8-hour road trip to Arizona to visit the only other family member I have on the West Coast—Ray Ray Whitaker. It's his b-day and he is in the federal prison there. He's more like a brother, since we were raised in the same house by Nana and Pop. More than 14 years in-and-out of prison since he was ten-years-old. We are one year apart, and slept in the same bed at times. On some birthdays, I received only a single gift: a card from him sent from whatever prison he was at. Growing up, he was actually the smartest Whitaker Boy. Despite his talent and intelligence, he's spent more than half of his 27 years on earth in a cage or cell. The system never rehabilitated or "corrected" him either. In some ways, it made him worse by introducing him to dangerous gangs and criminals. When he was 16 years old, he was charged as an adult and sentenced to his first prison stretch for years. After coming home and rendezvousing with some ruffians he met in prison, Ray Ray was shot in the head. I was at Rutgers at the time, and it shattered our family. The doctor said that, had the bullet gone an inch to the left, he would be dead.

Part of the untapped potential of brilliant minds like Ray Ray's is the reason why I want go to law school now. I'm certain he coulda been a Dr. or lawyer too, despite what we grew up in. Likewise, my path coulda easily led me to spend years in prison instead. I'm hoping to use these wings I've grown to help correct this criminal justice system somehow. Thanks for the second wind, Ray Ray—The Rugged Child. Something tells me I'll need it.

I'll be making a pit stop at the Grand Canyon on my way back from seeing Ray Ray. Camping and jumping pictures to help me stop and smell the flowers. Speaking of which, bout to head to Hollywood to celebrate my 26th Birthday tomorrow! 10-10-10 is a special day! It's the first date to have eight digits in many years. This October is also the first month with five Fridays, Saturdays, & Sundays in over 800 years. Best of all, during my 26th year, I become Dr. Whitaker.

The stars are indeed aligning.

***

November 11, 2010

Got the day off from work today, so I'm trying to pull a dime: ten hours of studying and research. Can't believe President Obama is visiting my school tomorrow! The first thing I'm gonna tell him is: "Stop cramping my style!"

This year I also saw the Dalai Lama and Angela Davis speak just a few days apart. These are the people hanging on my wall in pictures.

Also went to the barbershop for the first time in YEARS in preparation for tomorrow's graduation pics. Found a good, but overpriced, shop on Crenshaw. Loving my new lil' Afro, my fresh can of Afro-Sheen, and my afro pick with the black fist! Letting my SOOOOOULLL GLOW! Haha.

Thank you, LA.

***

December 1, 2010

Finished up with my last class teaching at USC today. It was a pleasure contributing to the growth of over 100 future scholars, leaders, and athletes during my teaching fellowship here. Can't wait to see them do BIG THINGS! Gonna miss em'. Still got those high school brats to deal with. ☺

***

December 11, 2010

Last day in LA for four weeks, and it was a rough one. Received terrible news while waiting in line to take the four-hour exam (LSAT) to gain admission into law school this morning. My homey Sahaad was murdered last night back in Jersey. This is the third time this year someone I grew up with won't be able to grow old...all because of violence. I couldn't even focus during the exam thinking about him and his family. Days like this make me not wanna return to Jerzy.

$$***$$

December 13, 2010

About to fly to Honduras to start my 4-week journey through Central America. Let's see if I can do three or four days in each country like I plan. Got about 100 pages of grading to knock out on this flight. Then it's Honduras, Belize, Guatemala, El Salvador, Costa Rica, Nicaragua, and Panama for the next 25 days.

$$***$$

December 28th, 2010

Explored 1200-year-old Mayan ruins in Honduras. Climbed an active volcano in Guatemala. Caught a boat to Belize to snorkel with small sharks. Fell in love with Nicaragua and all the nicknames the people yelled at me. Chico Moreno, Papa Negro, Will Smith, Kobe Bryant, etc. Heading to Costa Rica for New Year's. I sang "Feliz Navidad" in El Salvador to celebrate Christmas. It makes me miss my fam and friends. Was good to be in Jerzy for Thanksgiving. I'll be back before you know it, with gifts a-plenty from around the world.

$$***$$

January 1, 2011

I will never forget the year 2010 for a few reasons related to the number "10":

1) My birthday was on 10-10-10. A memorable way to turn 26-years-old.

2) I visited ten countries total: Japan, Brazil, and the seven countries on my Central American backpacking trip.

3) The number "2010" is three 10's, like my birthday (the "20" is 10+10).

All of this is quite mystical. I doubt 2011 will top it, but it is the year I become Dr. Whitaker. New Year, new day. Let's see what it brings.

***

January 11, 2011

Entering what could be my final semester of college after nine years straight. Got butterflies. Staring it down like Mike Tyson does his opponents before a fight. Tossing chalk like Lebron does before a game. Ripping off my shirt like Hulk Hogan before a wrestling match. Yet, still calm like a ninja meditating. The 20+ semesters have prepared me. Time to assassinate my dissertation.

Already planning a trip to Las Vegas for a 3-day weekend. It's only a four-hour drive from LA, so it's not traveling, per se. I'll bring my laptop to work on my dissertation and law school applications. A man needs something to do between the strippers and cocaine. Kidding! A gram of cocaine costs more than a trip to Mexico from LA. Don't do drugs. Feed your travel habit instead, you fiend, you.

I left my dissertation at home. Who would bring that to Vegas? Haha. Ok, ok...I'm kidding again. Over the past year, this dissertation has been like a clingy girlfriend that has followed me across ten different countries. Can't wait to dump her soon!

***

March 31, 2011

Going to the University of MIAMI for law school! You might be thinking…

"Ain't you graduating college for the fourth time soon and becoming Dr. Whitaker? Ain't you tired after nine years of college?"

No. I need to master our legal system for my master plan. I have to dismantle the Trap. My generation is getting shredded by systems that relate to law: mass incarceration, the War on Drugs, the School-to-Prison-Pipeline. Aside from that, what's wrong with spending the rest of my 20s in Miami?!

Just won an award reserved for the "most outstanding students." It's only given to a small handful of the 1,000+ USC graduates annually. You have to be nominated by a faculty member. Also received the "Outstanding Senator of the Year Award." Me? Out of the 77 senators representing the nearly 20,000 graduate students at USC? I represent a few thousand in the School of Education. Every graduate student pays a $26 fee to USC to create a million-dollar budget for our organization (Graduate and Professional Student Senate). I just voted on things, joined committees, and attended monthly sessions. We hosted field trips to places like Big Bear Mountain (with ski lift ticket included), Hollywood clubs (with free entry), and Malibu beach-front properties. We put on events like black-tie casino nights, speed dating, and countless lectures from leading scholars from all over the world. I'm pretty sure my "Outstanding Senator of the Year Award" came from my notorious Michael Jackson dance moves at our getdowns. I moonwalked away after getting the award.

This temporary recognition calls for a celebration. In 1,000 years, my name will be forgotten. In 100 years, my body will be beneath the Earth becoming rotten. In 60 years, my heart may be close to stoppin'…but as for TONIGHT, my temporary time of youth will be spent getting my Boogie on.

— 191 —

Look out LA, here comes The Most Outstanding.

***

April 8, 2011

<u>California Growth</u>

Hard to believe I've been growing here with these students at HPHS for four years. They've grown smarter, taller, and emerged like butterflies from their socially-awkward teenage cocoons. Pleasure knowing I've been a part of that growth. We're on our way to the senior camping trip in the forest just north of San Diego. This is my third time doing it.

The class of 2011 is my favorite class. They were in my after-school program as freshmen and sophomores, in my human and social services course as juniors, and I served as their college counselor during their senior year. I supervised 1,000+ of their hours working in their community youth programs and the nursing home. They are young adults now.

At the end of this California journey, and Miami is next. Who knows what that holds, or the growth I may experience there.

So how have I grown in Cali? How am I different?

1. More disciplined—from the balancing of three jobs at once with school.

2. Wiser—from overall experience and maturity.

3. Better understanding of relationships—from being forced to start them from scratch.

4. Better understanding of the world—from travels and cross-cultural interactions.

5. Somewhat better understanding of education—it's complicated.

6. Somewhat better understanding of the "system"—social, political, whatever. Equally complicated.

Still conundrums, though. Hence, law school.

***

April 23, 2011

Extremely hungover and sleep deprived from drinking until 4 a.m. with Morales. Spent most of Saturday in the Compton Public Library working with students one-on-one. It's the off-season for the Coliseum, so I got this gig to help me save up more for my move to Miami. A part of me wants to stay in LA with the phenomenal people I've met here. The other part of me wants to explore and grow. Wish I had more time to let these sides debate.

***

May 6, 2011

I knew having a Cinco de Mayo party at Casa de EDSA was a bad idea. I may not be Mexican, but my roommate, Morales is, and we somehow managed to go through gallons of tequila.

Next week, I will have to take three trips to the airport to pick up all of my family and friends coming to town for graduation. We'll be comfortably cluttered in my apartment. I'm cleaning up from the endless parties we've had over the past two weeks. Piñata candy still only the floor, BBQ utensils still in the sink, beer bottles still on the counter. Momma can't see this. She raised me better than this!

Also went to the Senior Banquet for my high school students. I've known them since they were freshman. Their beautiful speeches and a going-away award for "Dr. Whitaker" left me speechless and teary-eyed. Can't believe I'm approaching my last day at Huntington Park High School after four years, hundreds of students, and numerous priceless experiences. It's a part of my California experience that I'll never forget. Can't wait to see all the students who've inspired me throughout the years, tomorrow at graduation!

***

July 14, 2011

Finally defended my dissertation. Over 230 pages of groundbreaking, mixed-method (qualitative and quantitative), in-yo-face research. I'm in another league, chief. Now off to Las Vegas for the weekend for a bachelor party...then off to Jersey on Monday.

While conducting my research, I found less than ten percent of Black male students in LA would be eligible to enter a university when/if they finished high school—pretty bleak and familiar. At times, I feel I am not ready to leave this pursuit behind, but I need a bigger sword for this battle—The J.D. The Esquire. May all future foes and perpetuators of injustice quiver at the sound of the name ...

Dr. Amir Whitaker Esq.

***

July 2011

First Page of Amir's Dissertation

DEDICATION

To the hopes, dreams, and aspirations of the youth in environments where unfavorable conditions often prevent dreams from becoming a reality. To the memory of those who have struggled to create a world with less struggles. To the ongoing struggle for equality, peace, and true justice. To creating a more rehabilitative and quality criminal justice system through education. To my family back in New Jersey who have supported me throughout this process. To breaking cycles.

***

July 30, 2011

Legs tired from the Boogie. Heart emotional from the goodbyes. Mind wiser from four of the greatest years of my life. House trashed from the party. I'm fortunate to have met such amazing people on this journey. Thanks for the memories. We ain't done yet, LA. I'll keep waving goodbye until I'm waving hello again.

Joy Yo Self.

Endlessly.

Chapter 8: University of Miami

The four years Amir spent at USC were in the pursuit of knowledge. In actuality, graduate school and his dissertation ended up creating more questions than answers. After reading Michelle Alexander's *The New Jim Crow* in search of these answers, Amir enrolled in law school to gain an understanding of justice. This was one of the biggest mistakes and misunderstandings in Amir's academic career. Law school is not the least bit concerned with justice. Law is simply the rules that govern a society. Justice deals more with morality, and determines what is right or wrong.

Most believe all laws are created with the intent of establishing justice. Descending from people forced into slavery and oppression under the law, Amir knew better than that. Throughout law school, Amir learned that law was usually whatever the old white guy with the robe said it was. The words of judges (the primary readings in law school) became more sacred and infallible than the Holy Bible. Amir sat sourly at his desk for hours listening to lectures that he felt were worthless, waiting for a real conversation to happen.

How did we end up in Miami? Well, fully feelin' himself after visiting ten countries in a single year, 26-year-old Amir asked himself an essential question: "Where do I go next?" He knew he wanted to go to law school, and knew he could pretty much do it anywhere. Despite the love he was developing for LA, he wanted to venture outside of Cali. While stuck in LA traffic pondering his next move, the party/dance song by LMFAO, "I'm in Miami B*tch!" came on the radio. Instantly annoyed, Amir quickly changed the radio station. After cycling through radio stations with commercial breaks or even worse pop songs, Amir turned off the radio and sat in silence. The monotone, zombie chorus of the LMFAO song echoed in his head—the same way all catchy, but irritating songs do…

Drink all daaaay
Play all niiiiight
Let's get it poppiiiiin'
I'm in Miami triiick!

At that moment, Amir realized he had never even been to the "Magic City." He had heard it personified as a paradise by Will Smith, and seen its tropical goodness in movies like Scarface and Bad Boys. The LA weather had spoiled him as much as the Blizzard of 2003 had scorned him, so Amir was not even considering places with chilly climates. Having studied and worked in schools on the East and West Coasts, there was also an urge to see what the South was all about. If he could gain the same experience and establish a network in the Dirty-Dirty, he'd be the perfect candidate for national or federal government positions. However, being well-aware of American history, he wasn't open to living in most southern cities as a Negro.

"If I could live anywhere in the country, where would I live?" Amir thought.

This is how he analyzed the options of continuing his education. The superficial, warm-weather-loving, party-animal, bachelor side of Amir won out—as Miami became a top choice. The University of Miami ("The U") is Florida's leading university and is one of the Top 50 colleges in the country. It has produced world-class researchers, and celebrities like Dwayne "The Rock" Johnson, Sylvester Stallone, and Gloria Estefan. The campus sits on 239 acres of vibrant greenery, with a lake and canals that flow to the Atlantic Ocean. Campus wildlife includes crocodiles, blue crabs, manatees, giant barracudas, ducks, parrots, and an array of exotic birds. The school resembles a resort or posh Caribbean island. Some of the best beaches in the country are only a few miles away.

"Shut up and take my money!" Amir thought, after skimming the website.

With Miami being one of America's newest cities, The U is also relatively new. Starting in 1925 with a few hundred students, the Great Depression and hurricanes caused the school to struggle throughout much of its early years. Despite its location in an international and metropolitan city, The U still began in a southern state during the Jim Crow era. In 1905, the Buckman Act segregated Florida's three major colleges by gender and race. For white men, there was today's University of Florida; for white women, there was today's Florida State University; and for black women and men, there was Florida Agricultural and Mechanical University. The U started out as a co-ed university for white students. Hey, for the 1920s in the American South, that puts it ahead of its time! The Jim Crow policies that segregated Miami's schools also segregated its beaches up until well into the twentieth century. Throughout much of Florida, Negroes were not to allowed to share the same sand or ocean as whites.

In the 1940s, The U had a policy forbidding black football players from entering the "White Man's stadium." When schools like Penn State refused to bench their black players, games were canceled. In response to one cancellation, the Dade County Civil Rights Council wrote a letter to The U stating; "Negro and white soldiers fought together during World War II, and many of them died together. They should certainly be good enough to play football together."

Like many other Southern schools, The U overcame segregation and opened its doors to black students in the 1960s. In 1966, they became the first major college in the Deep South to award a black student a football scholarship. By the 1970s, their law school admitted its first generation of black students. Amir's mentor, D.W., was among the first black students—and he is only 10 or 15 years older than Amir's mother. While Amir attended The U, the campus banners proudly boasted "The University of Miami Commemorates 50 Years of Desegregation."

"As if that's something to be proud of!" Amir said. "That basically means my grandparents were unworthy and without the liberty to come here."

The banners reminded Amir of the "other" Affirmative Action that existed for centuries: the preferential racial treatment provided to Whites in America since its inception. It explained why he was one of two Black males in his law school cohort of nearly a hundred students. It also explained why most of the youth he met in Miami's juvenile detention center during his internship were Black. And it explained why both his brothers were locked up on one side of the law, while he studied the other side the law in a university. All of these things provided a unique lens, as he learned about the law and contemplated justice.

Law students at the expensive, private university in Miami were the most fascinating and contrasting group of classmates Amir had ever encountered. It made for exciting competition among the students, since graduating near the top of the class guaranteed six-figure salaries at major law firms. The students came from 30+ states and 120+ universities. Some of them were the kids were the kids in debate club in high school, and always reminded everyone that they wanted to become lawyers when they grew up. Many graduated as valedictorians—or very near the top of their previous classes. Some had already worked in law firms, or were the sons and daughters of lawyers. Some attended Ivy League schools, and drove luxury cars they didn't pay a dime for. Then there was Amir, the kid from Jersey who was kicked out of high school and stumbled into law school through a mistake and confusion. His classmates, on the other hand, had been preparing for this moment their entire lives.

The captivating blend of law students Amir encountered helped explain why the University of Miami has more graduates hosting courtroom TV shows than any other school. Alumni Judge Milian of *The People's Court* became the show's first female judge, and America's first Latina judge. Judge Alex Ferrer handled a few high-profile cases in Miami before having his own show for nine seasons. Emmy-nominated Judge David Young became TV's first openly gay judge. Lastly, Dr. Ana María Polos, host of *Caso Cerrado* (the most popular courtroom-based show in Latin America), is also a University of Miami Hurricane. Amir often wondered if any of his classmates—ample in personality, brains, and attractiveness—would end up with their own show.

Amir's main man during law school, and the person he'd nominate to have his own judge TV show, was his roommate, Rick. The two were an odd couple: the Brotha and the Bro. Rick was a 22-year-old kid from Chicago, lean with memories from the years he just spent at Purdue University. He was a frat boy, Division-I wrestler, and frequent know-it-all. His 5'1 frame was stacked and chiseled with muscle, and he was armed with an arsenal of tank tops to show it off. Rick could chatter your ears off for hours about typical "bro" stuff. One minute he's in your face forcing you to watch a trifling viral video, the next he's walking you through his new banana protein pancake recipe. Soon after that, he's telling you to "Shut your whoremouth!" because you have a slight disagreement. Shortly thereafter, he's using Axe body spray to kill a small pile of ants in the house.

Their crib was a cross-cultural clash of Rick's fraternity paddles and pro wrestling memorabilia, and Amir's guitars and relics from around the world. When Amir wanted to watch presidential debates or important Obama speeches, it was often out of the question, because Rick was on the couch watching the Disney Channel or some show about teenage werewolves. When trick-or-treaters surprised them on Halloween, Rick gave them protein bars. For his professional physique and fitness competitions, Rick transformed from a blonde-haired, blue-eyed white guy into a shredded, ripped black guy with his three layers of spray-on tanner. Styled his skin-tight purple pants and a crisp white V-neck shirt, he and Amir spent many a nights partying until the Miami dawn broke. During one drunken ramble, Rick started vomiting mid-conversation. He caught his breath and continued chatting as if nothing ever happened.

"I just don't let small issues get in my way, bro. Not about that life!"

Rick had a reputation for being an intense dude with damn-near no filter, and this rubbed people the wrong way.

"How can you live with that guy?" asked fellow law students.

The Brotha and the Bro got along well because of their similar struggles. Both grew up in poverty, with families devastated by drugs. Rick had recently lost his mom, and couldn't remember the last time he had talked to his sister. When administrative problems delayed their financial aid checks, Rick and Amir combined every dime they had and lived off $52.17 for nearly ten days. Rick was trusted to do the food shopping and racked up on tuna, peanut butter, pasta, tomato sauce, ground turkey, eggs, cold cuts, and two pack of turkey bacon. It was Rick's idea to go on welfare (Temporary Assistance for Needy Families) after graduation, since they couldn't work due to the 60-hour study weeks required for bar exam preparation. He convinced Dr. Whitaker to give "zero-fu*ks," and perpetuate the cycle of poverty they were born into. Being on welfare with five college degrees was a low point for Amir, but Rick thought nothing of it.

**

After completing law school in 2014, Amir graduated as part of the most indebted college class in US history. When he started college in 2002, it was the first time that more than a million college students graduated with student debt. The average amount then was around $17,000. By the time Amir graduated from The U in 2014, that number nearly doubled—with the average graduate more than $33,000 in the red. You can triple that amount for the average law student—and multiply it by ten for Amir. Two years earlier in 2012, the total amount of student debt surpassed one trillion dollars. I will write that number out so you can see how much it actually is. It is one million, millions...or one thousand, billions:

$1,000,000,000,000

God bless America. The only country brave and capitalistic enough to do something like this. Countries like Germany have higher education systems that are entirely publicly funded, therefore, millions of students pay absolutely no tuition. Not in 'Merika, though. Here, lawmakers give banks loans with interest rates far lower than those given to the students investing in a college education.

Student debt is just one of a few ways the American educational system punishes people for the symptoms of their inequality. Millions of students like Amir had to rise above unequal access to educational opportunities and resources throughout their life. They were never prepared for college, and the ones that make it often never finish. Amir was fortunate, and was able to transfer from community college to a university. This allowed him to avoid the college entrance exams that often perpetuate privilege and inequality. These exams are designed to predict how well a student will perform in college, but are often more predictive of family income and resources available to prepare for the test.

Despite America being the richest country in the world, we have the world's second highest poverty rate for children. Sure, American poverty looks luxurious compared to third-world poverty, but poverty is still punishment here. Some Americans are able to "pull themselves up by their own bootstraps" and escape poverty. Unfortunately, not everyone has bootstraps to begin with. Far too many of those born poor will die poor. Access to quality education and college preparation is not within everyone's reach. The limited opportunities to earn a livelihood resulting from the inequalities can be a life sentence.

After completing his 12 years of college, the greatest challenge in Amir's academic career took place at the Tampa Convention Center. This was the Florida Bar Exam—the 16-hour test held over a two-day period that's required to become a lawyer. Rumors of its difficulty frightened people away from the profession. For weeks, Amir drilled dense and deliberately complicated information into his head, studying for 10-14 hours per day.

On the day of the exam, Amir called his grandmother for a prayer session that shook the foundation of the earth. He then entered the hallowed convention center, crammed with 3,331 anxious and overworked fellow zombies. Endless rows of cheap wood grain tables filled the structure, each seating two adults—each adult pretending the other was invisible for hours at a time. Ample paramedics and ambulances were on deck, fully expecting a few people to faint or freak out. That $120,000+ you spent on law school better come in handy, Amir. It all comes down to this moment. After the test, the mass of people exited lethargically in a most awkward silence.

At its core, the Florida Bar Exam and similar exams are tests of self-discipline and mental endurance. Amir's primary struggle was mental. He had to rebuild his confidence after a few devastating defeats. First, he had a below-average GPA and was in the bottom half of his law school class. The GPA hysteria among his fellow law students suggested he wouldn't be able to get a decent job—and he half believed it. He failed to keep up with the gunners spending extra money on supplemental course materials. He didn't have access to the academic steroids, like Adderall, which nearly 35% of law students are estimated to use. Many didn't need it for diagnosed medical purposes, but instead used it to study for over 70 hours per week. Some used it after partying until 6 a.m. in order to get in a few hours of focus on the rocket fuel. Some got it by prescription, but most scored it from an underground black market that was making a few law students filthy rich. Pills were popped in plain sight, as Amir experienced what Bruno must have felt every time he saw Popeye eat his spinach.

The other defeat destroying Amir's confidence before the bar exam was the fact that he had failed the easier exam to become a lawyer—twice. This was a three-and-a-half-hour exam on lawyer ethics and professionalism. The first time he took it, he was preoccupied with his new non-profit and the keynote speech he was to give at USC's graduation. He also underestimated the exam's difficulty, because 98% of students usually pass it. This didn't help his confidence when he was part of the meager 2% of his class. He took it for a second time on less than two hours of sleep because of an all-night argument he had with his girlfriend.

"What kinda dipsh*t fails the MPRE exam, bro?" said Rick. "Like, only one person out of 50 fails it!"

Amir never told anyone that he failed it… twice, but he began to wonder if he was just irreconcilably unprofessional and unethical. He was scheduled to take the MPRE exam again two weeks after the real deal bar exam. Going into the two-day bar exam "0-2" multiplied the difficulty faced by our Welfare King.

After failing the first exam twice, one the law school deans "strongly suggested" Amir take an "exclusive" weeklong bar prep class offered by the university. Whenever Dean Strickland "strongly suggested" something, you pretty much had to do it. Despite the success he experienced in graduate school, Amir sucked at law school. To compensate for these challenges throughout his eight weeks of bar preparation studies, he stuck to the strictest ninja regiment of his life. Rise at 7:00 a.m., study for four hours, eat lunch, study for four more hours, workout/gym time, then study another four hours. He allowed himself to take 15-minute breaks after two-hour studying blocks to get some fresh air or make music.

During the prep period, Amir disappeared from social media and most worldly interactions. He turned off his phone two days prior, fully anticipating the drama that occurred before every major test. When he took the GRE to apply to graduate school in 2007, his aunt left a brief message saying his mom was in the hospital, but no one knew why. While standing in line to take the LSAT exam to get in law school in 2010, he received a call from his brother informing him of the murder of a childhood friend. As he turned his phone on while exiting the bar exam, two messages were waiting. One was from his father informing him of a "hit" was put on his little brother Tyson's life. The other was from his sister about a domestic violence dispute that included a slight stabbing.

Amir barely passed the bar exam, the same way he barely met the character and fitness requirements to become a lawyer. The Florida Board of Bar Examiners requires prospective lawyers to "produce satisfactory evidence of good moral character ... and proof that the applicant is otherwise fit to take the oath." The drug arrest Amir picked up when he was 15-years-old had come back to haunt him. He had to pay an extra $250 to appear before a panel of three judges and explain why he was trappin' half a lifetime ago.

"Mr. Whitaker," said one judge, "What arguments would you like to present to demonstrate your rehabilitation?"

"Aside from the fact that I've stayed out of trouble in the 15 years since," Amir said, "I have started a nonprofit organization to prevent youth who are misguided—like I was—from making the same mistakes. I'm also a few months away from receiving my fifth college degree. In some circles, I'm known as Dr. KnuckleHead."

The panel of three deliberated for months as Amir wondered if the $180,000 and three years' time he invested in law school would be in vain. Here are the journals chronicling that turbulent investment.

Chapter 9: The Hurricane Chronicles

Ages: 26-29

August 4, 2011

Driving across the country from Cali to Florida with just about everything I own in this 2003 convertible Chrysler coupe. In New Mexico now. Roughly 736 out of the 2,817 miles completed. May stop in Roswell tomorrow to dive into the Area-51 tourist traps. Paused in Arizona yesterday for a 5-mile hike through Chiricahua, the ancestral land of Geronimo and the Apache Indians. The mighty Buffalo Soldiers used to roam there, too. Must have had the entire trail to myself. Majestic natural beauty and seclusion.

***

August 6, 2011

Been partying in a different city/state EVERY weekend for the past month. Las Vegas, New York, New Jersey, LA, Dallas, and now NEW ORLEANS?! Miami next week. Covering 3,000 miles—east, west, and south. Which was best? This is Amir-I-Can Summer 2011.

I gotta spend an extra day in New Orleans because my car broke down. Was going strong for over 2,000 miles and 28 hours, until the axle snapped. My wheel almost popped off! I'm just happy I'm safe, and in one a hell of a city. Crashing on the couch of a former student who is attending Tulane University!

***

August 10, 2011

Reached my new home after 44 hours of driving through despite 2,937 miles. Thankful for my 10-year-old car with no AC... wheel almost popping off on the highway because of all the weight from my books. It's resilient, like the person driving it. I've had it for two years since selling that gas-guzzling Audi A6. My grandmother's prayers must've worked.

Now, it's Hurricane season.

***

August 20, 2011

Was just kicked out of The U (University of Miami) Law Library because it closed at 10 p.m. Still got so much read though. Walked past a foam party on campus with hundreds of half-naked students partying in bathing suits on a summer Miami night. They had water slides and rides, too. Wish I could join them...almost. Good to know the 45K we are spending a year here is well-spent.

***

August 27, 2011

Finally made it The U's gym. This is my third Division I school, and all of them have had flawless facilities. The U's gym is by far the largest, cleanest, and most advanced. Almost 20,000 square feet, an inside track, etc.

Made my ninja schedule for Fall 2011 below. Aiming high with 45 hours of studying (green), 20 hours of class (blue), and eight hours of fitness (red). It will be 73 hours a week, total. Damn straight I'm gonna party hard on the weekend! Damn straight I'm gonna travel every break I get! Call me crazy, but I hope to enjoy every minute of it. Guess it's why I've been in school for 22 years straight.

Goal 1- Get straight A's				DISCIPLINE is WISDOM. Vice versa		Study-45hrs	
Goal 2- Lose 5lbs(fat) & add 5 lbs(muscle)				Fall 2011 Ninja Schedule		Class- 20hrs	
Goal 3- Sleep 7-8 hrs a DAY!!						Fit-8hrs	
Goals 4-6- Become better at dancing, guitar, & spanish							

Time	Monday	Tuesday	Wednesday	Thursday	Friday	Saturday	Sunday
8:00		Lcomm		Study-Torts	Study-Torts		
9:00	Property	Lcomm	Property	Study-Torts	Study-Torts		
10:00	Property	Study-Torts	Property	Breakfast	Breakfast		
11:00	Study-Civil	Torts	Study-Civil	Torts	Torts	Study-OL	Study-CP
12:00	Study-Civil	Torts	Study-Civil	Torts	Torts	Study-OL	Study-CP
1:00	Home/Gym	Study-Elem	Home/Civil	Study-Elem	Gym	Study-OL	Study-CP
2:00	Civil	Gym/Lunch	Civil	Study-El 1:40	Lunch	Study-OL	Study-Pr
3:00	Civil	Study-Elem	Civil	Home/Gym	Study-Elem	Study-LC	Study-Pr
4:00	Lunch	Elements 3:3	Lunch	Elements	Study-Elem	Study-LC	Study-Pr
5:00	Study-LC	Elements	Study-Torts	Elements	Study-LC	Study-LC	Study-OL
6:00	Study-LC	Study-Pr	Study-Elem	Study-Torts	Study-LC		
7:00	Study-Torts	Guitar	Salsa Dance	Espanol	Salsa Dance		
8:00	Dinner	Dinner	Study-Torts	Dinner	Study-LC		
9:00	Zumba Dance	Hiphop Dance	Dinner	African Dance	Boogie!	Boogie!	
10:00	Study-Torts	Study-Pr	Study-Torts	Study-Torts	Boogie!	Boogie!	
11:00	SLEEP!	SLEEP!	Guitar	Study-Torts	Boogie!	Boogie!	SLEEP!
12:00	SLEEP!	SLEEP!	SLEEP!	SLEEP!			

9am-Smoothie	8am-Smoothie	9am-Smoothie	10am-Breakfast	10am-Breakfast	
11am-Fruit	10am-PBJ/Fruit	11am-Fruit	2pm-Lunchpak	2pm-Smoothie	
1pm-PowerBar	2pm-Lunchpak	1pm-PowerBar	6pm-Fruit	9pm-Booze!	
4pm- Lunch	6pm-Fruit	4pm- Lunch	8pm- Dinner		
8pm- Dinner	8pm- Dinner	8pm- Dinner			

***

September 10, 2011

Noticing two reoccurring patterns in my weekends:
1) Each weekend for the past ten weeks, I've had at least one night where I was up until at least 6 a.m. partying. I blame this on Vegas, NYC, New Orleans, LA, Jersey, and Miami.
2) Each weekend for the past four weeks, I was told by the librarian, "Please leave. We're closing."

One of these traditions has to stop. Guess I gotta find a new library. Haha.

In other news, I'm 4% done with law school.

***

September 17, 2011

On my way to my first tailgate and football game as a Miami Hurricane. Hungover from my first night clubbing in South Beach. Reminded me of Hollywood: overpriced, overrated, stank attitudes, and oversaturated. I wasn't missing much. But oh my, the sculpted goodies of the women walking Ocean Drive. It almost makes you understand why the stunnas rent luxury cars and slowly cruise the strip.

***

September 20, 2011

For weeks I've dedicated more than 65 hours a week to studying the law. I've made a commitment to do this for the next three years. I constantly find myself foolishly twiddling my thumbs waiting for conversations about justice to take place in class. The federal government recently released a report showing Black men are 46 times as likely to be in prison than white women (46 out of 1,000 rate for Black men vs. 1 per 1,000 rate for white women).

I recently toasted my first drink on South Beach to my brothers and childhood friends piled in cages. Afterwards, one of the white girls in our entourage generously offered folks Molly. She'll be aiight though. The U actually has a policy that allows students

— 209 —

caught with drugs on campus to avoid an arrest completely by attending counseling. If only policies and opportunities like this existed where I came from, a few friends would actually be free.

I'm starting to feel like an iceberg with mountains of frozen rock beneath it. I'm trying to channel this cold and massive anger. Anger is what transformed Bruce Banner into The Incredible Hulk, multiplying his strength 1,000-fold. Anger transformed Malcolm Little into Malcolm X, before he elevated the consciousness of the nation and world. Anger transformed Goku into the invincible Super Saiyan. I'm not them…I'm still trying to channel this anger into strength. But I am starting to fear nothing and no one. My only fear is the ferociousness of my true strength once I finally reach it.

6% done with law school.

Undergoing transformation through anger.

***

September 23, 2011

Forced to leave campus again. Why is the gym open later than the library at the University of Miami? It shows the priorities. Indeed, a healthy body is important, but a sharp mind should be Supreme. Libraries were 24-hours at USC, and open until 2 a.m. at Rutgers for us dorks. I'm feeling like transferring.

Just realized I have a lot in common with Lebron James & Reggie Bush:
1) All three of us are 26 years old.
2) We all recently moved to Miami to pursue bigger dreams.
3) We're all Black males, who overcame odds to make a bit of history.
4) I went to the same school as Reggie Bush (USC), and Lebron lives less than 2 miles away from me in Miami.

5) All three of our Miami careers are starting out rough. Lebron is a former MVP struggling to get in a rhythm with the Miami Heat. Reggie Bush just took his last team to the Super Bowl, but he and the Miami Dolphins are 0-3. And me? A few months ago, I graduated as the youngest in my doctoral cohort, but I'm struggling like a muh to stay alive in law school. I'm putting in the work, just not getting the results I want. Studying and in class 70 hours a week. They say it'll make sense at the end of the semester. I pray to God this is true.

***

September 30, 2011

Exactly one week before Amir-I-Can Travels Volume 16-17: Dominican Republic and Haiti. A trip is needed now more than ever. Transitioning to Miami and law school studies have worn me down. Can't wait to see these countries for myself. If I've learned anything from traveling, it's that people exaggerate differences and underestimate the kindness of the human spirit. People are the same everywhere.

"The World is a book, and those who do not travel read only a page," to quote Saint Augustine.

***

October 6, 2011

Midterm complete. Longest week ever. Little sleep, little exercise, whole lotta stress. I'm certain they're related. After a 14-hour day of studying, classes, and exams, there is nothing I want more than to Boogie. Gotta pack for my trip tomorrow though. It's all good...tonight I'll sleep in Miami, but tomorrow I'll sleep in Santo Domingo.

Roughly 8% done with law school, and getting ready for my first fall break.

***

October 11, 2011

Traveling through Hispaniola. Spending my birthday relaxing on a beach in the Dominican Republic was chill, but nothing compares to the moments I've shared with friends and family throughout my 27 years. Damn...I'm 27! For whatever reason, that sounds so much older than 26. Now I'm in my "late 20's."

Heading to Haiti tomorrow despite countless warnings. Apparently, UN Peacekeeping troops from Nepal (South Asian country that borders India) brought the deadly cholera disease to the island, and it's killed thousands of Haitians. Nearly 10% of the population has gotten sick. The country is also still recovering from last year's earthquake. It left over 300,000 dead, a million homeless, and was one of the worst in recent history. But travel warnings ain't enough to stop this Knucklehead. Not when he is in Miami and can fly into the Dominican Republic and out of Haiti for less than $280!

***

October 16, 2011

Back in the USA after one of the greatest and most memorable trips of my life. Gained a new perspective...more humble, grateful, open-minded, more impressed by the resilience

— 212 —

and compassion of humanity. Gaining a better understanding of myself through a better understanding the world. Gracias, Dominican Republic. Merci, Haiti. Stepping out of my comfort-zone and being open to new experiences has paid off. Most def gonna continue to experience things first-hand instead of listening to other people's jive. Officially halfway through my passport too. Been to 17 countries and counting.

It didn't take long for law school to assassinate the vibe. The first day back from fall break, a professor told our class of 80+ students...

"Your performance on the midterm was underwhelming...AT BEST...on a good day...and I'm in a good mood."

The statement included four layers of intellectual insults. Some law professors take themselves far too seriously. I've had nearly 100 professors in my ten years of college, but I've never encountered the arrogance and lack of respect for students some law professors display. Who cares how fancy your education is, especially when you didn't learn the basic lessons of respect and humility? Why do they subject us to these attitudes during our roughest years? And very few of these know-it-alls are practicing attorneys. Just "scholars" is all they are, yet they are teaching us how to become lawyers. Perhaps they know the rules, but seem clueless as to how they play out in the real world. That's part of the reason why 30% of us fail the bar exam here. And we are paying them more than 40 grand a year for this torture.

***

November 7, 2011

Tired and was about to go home after 13 hours of class and studying, but a book caught my eye as I was leaving the library. Started reading it and became enlightened about my school's dark history. They refused to let Blacks in until the 1960's... years after the Brown v. Board Supreme Court decision found segregated schools unconstitutional. Also, despite 80% of some UM teams being Black, a few decades ago they refused to play colleges with Black players.

Hitting the gym, then going back into the library. I'll do it for all those who had no opportunity to do it for centuries. Those who died for me to have this opportunity didn't die in vain.

To add to the weight on my mind today, one of my fav professors insinuated (in front of our class of 90+ students) that I would be taken more seriously/be less threatening if I cut my Afro. I responded to the professor by asking my neighbor, Michael, what he did to his hair this morning.

"Comb it?" he said, in a confused voice.

"Really?" I responded. "I did the exact same thing."

I won't hate myself because of the way the gods made me. As offensive as it was, he was well-intentioned, and I'm already over it. I don't have the luxury of clinging to undying anger. My energy is needed elsewhere. What he said is sadly true, though. Still, the fro will never go! If I put a dollar towards my student loans every time someone suggested I cut my hair, I'd probably be out of student debt.

Truth be told, I don't even love the fro like I used to. However, it's a political, artistic, and social statement. It's the natural texture of my hair, and I'm not ashamed of it. I won't conform to Eurocentric views of beauty and keep my hair cut low to make them comfortable. Their lack of comfort with my hair is probably the result of deeper insecurities within themselves.

I'm too liberated to be concerned with others' thoughts…even the women who tell me I looked more handsome with low-cut hair. I only want to please myself and the ancestors who blessed me with my uniqueness. Uniqueness is beautiful. The gods made me different and beautiful.

***

November 29, 2011

One semester, or 16 weeks, into law school. Still no class discussions on issues similar to what the Supreme Court of the United States just heard arguments on: the uneven and unfair crack-to-cocaine sentencing laws. Law and justice are so separated in this country. The highest court in the land is just now addressing an overtly racist law that has destroyed thousands of lives over decades. In law school, we're too busy learning about stuff like "Rules Against Perpetuities." I'd explain what this is, but I'd probably just confuse myself even more.

Cocaine and crack are the same drugs. Crack just adds baking soda and water. Think of it as a cocaine cake. Trust me, I whipped up a few batches in my teenage years. They share the same side-effects, too. Research actually demonstrates that regular cocaine use:

1) Causes more people to overdose and die than crack
2) Causes more permanent physical damage to the body than crack
3) Is used by a larger percentage of the population (2-3 times as much as crack)

Despite the increased danger of cocaine, crack drug charges carried literally 100 times more prison time than cocaine charges until late last year. The new law, the Fair Sentencing Act of 2010, reduced this disparity to 18 to 1 last year—at least for people who committed their offenses after the law became effective. Usually, new legislation does not apply retroactively unless Congress says so, and they didn't here. So people like Edward Dorsey, who pleaded guilty in June 2010 to possessing 5.5 grams of crack cocaine, with an earlier conviction were subjected to a mandatory federal prison sentence of ten years. Under the new law, the sentence he received would be three or four years. Still a lot of time for a couple rocks, but much better.

Crack is also the only drug that comes with mandatory prison time, if the charge is federal. Although crack drug charges are now "only" 18 times higher than cocaine charges, it is still very unfair. Tens of thousands of people of color are still without freedom because of the original unjust and extreme sentencing. Luckily I watch the independent news, like "Democracy Now," to learn about this being challenged in the Supreme Court. Law school lectures are too busy focusing on "Rules Against Perpetuities" ... and my funky-fresh Afro.

***

December 13, 2011

Tomorrow is my first law school final exam. Playing LL Cool J's "Mama Said Knock You Out" in preparation. My USC dissertation was also finally accepted and officially published. I've had to do quite a few tweaks on it over the past few months. I was probably one of the few people in the universe working on two doctorates at once.

This is just one of many things that made this the most stressful semester ever. Heading to Key West after final exams with a few crazy law students. Heading to the Olde Country after that, only to be greeted with a funeral of a friend and neighbor of more than 20 years. R.I.P Ruben. You were a good dude. Also the one-year anniversary of Sahaad. We are an endangered species, dying too young. Life is too short. Go everywhere and see everything while you can. Stress is inevitable, so just smile in between. I'll pour out a lil liquor for the homies in Key West. Ya'll are forever remembered. I'll continue the struggle for a world with better conditions for us.

17% done with law school. One semester down, five to go. Rocking my FroHawk, too. Warrior mode. Grateful for the day and opportunity. R.I.P to the fallen.

December 31, 2011

Goodbye, Olde Country. Love the Jerzy fam and friends, but I can't risk another New Year's in a jail cell. Haha. Bout to fly home to Miami. My flight lands at 11:57 p.m.—three minutes before 2012! It was the cheapest flight available, but landing at the same time the ball drops might have a deeper meaning. Not sure what it is, but I'm looking forward to a new year with new goals to reach, new mistakes to learn from, and new challenges to conquer.

I'm pregaming on my flight so I can head straight to the party once I land in Miami. So what if the Department of Homeland Security does not allow more than three ounces of liquid? Just get a bunch of lil 1.5-ounce bottles of booze for the Miami Turn-Up. It's the only way I can actually afford bottles of Johnnie Walker whiskey. Meanwhile, at the club we are trying to go to tonight, you can spend $10,000 on a single bottle of champagne.

March 11, 2012

I took a study break for the annual Calle Ocho Festival in Little Havana. Over 20 blocks of Miami are closed off for the festivities. Hundreds of thousands of people are partying in the street. Food, music, dancing…11 different stages with performances by folks like Fat Joe and Flo Rida. It's free, too.

With all of this golden freedom, I can't stop thinking about my brothers...both of whom are locked up right now...like countless others—Black and Brown. They are deprived of their freedom the same way our ancestors were stripped of theirs for more than 80% of American history. While their actions contributed to them getting locked-up, I'm certain they would have freedom if their circumstances were different. Poor, Black, substance abuse issues—pick one.

Now the middle brother struggles to enjoy his golden freedom and youth in Miami. We are still being hunted down like animals, too. Look at what happened in Tulsa a few months ago. Two white guys went on a killing spree in a predominantly black neighborhood. They pulled drive-bys on random residents from their pickup truck. They left three strangers dead, and another two critically wounded, for no reason other than their skin color. Millions of my people died without freedom. Many millions more died or struggled fighting so that we could have freedom, equality, and opportunity. I'm grateful for their sacrifice, and will take advantage of the opportunities I have that they could only dream of.

I will never impose any limits on my potential, goals, or dreams. Where there are limits, there cannot be freedom. Just wish I was capable of enjoying my freedom, and things like the Calle Ocho Festival, without feeling guilty. But hey, at least the guilt serves as motivation to do something about these conditions.

***

March 2012

So much going on in Miami today. WrestleMania 28 is happening here live—with my high school here The Rock fighting for the first time in years. Also, thousands are marching for Trayvon Martin with his family. He's is the unarmed Black teenager who was murdered while going to the store to get Skittles, a few weeks ago. No charges filed against the "neighborhood watch leader" who killed him. Because he "reasonably" believed he was threatened, Florida's "Stand Your Ground" law allows him to walk around freely. Trayvon was visiting his father in Central Florida for two weeks because he was suspended from a Miami school for ten days. His Mom couldn't supervise him while he was out of school for two weeks in Miami, so she sent him to stay with Dad. Because a grown man felt threatened by him—a teenage boy—she'll never speak to her son again.

Meanwhile, I'm in the law library wishing I could be at the March for Trayvon, or Wrestlemania. Or at least discuss what happen to Trayvon in my law classes, especially since he's from here. So happy the semester/year is almost over. 28% done with law school.

***

May 14, 2012

Hello, first week of summer! This one might be the greatest. I start my internship next week at the juvenile courthouse. I'll be working for the Miami-Dade Public Defender's Office. We handle 85% of the thousands of arrest cases involving Miami's youth. Got a part-time job working as a research assistant for a top scholar/professor, too.

After five weeks of summer in Miami, I'm headed to Europe for 40+ days. Mostly will be taking classes at the University of Amsterdam, but also gonna try to street-travel through ten or so countries.

But while I'm here in the USA, I'll be grinding at two jobs, taking a law school class, and taking several classes at Miami-Dade

College to help start a non-profit. Betz believe the Europe trip will be well-earned!

***

June 22, 2012

The City of Miami was on FIRE last night after the Miami Heat won the NBA championship! Put on my black and red wingtip shoes with a matching Lebron James jersey to go celebrate. There was madness in the streets and on South Beach. A few homies from the Olde Country were down in Miami, too. Foxx, Marvelous Mar (R.I.P), and Killa.

I've been lucky enough to see many championships over the past few years. The LA Lakers won three championships while I was living in LA. The Heat just won a championship my first year living in Miami. USC has been to the National Championship more than any other team in the past decade. The University of Miami has won more championships during my lifetime than any other college football team. Rutgers had their greatest season ever when I was a senior there. Each city celebrates differently. In Los Angeles, they burn stuff and flip over cars. In Miami, they bang pots and pans, and march in the street. Not sure which I like best. I'm not a gambling man, but if I were, I'd put my money on the team of the city I'm living in. I know how to pick em!'

Los Angeles and Miami are alike in many ways. Keep the sunshine and palm trees, just add rain. Replace Kobe with Lebron James, earthquakes with hurricanes, smog with humidity, pretentious Hollywood scene with ostentatious South Beach scene, Mexican zest with Cubano spice, the Pacific Ocean with the Atlantic, Converses with boat shoes. If I develop relationships and experience growth here, like I did in LA then look out world!

***

July 23, 2012
Amsterdam, Netherlands

Euro-Mir, live and direct. Just turned in a 21-page final paper for my American law school class. Wrote it on juvenile rehabilitation and education...basically re-exploring my dissertation, from another angle. Now, all that stands between me and "summer" is an International Human Rights Law exam on Wednesday, an International Criminal Law exam next Saturday, a 10-page paper on Gender and Human Rights due next week, a few assignments for my online classes, and a few more weeks of work doing paid research for my professor. Still trying to stop and smell the flowers in between the grind.

Completed Amir-I-Can Travels 22 and 23 this past weekend in Scotland and Wales [Story in "Street Traveler"]!

***

August 5, 2012
Amsterdam, Netherlands

I submitted the paperwork to incorporate my non-profit organization a month ago. Chose to have it go into effect today, though, because I didn't want any distractions from the three exams and 30 pages of papers I submitted over the last two weeks of class in Amsterdam. Now that I'm done with that, I'll shift focus to the more than 100 pages of curriculum, business plan and proposals, grant applications, etc... that I will be writing over the next few weeks in Europe for my non-profit. Even though the work will be ongoing, it feels great that my organization is officially incorporated as of today!

PROJECT KNUCKLEHEAD

EST. 2012.

Project KnuckleHead will work to create programs for youth to help them stay in school and avoid incarceration. We'll have numerous programs to provide the motivation and support required to stay out of trouble and succeed in school. It ain't easy, ya know. Each finger in the fist of the logo represents one of the five core areas we will focus on: mentoring, employment, community service, youth empowerment, and education. It is a non-profit based off of ideas I've been developing from:

1) More than four years of graduate school research and my dissertation.

2) Professional experience from teaching in New Jersey and California for more than six years, working and volunteering for numerous non-profits for five years, and working with youth for more than a decade.

3) My personal experience as someone who grew up "disadvantaged," like the youth we will serve.

The ultimate aim is to take vulnerable youth like me (and those who were arrested, kicked out of school...you know, the "Knuckleheads") and give them the support the need to be successful. I hope to incorporate music and art into it, too.

In our darkest days, Project KnuckleHead will draw inspiration from three wise heroes of mine.

"It is easier to build strong children than to repair broken men."

-Frederick Douglass

"They say it ain't no hope for the youth, then the truth is...it ain't no hope for the future."

- Tupac Shakur

"Wu-Tang is for the children."

-Old Dirty Bastard

Anyways, about to catch some sleep on a night bus to Berlin, Germany…but as you can see, I stay dreaming, anyways.

***

August 24, 2012

I just started my 11th year of college and 24th year of school. It was a very rough first week, to say the least. Long story short, confusion over my lease caused my landlord to move out all my stuff while I was away in Europe. Now a lot of stuff is missing or stolen. All three of my guitars, the samurai swords I got from Japan, a painting I got from South Africa, my Xbox 360, laptop, hookah, iPod, and several other things. I just want Natalie back. She was my favorite guitar of all time—a custom 1972 Fender Telecaster. She was what I missed most while I was traveling over the past six weeks. I had her for almost ten years. She was all I had when I moved to LA five years ago. She rode shotgun with me when I drove 3,000 miles across the country to Miami. I fell asleep playing her on countless nights. Whenever I was feeling down, all I had to do was touch her to feel better. In the only picture I have of my guitar teacher, who just died, he was playing her (Rest in Power Billy Spruill AKA Uncle Bilal). Yea, I cried for the first time in a very long time when I learned she was gone.

To make things worse, my financial aid for the semester is late, so I haven't been able to get any of my books for school. Maybe I shouldn't have spent most of my savings in Europe, but I was banking on my financial aid coming through like it had the previous ten years. At one point, my bank account only had $0.16 in it. Haha.

Behind on my studies for the first time in recent history, too. Most def not starting off year 11 on the good foot. But if there is one thing I know, it is struggling…it is adversity—the story of my life. I just take the lessons and wisdom that come from it. I can think of at least three things to take from this:

1) Never grow too close to material things—they come and go.

2) Savor the flavor of the good times—like the memories of the past six weeks in Europe.

3) Sh*t happens. You are not invincible. You aren't always responsible for what happens.

Through this pain, I'm stronger, wiser, and more prepared for the future. A few years ago, this would have been handled in the streets, but I got too much to lose now. I'm going to sue the pants off my landlord for this, though.

Miss you, Natalie. You can never be replaced.

***

August 25, 2012

Made it to the advanced level in The U's Salsa Club today. Might have been the first time I experienced joy and happiness during my first week back in the US. Dancing always makes me forget about my troubles. You can take away my material things, but you can never deprive me of my BOOGIE!

The best things in life are truly free. I was part of the Salsa Club at USC in LA too, but it was nothing like this Cuban-Miami-Rueda style stuff. We dance in a circle, or "rueda," as we switch partners. The moves they teach us retain their original vulgar Spanish words (Adios con la Hermana!). I get to lock hands with women of all races, some barefoot, some in heels. Touching each in the gentlest, most delicate, I'm-not-a-creep fashion. Neglecting my studies for the sake of my weary soul.

In other news, I desperately want to punch this dude named Seth in the face. He's a fellow law student who calls me every single word he can think of with "swag" as a prefix or suffix... swagmaster, swagadelic, swagnificent, swagtastic, etc. He's usually tolerable for two to three minutes, then it all gets really annoying. Sometimes I imagine myself headbutting him with a helmet. But this trust-fund kid has thousands of dollars in guns, including an M-16 assault rifle. You need a friend like him just in case there is a zombie apocalypse. He also educates me on the Miami glitz life.

"I don't need much more to drink, Señor Swaguerro. Everybody knows that in Miami, we only drink until 11:30 (PM). We turn up the party with coke after midnight."

***

September 20, 2012

<u>Much-Needed Second Wind</u>

I FOUND IT! Thought it got stolen with all of my stuff in last month's burglary. It's a picture that has been my motivation for 14 years. I painted it when I was in 8th grade. It has the names of my 17 closest friends back in Jersey placed around a two-faced, half-skeleton character. Despite what people thought and how we were treated, we weren't a gang or anything. Just snotty-nosed kids from the same neighborhood. Wasn't the beautiful part of town either. Out of the 18 of us, only three survived the storm to graduate from Plainfield High (that's 17% of us). All but two of us were arrested as juveniles (89%), 11 of us entered the adult jail/prison system (67%), at least five of us have been shot (27%), and I am the only one to graduate college (6%). This means I am from an area where people are more likely to get shot than to finish high school.

This picture will be my motivation because I still believe that any of my boys could have, and STILL CAN, do what I did. I still think some of them are smarter and more talented than me. If anything, I'm just more disciplined and focused. Their untapped potential is the reason why I started Project KnuckleHead in the first place. All potential needs is guidance and support. We have to save the next generation of Knuckleheads from learning the hard way— from falling victim to the Trap. They deserve the same support and opportunities available to those who are more fortunate.

Despite the bleak statistics, the people identified in the painting have come a long way today. Most have gone back to school and are trying to stay out of trouble. This is extremely hard coming from where we are from. I love all my boys like brothers. We survived a warzone together. Actually, a higher percentage of my friends have been shot than soldiers fighting in Iraq. And don't get me started on the post-traumatic stress and depression that our environment has given us...

So many people fall victim to the system where I'm from, it makes you wonder. I know we often call areas that openly sell drugs "The Trap," but there is something more complicated at play. The system may not be so broken after all. Perhaps it's doing exactly what it was designed to do. Mass incarceration, the War on Drugs...all traps waiting to catch you. Mass incarceration in America has created a system unlike anything previously seen, yet strangely reminiscent of our darkest era.

The Land of the Free has a peculiar obsession with taking away freedom. We are one of nearly 200 countries, but we have 25% of the world's prison population. We have more people in cages than Russia AND China...combined. More than any country in the history of the world. Up until last year, we were the only country that sentenced 13-year-olds to die in prison until the Equal Justice Initiative won the Supreme Court case. This ain't cheap either. It costs about a million dollars to keep someone in prison for 25 years. This addiction is the reason why many states spend more on incarceration than education. It is the reason America spends more money taking away freedom than most of the world combined.

Mass incarceration is fueled by its fraternal twin, the War on Drugs. This trap has cost the government more than a trillion dollars over the past four decades; yet drugs are cheaper, more accessible, and more dangerous. This trap is the reason there are more Black people under correctional control (jail, prison, probation, or parole) today than there were enslaved a few years before the Civil War—millions of modern-day captives. Most of these incarcerations are related to drugs, and are casualties of the war. Addiction and substance abuse aren't crimes. They are an illness of the mind that must be healed and rehabilitated, not criminalized.

My little brother, Tyson, picked up his drug addiction after getting shot. He ended up addicted to the opiate painkillers that were prescribed to him. It probably sedated his mind and helped him cope with the trauma and hopelessness of our city. Putting him in a cage hasn't helped him recover from his new-found addiction either. I've seen the Trap make several loved ones worse. My big brother, Jamal, was never on "meds" until he served that 9-month juvenile boot camp sentence at age 16. They shut down juvenile boot camps like that here in Florida, after 14-year-old Martin Lee Anderson was murdered by detention guards in Panama City, Florida.

The cost of incarcerating and traumatizing (and possibly killing a kid) for a year is equal to the cost of hiring a teacher, a social worker, or a police officer. In some places, teachers are getting laid off, while prison guards are getting hired. Our generation is the first in history to deal with this.

Drugs and addiction have been around since the beginning of time. Unfortunately, today's Trap causes countless Americans to lose their freedom, instead of receiving the support and treatment required to overcome their addictions. Systematic racism in all in The Trap. Minorities are about 30% of the population, but roughly

70% of all drug arrests. Research proves people of all races use drugs at about the same rate. I have many friends from different races and have seen this to be true, first-hand. But Blacks are up to than ten times as likely to be arrested for drugs than whites. The War on Drugs also fuels traumatizing police tactics in our communities. I've had the misfortune of having many guns pointed at my head in my life, but I will never forget the 9mm pointed at me by a jumper Narc in that drug raid when I was 11-years-old. These tactics cause us to further dehumanize each other. No wonder more of my boys have been shot than finished school.

The War on Drugs has had a catastrophic impact on my life, but it's counterpart—mass incarceration—is on par with slavery because of five qualities. I've become far too familiar with them through my personal experiences, and the experiences of my family:

1) <u>Deprivation of freedom and rights</u>: like slavery, mass incarceration takes away your freedom in many ways. This is much deeper than people in cages being told when to sleep, eat, and talk to loved ones, or having their physical movement restricted. A criminal record in America brands you for life. Discrimination is legalized when people must "check a box" on applications for jobs, housing, education, public benefits, licenses, and more. My juvenile charge from 15 years ago might actually prevent me from becoming a lawyer. I have to pay an extra $250 to appear before a panel of three judges and make a case for me "rehabilitation." Felons are also deprived of essential liberties like the right to vote or own a gun. Most of my loved ones have to check boxes and consent to the discrimination against themselves.

2) <u>Destruction of the Black family structure</u>: like a child whose family was sold to another plantation in the 1800s, I was ripped away from my parents for years at a time while they were incarcerated. We missed many Christmases and milestones together. The cycle repeats as Jamal's kids wonder "Where's

Daddy?" while he is in a cage for his drug charges. Jamal is still bitter with resentment from being locked away during the birth of his first born. In the 1950's, U.S. Census data revealed that less than 20% percent of Black children were born out of wedlock. Today, more than 70% of Black children are born to single-parent households. It's fair to say that millions of Black men in the Trap contributes to this, too.

3) <u>Devastation of one's psychological state</u>: like slavery, incarceration causes post-traumatic stress and emotional trauma. Research by Dr. Joy DeGruy highlights the ways slavery contributed to the violence, anger, self-destructive outlook, and feelings of hopelessness felt among many Blacks today. "Post-Traumatic Slave Syndrome," as scholars call it,is the consequence of generational oppression and is perpetuated through institutionalized racism (i.e. mass incarceration, the War on Drugs). So the survival behaviors prevalent in Black communities today are a result of this history.

   Similarly, incarceration can leave a traumatic scar on current and future generations. I still remember moments when my father woke up on the couch startled, confused, and in a cold sweat, until he realized he was no longer in a cage. Ray Ray was forced into incarceration for so long, he is "institutionalized" and struggles with basic daily interactions. Mass incarceration has created illnesses, like "Post Incarceration Syndrome," that lead to antisocial personality traits, substance abuse, and post-traumatic stress. I see this among many kin who are struggling to re-adjust, while carrying resentment from being subjected to conditions no one should experience.

4) <u>Forced and exploited labor</u>: in 1865, the 13th Amendment abolished slavery "except as a punishment for crime." Businesses and entrepreneurs have been exploiting this loophole ever since. Prison labor is utilized to manufacture products for many of the world's top corporations, like Wal-Mart and McDonalds. Prisons generate billions of dollars in revenue from

this exploitation. On average, prisoners work eight hours a day and make between 23 cents to $1.15 an hour, and is illegal for any other citizen. This is six times less than minimum wage. Ray Ray told me plenty of stories about working long days in the Arizona sun for roughly $2.00. Sadly, this exploitation is legalized, constitutional, and nearly impossible to challenge because of the 13th Amendment.

5) <u>Lucrative financial incentives for the system to continue</u>: slavery was the most profitable industry of its time. Its wealth built empires, like America, and fueled industrial revolutions around the world. Today, the private prison industry is one of the fastest growing sectors of our economy. People are making millions off of others' suffering and loss of freedom through the Prison Industrial Complex. One of my classmates shamelessly bragged about the money he is making off of his private prison stocks. In 2011, two Pennsylvania judges were sentenced to decades in prison because of their "Kids for Cash" scheme. They received over two million dollars in kickbacks from companies for sentencing thousands of kids to do time in privately-run juvenile facilities. The children spent months in these facilities for "crimes" like stealing toilet paper. Some of the kids committed suicide because they couldn't take the confinement and torture. The Trap runs so deep, "honorable" judges who take an oath to administer justice are actually profiting off of America and eating up its youth. The Juvenile Law Center filed a class action lawsuit against the judges because of the injustice, but I guarantee it's happening all over the country.

The parallels between slavery and mass incarceration provide evidence that many things have not changed for Blacks over the centuries. The institutions of mass incarceration and the War on Drugs are the most impactful systems on me and my generation.

Dafuqem-I gonna do 'bout it? I'm in my second year of law school, and these injustices haven't even been mentioned yet.

Do I really think I can change them? I feel like I'm looking at a fire that has been burning strong for centuries. I still have the physical and psychological scars from when I was in the fire, myself. Now I have to decide on whether I will reenter the fire, or watch it burn my people. I'm far from fire-proof, but I have a few extinguishers with me now—in the form of experience and education. You think sh*t is hot now? Get ready, son.

It took a Civil War to end slavery.

You ready for war, Dr. KnuckleHead Esq?

***

October 10, 2012

Montego Bay, Jamaica

God Bless the fall break that law school gives you! It falls on my birthday week every year. Never thought I'd celebrate my 28th birthday in my 28th country. Didn't think I'd still be in school at age 28, either. Didn't reach that childhood goal of having a wife, kids, and house by this age. Those will come in due time though…hopefully. For now, I'm in Jamaica, and single like a dolla bill!

Flight from Miami was just $250, and since I'm couch surfing, I'll probably spend less than $250 while I'm here for my birthday. Just half the monthly check from my part-time job. Had to choose between this trip, and a trip home for my 10-year high school reunion.

Sorry PHS, Class of 2002. I'll catch you at the 20-year mark.

***

November 1, 2012

A few hours ago, I was dancing in a Miami club in a Halloween costume. The sun hasn't risen yet, but I'm already up, suited, and ready to go. This attire is slightly different. Important business meeting for my non-profit before class. A few hours ago, I was Vegeta from the Japanese anime show "Dragon Ball Z." Rick's excuse-to-be-shirtless costume this year was "Magic Mike." We drank with Ninja Turtles and cowgirls at an outdoor Halloween Full Moon party. We grooved to the pulsating music that plays so much in Miami, it's starting to sound like the city's heartbeat. You hear it in the coffee shops, supermarkets, restaurants, and blasting from luxury cars next to you in traffic. It starts out like...

BOOM
BOOM
BOOM
BOOM

Then it elevates to...

BOOM-chigg
BOOM-chigg
BOOM-chigg
BOOM-chigg

Occasional breakdowns, climaxes, and explosions are interwoven. Maybe some soulful singing if you're lucky. Either that or Reggaetón...

BOOM...chi-BOOM, chi—BOOM
chi-BOOM...chi—BOOM
chi-BOOM...chi—BOOM

Preparing to vote again for Obama. He aiight, but this two-party voting system is starting to feel like a sham. It's not a true democracy, and it makes me not want to vote. But because of the harsh disenfranchisement laws in Florida, 32% (or nearly one out of three young Black men) cannot vote. That doesn't sound like a democracy to me. Millions marched, thousands were harmed, and many were killed in the struggle for me to have a voice. I appreciate their sacrifice enough to make certain my voice is heard, even if I don't agree with the system.

***

November 18, 2012

<u>Death of The Convertible Coupe</u>

I just got back from a free trip to Chicago. Got my law school to pay for me to present my dissertation at the annual conference of the American Society of Criminology. Just had to submit a proposal to the student government folks so they'd cover my flight and hotel. They wrote an article about it, which I put on my resume.

Took a Jumpman picture next to the Michael Jordan statue in front of the arena the Chicago Bulls plays at. But, unfortunately, my Chi-town glory is overshadowed by the drama and disaster I am returning to in Miami. My car was in a horrible accident while I was in Chicago. I left the keys with a friend, who had a job interview while I was away. Someone ran a red light and hit her in my car. Thankfully (and most importantly), everyone is ok. Unfortunately, my car is totaled—gone forever. Pegasus, the white Chrysler convertible that held me down for years. She was the most dependable car I ever had. I drove her across the country. I proudly paid for her with my own money. I was just thinking about how I wanted to give her to one of my brothers when I got a new car.

Humbled again by another loss, another lesson from the gods. Remember: don't grow too attached to material things. Take NOTHING for granted.

I am now without a car for the first time in ten years. But if there is one thing I know, it is struggle…it is adversity (ok, that's two things). That's why I stay jumping, to remind myself that not even gravity can keep me down. It seems the gods like to test me most when I'm at my best. It happened three months ago when I returned home from Europe to find $2,500 worth of my stuff stolen. Now my faithful and necessary car has been taken from me. Neither of the disasters were my fault.

For whatever reason, the gods are preparing me for a greater struggle to come. Setbacks can occur at any moment, so thick skin is required. I know this experience will make me stronger. This pain is temporary. Take it in stride, lil homey, and let it go. Focus on changing the world instead of these temporary and material losses.

Yesterday I was leaping around Chicago enjoying my youth. That seems so distant now. I'll jump again tomorrow. Not even gravity can keep me down. I'll get another car somehow. That is the thing about the gods, they come through, always…somehow.

***

November 28, 2012

Victory in my first independent case! Just left court from the case against my landlord. Judge awarded $2,559.50 in my favor! Of course, my guitars, swords, laptop, and world art cannot be replaced and are priceless. Still, this money will help me get a sweet new G-ride. Landlord gon' pay what he owe! I'll garnish his wages in a heartbeat! But for now, I have to catch two buses to get home, then bike to campus for class.

I'm slowly rebuilding back to where I used to be. Rising from the ashes. Feeling like Dwayne "The Rock" Johnson. As the only freshman in his starting lineup at The U, The Rock tore every ligament in his shoulder, benching him for the season. He soon fell into depression and quit The U. He eventually bounced back, recovered from academic probation, and helped the Miami Hurricanes become National Champions. Now he's one of the highest paid actors in the world. Time to get on this Rock shiznit.

***

December 12, 2012

<u>Lucky Number 12</u>

We just finished the 12th hour of the 12th day of the 12th (2012) year. I visited 12 countries in 2012 (Mexico, Jamaica, Europe backpacking trip). I'm preparing for my 12th and FINAL year of college.

I've visited 12 different schools and juvenile facilities in Miami in 2012. Jesus had 12 disciples, and there were 12 tribes. I'll be flying 1,200 miles home to Jersey soon. And after paying more than $600 to this tow company, I've only got $12 to my name. Haha.

But after all I've learned and experienced this year, being broke again just dust on the shoulders. Indeed 2012 was one for the record books, in both losses and gains. Just enjoying the ride.

What you got 2013!?!

***

February 6, 2013

Crying like a baby right now.

I initially set the goal of having at least 70% of students say Project KnuckleHead's D.I.G. (Dreams into Goals) Youth Summit increased their motivation to stay in school. This is important because half of the students who attended our summit are "at-risk" for dropping out. But 100% of the students said they are more motivated to stay in school because of D.I.G on their surveys!

The Youth Summit cost over $1,000 of my own money, but it was well worth it to be able to inspire the 120 students.

***

March 15, 2013

We just finished a hugely successful D.I.G. Youth Summit in Los Angeles at USC. Got over twenty of my former students from HPHS and USC to come out and volunteer. Makes me feel old when students I had as freshmen in college are now in graduate school. Or the students I had as freshman in high school are now well into college. Now we are changing the world together.

Feeling like James Bond during this West Coast spring break. Watched the sunset on Venice Beach. Hiked to my secret spot for the best view of the LA skyline and Dodger Stadium. Trekked a path to see the Hollywood sign close-up. Saved the world through Project Knucklehead. Went with my boo-thang, Shakirah, to a beach-front hotel in Mexico. Wrapped things up in Las Vegas, where $100 quickly turned into $240.

Bond.
Worrrrrd is bond.

***

May 16, 2013

Never stayed in a 4-star hotel before, at least in America. Never really wanted to. I spent most of the last summer sleeping on couches throughout Europe. But to show their appreciation for me giving the keynote speech at graduation, USC paid for my flight to Los Angeles AND put me in a fancy downtown hotel for a few nights. It's like $400 a night. Of course, I trashed the room with Morales and the hooligans. Outside the window of my hotel, American Idol's Season Finale is being filmed live at the Nokia Theater. Across the street is the LA Kings playoff game at the Staples Center.

The dean of the School of Education sent me a personal invitation to deliver the keynote address after hearing about the work I'm doing with Project KnuckleHead. The communications staff that came by the DIG Summit to take pictures for an article heard my Knucklehead spiel. I was flabbergasted when I opened up the invitation letter, and thought it was Morales pranking me. USC wanted my 20-minute speech written word-for-word. Of course they told me in the middle of law school finals. Invited a few Miami peeps over for brunch to critique my keynote and practiced it with some of UM Law the deans. Still can't believe USC really felt I was worthy of giving a speech to thousands of people!

I nailed it and got a standing ovation. Who knows who was in that crowd. USC has history-making alumni including: Neil Armstrong (the first man on the moon), John Wayne, Reggie Bush, George Lucas, and many others. USC Trojans are the founders of companies like MySpace, Kinko's/FedEx's, and other Fortune 500 companies. The owners of the Lakers AND the Dodgers are both Trojans. Presidents, Prime Ministers, and Ambassadors of Japan, Egypt, Singapore, and Jordan are USC Trojans. Governors and Senators from states like California, Nevada, Virginia, and Kansas were USC Trojans. Two of the deans at my Miami law school are USC Trojans.

Dr. KnuckleHead is a Trojan, and he just gave the 2013 graduation keynote for the School of Education. Despite the all-expense-paid trip to LA to deliver a speech to thousands, my greatest rockstar moment came earlier this month. I put together a seven-piece band to perform for a Project KnuckleHead fundraiser at Tobacco Road—Miami's oldest bar. I convinced a few law students and undergrad friends to jam out for the cause. We sounded aiight, and raised a few hundred for the program. Met the chillest musician this semester, this cat name Ivan Malespin. He sat in with our band and headlined our fundraiser with his quartet. They were so good, that the best we could sound before them was "aiight." At least our set closed with "No Diggity." No doubt, baby.

Other highlights of the semester include camping and Mardis Gras in New Orleans. Drove there with Rick and a few law students in the new KnuckleHeadmobile. Got a used, bright yellow mini-SUV for a good price. Will need the space to carry the instruments for the music program I want to start with Project KnuckleHead.

***

July 17, 2013

Using my summer break to take Project KnuckleHead to the next level. We began weekly who have been arrested and are in the juvenile justice system. We take over their 90-minute group therapy time and do music, art, and self-expression activities. During my first session, I gave a general talk to the youth. After touring the facility and noticing the absence of music and art opportunities, I asked my musician friend Ivan if he'd go do a workshop with me. He got a few more musicians, and we created a four-piece band of inspiration. They were all professional musicians, so I couldn't keep up with the cats—but that's what a behind-the-neck guitar solo is for! After the performance, we let the students experiment with the instruments.

In the surveys we asked the students to complete after the session, more than 60% of youth said it was the first time they experienced any music instruction. On average, the youth rated the experience 9.2 out of 10. 100% of the youth said we helped them discover positive ways to express themselves. I know firsthand how expressing yourself through the arts can help you overcome struggles, become more patient, more creative, more open-minded, more courageous, as well as other things. Deciding to stay in the crib and play guitar or make beats kept me out of trouble on many occasions. Now Project KnuckleHead is about to give the same gift to Miami's youth. We are literally helping youth discover their soul! This is a gift they will never forget!

***

August 9, 2013

Just finished my last day doing civil rights work for my summer internship with the Southern Poverty Law Center. It was one of the most enlightening experiences I've ever had. I did many things, but I am most proud of two major cases I got to work on:

1) A complaint against the state of Florida on behalf of every Black and Latino student in our public schools. We are challenging Florida's race-based education standards, which set different test score expectations for students based on the color of their skin.

2) A class action lawsuit against a Florida county for its treatment and abuses of children. They shut down all of their juvenile facilities, and have been holding kids as young as eight years old in county jails with adults. For the kids, the experience is no different from the adults. They are frequently pepper sprayed, and tortured with solitary confinement, and receive limited education.

I leave the summer gig fulfilled, knowing that I have done things that will benefit millions of youth across the state. I think I'll like being a civil rights lawyer. We're not afraid to stand up to the gov'ment. We all know how Florida needs a serious foot up their a*s.

This is the Gun Shine state, after all.

***

August 22, 2013

Started my 12th and final year of college...or 25th year of education. Ironically, I received my teaching certification letter of eligibility from the state of Florida on the same day. Now I've been certified to teach in New Jersey, California, and Florida!

Reflecting on how this educational path has been one hell of a ride. I wish I could talk to that 18-year-old Amir, starting community college back in 2002. I'd share stories with him he wouldn't believe. I'd tell him education was the reason he:

- Met numerous friends for life.
- Spent his 20s living in Los Angeles and Miami.
- Was paid to travel to cities like Chicago, DC, and San Diego to present at conferences.
- Learned guitar and performed for thousands in six states across the country.
- Had more than 15 roommates: Black, White, Latino, Asian, Middle-Eastern, etc.
- Worked with and inspired thousands of students at seven schools across the country. Taught every grade level from kindergarten to college. Even worked at the high school "Grease" was filmed, and other high schools attended by people like Ice-T and Quentin Tarantino.
- Gave speeches to thousands and appeared on national television.
- Contributed to lawsuits to bring about justice and equality.

- Represented dozens of youth at the juvenile courthouse.
- Was able to travel to a dozen different countries.
- Started a nonprofit that will inspire thousands of youth from similar situations.
- Became braver, more open-minded, more resilient, more disciplined, and more patient.
- Can literally do anything he muthaf%@#$ wants to do.

I would tell that 18-year-old that time will pass regardless, no matter what you do. You may as well invest in yourself, and move closer to you dreams through education. Ironically, I recently found an old college assignment from 18-year old Amir from almost 11 years ago.

My major at UCC is Computer Science. After the completion of the Associate's degree program here, my plans are to transfer to Hawaii Pacific University. My career objectives begin with me starting with an internship...then maybe a couple of years later become a Technical Support Manager. My ultimate goal is to open a business with my brother entitled 'Chips & Whips' where we specialize in computers and cars.

-Amir, 2002

No chips or whips youngin'. You're still sharpening your sword for the battle, in your 12th and last year of college.

Final Round...FIGHT!

***

September 4, 2013

I'm over law professors to the max. I agree with President Obama: a full year needs to be shaved off the three years of law school. Luckily I'm able to take advantage of the many learning and credit opportunities available outside the lecture hall.

Officially back in two of my favorite elements. Started teaching today at Miami Carol City High. It's the school Trayvon Martin once attended, as well as Rick Ross and Flo-Rida. I teach a weekly Street Law course to students there. We're doing a lesson on "Stand Your Ground" in a few weeks at the students' request. Some of my students were friends and classmates with Trayvon, and they are curious to learn about this law used to justify his murder. Perfect time to teach the youngins' the difference between law and justice.

Also started working at the Juvenile Courthouse for the Miami-Dade County Public Defender's Office again. I'm learning from a fearless group of lawyers who ensure youth are given adequate legal representation after they are arrested. My first trial starts in a month. One of my first clients was a 14-year-old kid I had to write a motion for to get his bike back. The police wouldn't return it.

My favorite moment occurs when we greet a youth in court, recently handcuffed and coming out of detention custody. They timidly enter the room looking for us—the only ones on their side. We are their lawyers, their representation, and their voice. I recognize all the feelings I had when I was in their shoes. Confusion, fear, uncertainty—yet with an outer shell pretending to be hard and in control. If you look at the kids long enough, you spot the "I just wanna go home" glimmer in their eyes. All of them are in need of help and support, but none deserving a cage.

"We enter a general plea of not guilty, demand discovery," we'd say on their behalf before we even say a word to the youth themselves. We let them know that we must talk first before they plead. If something unjust or unlawful happened to them (which is frequently the case), we can get the case dismissed. Well, that depends on the judge actually. This one judge rarely rules in the favor of our clients, especially if they are Black. Funny how the same facts and situation can lead to different outcomes depending on the judge. Justice is supposed to be "blind" and applied equal to everyone regardless of color or income-level. Yea...aiight.

> That Justice is a blind goddess
> Is a thing to which we black are wise:
> Her bandage hides two festering sores
> That once perhaps were eyes
> -Langston Hughes (1932)

"Stand up next to your client!" the senior attorney and supervisor, Deborah would yell at the lazier PDs sitting in their chairs. We were required to assertively stand up next to our clients to let them know that we had their back. I always felt so empowered during this symbolic moment. The youth go from being alone and unrepresented, to having us to fight for them.

During my first year of law school, over 100,000 kids were arrested in the state of Florida. This is more than the number of adults arrested in several large countries combined. Miami is arresting less, but they have some of the hottest hotspots. Take Miami Gardens: it's where the high school I teach at is located, and it has 110,000 people total. However, over the past four years, over 65,000 citizens have been searched by the police. Our clients are often youth stopped on playgrounds, or on their way home from school. Children as young as five-years-old are being stopped and searched because they looked "suspicious." According to police records, a 99-year-old man near a nursing home was searched because he looked "suspicious." A store clerk named Earl was stopped 258 times over the past few years. On 62 of the stops, he was arrested for trespassing at the very store at which he worked. Of course, this was only happening to Black people. A new investigation by Fusion News revealed that officers stop and search random people frequently to fulfill quotas. At the public defender's office, we are often the last line of defense to fight these injustices and keep people like Earl free.

In my Criminal Procedure law class, I learned that these War on Drug tactics used by Miami Gardens and others are unconstitutional violation of our rights. The Fourth Amendment of the Constitution states every person has a right to be free from unreasonable searches. Searching someone randomly walking down the street is pretty f*cking unreasonable, but I never realized it was illegal until law school. Rights are violated far too frequently, and most of the time the injustices go unchecked. Had I known my rights back in 2008, I would have avoided that arrest with the Jersey comrades. I'm a member of organizations like the ACLU and NAACP that fight these unjust practices, but I have to do more somehow.

I wish I knew about the Constitution when my friends and I were getting systematically searched by police officers, years before we even thought about selling drugs. Frequent frisks by cops were weird at first. No man had ever touched me in those places. Eventually, it became a procedure, almost like paying the toll before a bridge, or turning on the light before entering a room.

Teaching at Carol City Senior High through Street Law, and representing youth at the Public Defender's Office are more than just internships—they are privileges. I'm grateful for the opportunity to empower and influence the youth. I grew addicted to it while teaching in Jersey eight years ago. I really haven't left the classroom since. Over 1,000 students...from South Central Los Angeles to South Africa to South Florida. And I don't see myself retiring anytime soon. This is an addiction. And like a true fiend, over the past year, I have depleted my savings and worked thousands of hours for free to get Project KnuckleHead off the ground. As if Miami ain't expensive enough.

***

September 25, 2013

Breath. Slow down. Relax.
Indeed, there is urgency.
Remember, you have always done so well with patience.
Your success is inevitable. The struggle is secondary.
I mean…you're Dr. KnuckleHead.
Mentally Numb. None of that sh*t matters.
I'm just getting old. Tired. This is not sustainable.
Hurry up, and get Oprah-rich.

***

November 27, 2013

So 23 semesters down, one more to go. Just spent four hours in a mock trial with my high school students. To make things interesting, we gave them a "Stand Your Ground" trial. We also had a Thanksgiving potluck at the Public Defender's Office. Yams, mojo pork, collard greens, rice and beans, jerk chicken, ham, turkey, wasabi eggs, parsley potatoes...only in Miami! After the table was fully set up, the staff just stood around and marveled at it.

"You may as well eat first, since we're not paying you anything," said John, one of the supervising attorneys.

I took Project KnuckleHead on a five-school tour in Los Angeles this semester. Tossed up the West Side sign in a photo with students at Crenshaw High, went back to USC for homecoming, and partnered with a few student organizations to host our first LA fundraiser. After all, Project KnuckleHead can't sustain itself on a budget of whatever its starving law student founder can afford to spare for the month. I persuaded the organizations I was involved in as a USC student to provide the food, and convinced the campus bar to offer drink specials. We had raffles and silent auctions. I got some former students, who are headed straight to the NFL, to autograph a few footballs. One sold for $170! We are going to use the extra money to start our after school program out there.

Lastly, this semester, I told my story on national television. It was late night TV, so I tried to be funny and laid-back. I ended up sounding dorky in the end. Haha. Always been the quiet, shy type who doesn't like attention. The only reason I accepted the invitation to appear on TV was to promote our fundraiser.

***

March 29, 2014

Never apologize for your ambition—it is a disservice to your dreams and a dishonor to your aspirations! Anything lost while pursuing your goals is not a real casualty—especially if it came to you after you set those initial goals. Sacrifices are inevitable…
It ain't nothin to cut this chick off—but, eventually, loneliness catches up to you.

***

April 10, 2014

Exactly one month away from my fifth and final college graduation! After 25 straight years of school, "senioritis" is an understatement. Reflecting on my struggle gives me strength. In just the 12 years of college alone, I've balanced academics while dealing with:
1) the humiliation of writing to financial aid, explaining why I couldn't provide either parents' taxes, since both were incarcerated.
2) the sorrow from phone calls informing me that my brother, cousins, or best friends had been shot.

3) the pain of losing friends and family members to violence.

4) the betrayal from friends mocking me for being "too good for the streets," because I was in college.

5) the frustration of having six of my cars break down.

6) the torment of a three-hour daily commute—two buses and a train—to get to the community college, just to take classes I wasn't getting credit for.

7) the disappointment from people closest to me telling me I was not in a "real college," while in community college.

8) the anguish of trekking through 15 inches of freezing snow to get to class.

9) the exhaustion from working 16-hour shifts just to the pay bills.

10) the fear of not knowing where rent money was coming from, because I was dead broke.

11) the devastation of having my apartment burglarized…TWICE.

12) the anger at the racist, insensitive, and ignorant comments made by classmates and professors.

13) the outrage and irony of starting law school with both my brothers in jail.

14) the financial responsibility of paying my family's mortgage and bailing several loved ones out of jail.

15) the embarrassment from professors and judges telling me to cut my hair—as if God made me ugly.

16) the animosity I held against my privileged classmates, who never had to deal with any of these struggles—but still complained.

17) the calamitous California earthquakes, Florida hurricanes, and Jersey blizzards.

Dust off your shoulders, kid. They don't call you Dr. KnuckleHead for nothing. Never let anyone tell you what you can't do. You are Infinite. If you can deal with 12 years of all that, future challenges will be inconsequential.

Still, for all the negative emotions I experienced, college provided many positives like:

1) the joy from interacting with and learning from people of many backgrounds and races.

2) the infatuation with knowledge and learning that came from taking 120+ different course.

3) the pride of doubling my high school GPA.

4) the opportunity to share my story and wisdom in speeches given to crowds of thousands of people.

5) the culture shock from studying in Africa and Europe, and visiting nearly 30 countries and 20 states.

6) the satisfaction of knowing my legal advocacy kept a few kids out of cages, and helped in the fight for a more equitable education system.

7) the indescribable feeling of starting Project Knucklehead—and inspiring hundreds of youth across the country.

8) and finally, the hundreds of experiences and people that I will never forget.

I now see that, aside from my grandparents, my greatest blessing might be my patience.

For whatever reason, I learned to never focus on the whole staircase, but to just take things one step at a time. Each day is an opportunity to get closer to your dreams…or regret wasting your time. I eventually accepted my struggles and viewed them as temporary pain necessary to break the eternal cycle. After 4,380 days (or 12 years) of work, I am about to be Dr. Amir Whitaker, Esquire. I told my mom this last week, and she wasn't even sure what an "Esquire" was. There aren't many licensed attorneys where we came from, so I didn't know what an "Esquire" was either until a few years ago. We got one now.

I'll never forget my doctoral graduation three years ago, when the "Congratulations Dr. Whitaker" sign confused the hell out of my little cousin.

"You don't look like no Dr!" he said.

"What does a 'Dr' look like?" I asked.

"White," he said, after briefly thinking about it.

"Well," I said, "they don't look so white anymore, do they?"

At that very moment, a cycle was shattered. Maybe you should consider sharing your story one day to help give Black children the permission to dream.

Uncle Sam: "And that's how you Escape The Trap!"

***

April 22, 2014

The morning was a bit awkward until I blasted Kanye West's *"Good Morning."* Yesterday I woke up, looked at myself in the mirror, and said:

"Damn son! You're 29-years-old, and you have not stopped going to school yet?!"

For nearly 90% of my life, I have had to anticipate school and class almost daily. But after 25 years, today is the first day in my life where I no longer have to do such a thing (excluding bar exam prep!). So GOOD MORNING!

The happy ending in Kanye's third verse almost brings me to tears every time!

Good morning, look at the valedictorian
Scared of the future while I hop in the DeLorean
Scared to face the world, complacent career student
Some people graduate, but be still stupid
They tell you read this, eat this,
don't look around, just peep this,
Preachers, teach us, Jesus
Okay look up now, they done stoled yo' streetness
After all of that, you received this
...from the moments of pain,

look how far we done came
Haters saying you changed, now you doing your thang.

I will always be a student, or at least someone who is curious to learn all that I can. Life is for learning. It's just one big lesson. But here's to not having to do it through school!

I know it's the morning, but I think I should have a drink. Can't get too comfy in the celebration, though. I still have a week of internships. They have actually been the best part of my law school experience. Through our Career Development Office and other initiatives, I've racked up nearly two semesters of credits working in courtrooms, communities, schools, and with a top civil rights law firm while attending The U. Education is infinite and cannot be constricted to the classroom.

I'm wrapping up my second year as a Street Law fellow, too. I've taught weekly classes on law to high school students and youth in juvenile detention all over the city. I'm also finishing up my second year as a fellow in the Education Justice Project—my law school's program to develop community-based lawyers. I'm mostly working with local churches, like President Obama did as a young lawyer in Chicago. Over the past four semesters with this "Historic Black Church Program," I've conducted a dozen Know Your Rights trainings, co-authored education rights materials distributed to hundreds of students and parents, protested in solidarity with students and community organizations to put pressure on the local school district, and helped mobilize a coalition of organizations for education. The professor of the program is a bit disappointed that we haven't completely obliterated racial inequality in our few semesters, so I don't expect my grade to be that high. Still, we took a chunk out of Miami's School-to-Prison-Pipeline.

There was a common thread amongst all the internships I held—they give as much as you take. You have one primary Internship Supervisor, and in law school this has to be an attorney. While in court, some interns just spend their down time on their cell phone. To avoid this and get the real value out of the internship, I just asked someone for something to do—or better yet, I created my own projects. Not just for the hell of it, though. I found gaps, filled them. At my civil rights internship with the Southern Poverty Law Center, I've added so much value to the organization that they are considering hiring me afterwards! My supervising attorney Stephanie Langer is starting her own law firm, and she recommended me as her replacement. Indeed, one of the primary purposes of internships is to get exposure for job opportunities.

The disdain I developed for law professors pushed me to maximize my out-the-classroom learning, and I'm eternally grateful I did. I've built my resume, networked with a group of lawyers and advocates, and made a difference—all while receiving academic credit.

***

June 10, 2014

Taking a study break and staring aimlessly at a few of the awards I've received over the past weeks. I never expected anything extra in return. But it does feel good knowing what I'm doing is appreciated and impactful. The awards are as follows:

1) The Roger Sorino Award: this award is given to the graduating law student who "best exemplifies leadership, dedication to the school, and service to the community." I would not have chosen myself as its recipient, but I am humbled that I was selected by the Society of Bar and Gavel. It is only given to one out of 300+ students graduating from the University of Miami School of Law every year.

2) The HOPE Innovative Service in the Public Interest Award: this award recognizes innovation through the creation of a new program that addresses the unmet legal needs of others. It is also only given to one law student in the graduating class.

3) An award from my old elementary school for "Valuable contribution to the lives of children and outstanding achievement as a Stillman graduate." They had an assembly for me and errythang. Proud Owl!
4) A plaque from Laura Saunders Elementary for my support and speaking at their graduation. I saw a few parents moved to tears in the audience.

Also, our Arizona D.I.G. Youth Summit for teens in from Ak-Chin Native American community and reservation was a huge success! We had mentors from the Navajo, Apache, Tohono, and other Native American nations. Most students experienced their first college visit. For many, it was their first major trip off the reservation. EVERY student who participated said they were more motivated and inspired to stay in school. Because more than 70% of the students we served are at-risk for dropping out of school, this is a HUGE success. This was also the first time Project KnuckleHead was paid for serving the youth we inspired. The Ak-Chin got that casino money, so they paid for my travel and provided a stipend. Just in time too, cuz a n*gga on welfare. I can't believe this ish. With all these awards and five college degrees, I applied for government support in May after graduation. What else can you do when you have to study 65 hours a week? I've taken out so many student loans, they refuse to give me another dime.

The "Esquire" swag is within reach. Just in time, too. Got my first post-school job as a lawyer with the Southern Poverty Law Center. I have several cases, on behalf of tens of thousands of children, waiting for me at work. The commas in the number of clients aren't the only commas coming my way soon. I'll have to start paying off my hundreds of thousands of dollars in student loans after graduation. More than half of it is from law school. I would be paying it for the next 40 years, if I didn't plan to enroll in this public service loan forgiveness program. Imagine being 60-years-old still paying for this!?

Was it worth it? OF COURSE it was. I know it's a serious risk. But people take out loans for cars that lose value, marriages that fail, businesses or investments that never take off. What I have can never be repossessed or divorced.

I've had the opportunity to spend my 20's learning great things, meeting great people, and living in great places. I think these 12 years of college have given me an unfuqwittable understanding of the law, education, the mind, and history. Combined, these disciplines have helped me make sense of the institutionalized barriers I've been fighting all 25 years of my education—and thirty years of my life. I realized I've been running up a reverse escalator, with its stairs mechanically pushing me back down. Meanwhile, on the other side, other people are standing-still on their escalator, enjoying a smooth ride up. Exerting no effort. Well, I finally hustled to the top of the stairs, but I'm out of breath. Inadequate preparation at inferior schools, emotional hardships, low expectations, limited financial support, family issues, community underdevelopment, the War of Drugs, mass incarceration, the School-to-Prison Pipeline…I've somehow managed to survive a warzone, with landmines and traps at every turn. Education is the cape I used to fly over it—my ticket out.

No matter where you come from, education can take you anywhere. Although I was resistant to it at first, education is simply growth and change. Once you learn something fresh, you are automatically transformed into a new and (usually) better person. But now that I have this knowledge and experience, what am I going to do with it?

This was just a journey to prepare for a journey.

This concludes 1/3rd of Million. The full book is forthcoming.

BOOK THREE — STREET TRAVELER

As a 22 year-old college student, Amir becomes the first person from his neighborhood to obtain a passport. An opportunity to visit Africa unleashes an addiction to traveling and culture shock that change him forever. He becomes obsessed with a goal to visit 30 countries before his 30th birthday, and embarks on an eye-opening quest throughout all corners of the globe. Realizing he does not know how to travel, he relies on "street smarts" to escape danger, explore forbidden places, and survive on a few dollars a day. Curiosity leads him to intriguing destinations across Asia, Africa, Europe, Latin America, and the Caribbean. In the process, Amir uncovers priceless life lessons through encounters with some of the quirkiest and most inspirational people in the world.

Chapter 1: The Departure

For as long as I can remember, I've felt a curious spirit residing within—longing to explore the unseen. Despite this feeling, I did not own a passport, or even leave the East Coast of the United States, until I was 22-years-old. I'm not sure I even knew what a passport was until college. Where I'm from, you were fortunate if you got to see anything outside the few blocks' radius of your hood. See the world? We were lucky to see tomorrow. Neither of my parents have passports, or the documents required for them to leave the country. Other family members and friends owe thousands of dollars in back child support preventing them from going abroad.,

I was born poor, and because of the work I want to do for the rest of my life, I have accepted the fact that I may never become rich. This reality is hard to come to terms with as an American. We have a culture that is oversaturated with social programming telling us to get rich, envy the rich, and even if you're broke, find ways to live like the rich. To be content having little money is almost un-American. All this freedom and the opportunity to get paid? Why not be the next millionaire or superstar?!

Aside from the reality that only a small percentage of our society will become financial rich, I recently accepted the idea that there is more to life than materially wealth. Seeing the world helped me discover this. The idea of not attaining affluence no longer bothers me because of how rich I am becoming with life experiences. And this didn't require a million dollars or rocket science to accomplish, either. It was as simple as saving what I usually spent on going out or eating at restaurants (about $40-$80 a month).

So far, most of my travels can fit into three categories: vacations, tourism, and backpacking. Vacations are for those who want to chillax in another country. Commercials showing those with perfect smiles and bodies playing beach volleyball lure you in. The world is often seen through the eyes of a resort—which is more than happy to provide all your meals, entertainment, and activities. Often strategically placed in a remote area, transportation off the resort and to other parts of the county can cost you quite a few bucks. I took a vacation once…and it was awful. When I'm in another part of the world, I'm too eager to explore to relax. I'm too curious be removed from the genuine experience of a country that comes from seeing it from a local's perspective.

Cruises are vacations on a massive ship with thousands of people. Relaxation is guaranteed because, in the middle of the ocean, there is not much else you can do. Cruise ships usually dock in different countries for a few hours or days, and let you have a taste of each locale. Although you'll enjoy the endless entertainment, activities, and top-notch service on the ship, if you're anything like me, you'll yearn to see more of each country. Port areas are also not the most authentic parts of a country because they are typically designed for tourists, presenting the most cliché and stereotypical versions of a country's culture. In some dockside areas, vendors scramble to change their sets like the crew of a Broadway play in between scenes as the many cruise ships arrive.

General tourism is the most common form of international exploration. It involves sightseeing and traditional activities. There are endless types of tourism to choose from: adventure tourism, cultural tourism, family tourism, volunteer tourism, sex tourism, food tourism, educational tourism, religious tourism, ecotourism, romance tourism…or some weird combination of any or all of these. Wise tourists secure hotels near a city's center or near the most popular attractions. This grants you easy access to tours, transportation, popular restaurants, and other experiences. However, areas designed specifically for tourists are usually the most expensive parts of a country. Hosting the most tourists, they can also wind up being the least authentic parts of the country. Nevertheless, they are well worth the experience.

Finally, for those want to have to shower four times to wash the funk of a country off, there's backpacking. Traditional luggage is swapped for a backpack, providing the agility required to explore the cracks and crevices of a new land. You're on a budget, and could rarely eat full meals in some places. You sporadically snack on cheap local street food instead, or one of the five turkey sandwiches you made and packed to hold you down for the day. You don't stay at hotels for $100+ a night. Instead you pay $4-$40 a night for hostels, where you share a dorm-style bunkbed with strangers from all over the world. I've been crammed in hostel rooms with up to 24 backpackers at a time—each of us an international mystery, slightly rough around the edges. Each of us possessing the hustler mentality required for backpacking.

Once I abandoned my suitcase for a large backpack, it felt as if I was liberated from a 60-pound ball and chain. It forced me to find ways to pack lighter and more efficiently. My travel evolved, as I became better equipped to cover more ground in less time. It became easier to jump on a crowded bus in Budapest, or climb up three flights of subway stairs in Paris. I could run top-speed in hopes of catching that last train departing for Cairo in two hours—or wander easily around a city for miles because I *just* missed that last train.

If you tap into it, the bravery and open-mindedness required to backpack introduces you to a new realm of life experiences. You become less hesitant to try new foods, because you're forced to eat whatever $3 gets you. You interact more with locals in markets and on public transportation. Best of all, you encounter priceless moments of a country in its rawest form—moments like eating sushi under a cherry blossom tree, surrounded by rambunctious school children jumping rope in Japan; or observing the 63-year-old grandmother hustling past you, while balancing multiple baskets of food on her head in Haiti. These are the moments too precious to spoil by taking a photograph. Instead, you cross-your-heart-and-hope-to-die you never forget them.

Backpacking injects steroids into your travel in five essential ways: audacity, mobility, time efficiency, open-mindedness, and effective budgeting. It is the primary reason I was able to visit dozens of countries before turning 30-years-old. It allowed me to experience these 30+ countries while spending what most pay to visit just 5 or 6 destinations. Even more surprising, I was able to visit all of these countries during an eight-year span, while in my 20's. Here are five of my favorite. More to come soon in blogs and a full publication.

Chapter 2: Guatemala, 2010

- Capital City: Guatemala City
- Population: 15,189,958 Demographic breakdown: Mixed: 41%, Amerindian: 38.9%, White: 18.5%, Black: 1%, Asian: 0.6%
- Currency: Guatemalan quetzal
- Exchange rate to dollar: 1 quetzal = 0.13 US dollars
- Cost of a meal: 100-130 quetzales
- Cost of a beer: 22 quetzales
- Language Name: Spanish [Many dialects of Mayan are spoken as well]
    - Hello = Hola (oh-lah)
    - Street Slang = "bolo" a very drunk person, "como no chon!" yes, of course
- Must See:
    - Natural Wonders: Lake Atitlan, Pacaya Volcano
    - Architecture: Mayan Temples, Colonial Antigua
    - Important Historical Sights: Ruins of Tikal
- Must Do:
    - Festivals: Semana Santa
    - Activities: hiking Mayan ruins, volcano treks

My most ambitious backpacking trip—a month-long journey through all seven countries in Central America—required a little over a year of saving. It cost the same as a 9-day tour through two countries in Europe booked through some travel agencies. Few believe me when I tell them it only cost me $1,500 to visit Belize, Guatemala, Honduras, Panama, El Salvador, Costa Rica, *and* Nicaragua. This included everything: flight, food, accommodations, transportation, and even souvenirs. Of course, there were compromises on the quality of a few things, but that's a bargain I accept in order to see more of the world. After dropping $500+ on a flight to visit a destination, I only allow myself to spend a couple of hours in my room sleeping and showering. This way there's no need for fancy accommodations. It encourages you to just get out and explore the place that you've been saving up for a year to visit. I also feel experiencing the raw authenticity of a country requires a voyage beyond the tourist traps and overpriced restaurants near the expensive hotels and city centers. Places where the locals eat are the most authentic and the cheapest, by nature.

Step one of planning a backpacking trip: choose the countries where you will enter and exit. I usually twirl my globe around for 30-40 minutes and ponder. I look for large landmasses and envision zigzagging trails across multiple countries. For my Central America trip, I chose to arrive in Honduras in the north, and depart from Panama in the south. It's usually cheapest to fly into the capital or one of the larger cities of a country. These cities also provide the best transportation to other parts of the country. In Honduras, it was cheapest for me to fly into San Pedro Sula (SPS). Later on in the trip, I discovered that SPS has the highest murder rate in the *world*, and that statistic may have contributed to the low priced flights! I'm overjoyed I was ignorant to this danger as I blissfully roamed the streets with Mahogany, my travel partner. Explaining the dudes with assault rifles in random places would have been harder to bullsh*t had I known the reality.

After you figure out an entrance and exit for your trip, you can move on to the fun part: planning the journey in between the two points. In Central America, the plan was as follows: start in Honduras, take a $50 ferry to Belize, followed by a few $20 buses through Guatemala, and then off to El Salvador for $17. Afterwards, a $44 night bus through Nicaragua, then off to Costa Rica for $23, before concluding with a 16-hour, $47 bus ride to Panama.

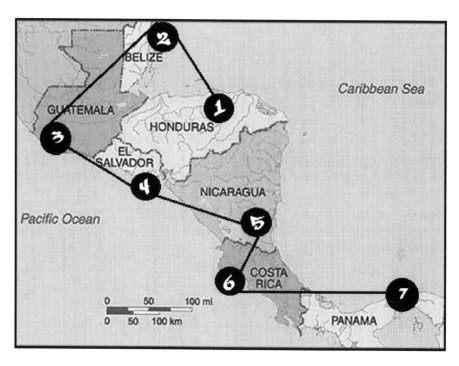

That was the plan. It didn't take long to realize that backpacking and plans don't work well together. Backpacking requires flexibility, and the occasional bout of irresponsibility. Maybe a detour to follow your new Australian friends to a rare, unheard of part of Costa Rica. Perhaps you'll end up kicking it an extra day with the petite French chick you met, because you loved the way she pronounced your name with her accent. As you told her on many occasions, "They don't make 'em like you, where I'm from, mon chéri."

My favorite country on the Central America trip was Guatemala. The country is lush in three of my favorite areas of tourism: adventure, nature, and ancient culture. With so much to do, spending five days in the country, and merely a single day in some of its cities, was painful. You can spend weeks exploring a town by itself. However, my current style of exploration rarely permits staying in a single city for more than a couple days. In my quest to devour worldly experiences, I viewed cities like dishes in a country's multi-course meal. Accept this as reality, and spending limited time in a place is no longer painful. Don't accept it, and you will never leave a country feeling satisfied.

The four-course Guatemalan meal filled me with inspiration. A major highlight was hiking 2,400-year-old Mayan ruins through the ancient rainforest capital of Tikal. This was the perfect contrast to Antigua, the colonial capital of Spain's "Kingdom of Guatemala," with its well-preserved 16th-Century architecture and historic churches. Antigua was my home base when hiking the Volcán de Pacaya—one of Guatemala's 22 volcanoes—which just-so-happened to violently erupt a few months before my arrival. Finally, my trip concluded in Livingston, where I discovered a different shade of black amongst Guatemala's Afro-Caribbean natives. Having no road access, the remote town is only accessible by boat. It seemed like an entirely different country itself.

The entire Central America trip was a seven-course meal with breathtaking attractions [full stories in next edition]. Clocking in more than 80 hours on buses and boats, I covered over 1,400 miles on the journey. The occasional train ride or short flight utilized in other backpacking trips was not needed here. The plan was: Start the trip accompanied by Mahogany for a week, drift solo for two weeks, then link up with my girlfriend, Tasha, for the last leg of the trip. Finding a travel companion for the entire duration of a multi-country backpacking trip can be a difficult task.

My quest began in Honduras, visiting the ancient Mayan temples of Copán. They were mysteriously abandoned in the 10th century. They were largely unknown and untouched, until Diego García de Palacio "discovered" them in 1570. In Belize, the only English-speaking country in Central America, I snorkeled with sharks and stingrays in the crystal blue waters of the world's second largest coral reef. In El Salvador, I chilled on the beach and celebrated Christmas with a local family with enough fireworks to launch my 45-pound backpack into outer space. Costa Rica, the most beautiful country I have ever seen, included unforgettable zip-lining and surfing experiences. In Nicaragua, I became a legend known as "Papa Negro" in a small town, and visited an island where the dually erupting volcanoes that created it made it the highest lake island in the world. Finally, in Panama, I peeped the Panama Canal—the historic shortcut between the Atlantic and Pacific Oceans, which took ten years—and 25,000 lives—to construct.

Between these activities, I managed to squeeze in salsa dancing lessons, biking, rainforests hikes, live music, parades, local cuisine, nightlife, and more. I was hoping to do all this for $1,500, while living out of a 2-foot backpack for a month. If I could pull this off, I was a "hustla" for real. My living expenses as a single guy in Los Angeles at the time were roughly the same if you included rent, bills, and food. If I could see the world for the same price as living in Los Angeles, that was an indicator that I needed to spend less time in Los Angeles—and more time in the world at large.

Guatemala's Tikal National Park is a 350-square mile jungle, containing thousands of ancient structures. Because of its biodiversity and archaeological importance, it is one of the few World Heritage sites recognized by the United Nations that is significant in both nature and culture. In the middle of a natural paradise, Tikal's pyramids stand erect and scratch the sky, reminding you of the greatness of Guatemala's ancestral heritage.

Tikal's construction began in the middle of a tropical rainforest more than 2,000 years ago. Every rock in its endless maze of structures was shaped and carried by hand. It was one of the most significant ceremonial cities for the Mayans. While Europe was entering the medieval Dark Ages, the Mayan empire and Tikal were thriving and expanding. Although it was one of the world's largest cities in its heyday with over 100,000 inhabitants, it was mysteriously abandoned a thousand years ago. Its demise remains one of the world's great mysteries.

My entry into the national park came a wicked walking tour.

"There are Mayan innovations in mathematics, astronomy, art, medicine, and architecture that are unmatched to this day," our tour guide informed us.

After a brief introduction, the tour guide provided us with two names to call him: "Xaman Ek," a reincarnation of the Mayan travel god, or "Carlos." He proudly explained how he descended directly from the people who built this ancient city. Throughout the tour, he'd swiftly climb trees and echo an array of wildlife calls. Aside from his ability to communicate with exotic birds and monkeys, Xaman (pronounced "sha-man") knew the answer to any question you could ask about the rainforest, Guatemala, or Mayan civilization.

"We developed one of the only writing systems in the early Americas. More than 20 dialects of the Mayan language are spoken in Guatemala today, with some originating thousands of years ago," he informed us.

At its peak, the Mayan civilization stretched through Mexico, Guatemala, Belize, El Salvador, and Honduras. The origins of its earliest villages trace back more than 4,000 years. The Mayans predate the Aztec and Incan Empires—two other great pre-colonial civilizations. Their hieroglyphic writing system dates back about 1,700 years, and catapulted the rise of city-states like Tikal. As we journeyed through our tour, ancient scripts dominated the sides of buildings like graffiti on a Bronx subway car. It's peculiar that a culture utilizing the written word so much left behind no clues of its demise—almost too peculiar.

Xaman explained how many of the buildings' construction and location were based on astronomy and alignment with the stars.

The cosmos also determined where the doors were placed in the dwellings. Perhaps this is why scenes from the first "Star Wars" movie were filmed here in the 1970's. Mayans used the stars to calculate and create calendars with unprecedented preciseness. They may have been the first civilization to document the calendar that most of the world uses today. Some of the pyramid temples have exactly 364 steps for you to climb into the clouds, symbolizing each day of the ancient year. Calendars were so important to the Mayans that people's names were often determined by the day they were born.

"You can climb steps people built over 1,000 years ago. Just be careful!" Xaman said.

"Tikaaaaaaal!" my travel companion, Mahogany, would say spontaneously, like the Wu-Tang rapper who used it as a nickname.

I was happy Xaman was speaking in English. Although my Spanish was improving, I wanted to learn everything possible, and I was certain much of this tour could not be explained in the few Spanish words I knew. I always knew flunking Spanish in high school would come back to haunt me.

With Xaman's explanations, our anticipation rose for the temple hikes. I felt like "Jersey Jackson," a young black version of Indiana Jones. In my mind, I had to ascend the forbidden steps of ancient temples to defend hidden treasures. Mahogany seemed to think she was Lara Croft from Tomb Raider, making our quest look supremely effortless in her tank top, shades, and stylish hiking boots.

We reached a temple that greeted us with a colossal stone head on the ground.

"You look just like that guy!" Mahogany shouted. "You make that face all the time!"

I was fully offended. The ancient head wasn't bad looking. He just had a mouth gesture typically seen on rap artist showing off their gold grills. Perhaps the sculpture was one of the Mayan nobility with jade teeth who Xaman had told us about. A mouth full of bling is the only thing to justify such a mean mug.

"I make THAT face?" I responded.

"All the time!" she said.

As Mahogany and I discussed my Mayan counterpart, Xaman appeared at the temple and translated the hieroglyphics.

"This says 'Ah Cacau,' or 'Lord Chocolate,'" he read.

"Divine ruler of Tikal."

I felt a slap on my back, and heard a roaring laugh echo through the hollow chamber.

"Oh my gosh! That name is perfect for you!" she joked. "Lord Chocolate! Ha!"

"That sounds like a friggin' stripper name!" I said.

Ah Cacau, the divine Mayan chocolate ruler, took the throne in 682. He restored Tikal's prestige after the damage wrought by a war with the Caracol people from modern-day Belize. His elaborate 154-foot temple pierces the clouds at a height taller than all the trees in the rain forest. Legend has it, he's buried somewhere around here in ceremonial robes, adorned with 200 pieces of jewelry, and surrounded by pottery given as grave offerings. This tempted Jersey Jackson to scheme on a come-up. Payback for the stripper name he cursed me with 1,500 years after his death. Thanks, Lord Chocolate.

We trekked through the rainforest for hours, as temples mysteriously revealed themselves through the trees. A sea of plants and foliage decorated the Tikal landscape. I kept my ears open for the hundreds of animal species present. We heard the piercing screeches of howler monkeys mixed with the serenades of tropical toucans. Xaman warned us of occasional bats in the ruins. We evaded the jaguars, pumas, snakes, and crocodiles that can be found in the region. However, a few flamboyant peacocks occasionally blocked our path and forced detours. Wild turkeys also roamed around comfortably, as if we didn't exist.

"I swear it smells like someone was blazing some ganja in here!" Mahogany commented, after leaving a secluded ancient dwelling. "Guatemala got that sticky-icky!"

Mahogany was a school counselor from South Central LA in her early thirties. She was a seasoned traveler with trips to Europe, South America, and the Caribbean under her belt. Many travelers have that one thing they must get in every country, and I've always found Mahogany's most peculiar: a picture with a chest-naked man, and her hands resting on his chiseled abs. She was in great shape herself, which made her a great adventure travel partner. After hiking ancient ruins, we anxiously anticipated conquering an 8,000-foot volcano on the trip.

I had never traveled with a woman before. Mahogany was so down-to-earth, I figured she was probably a better travel partner than most guys. However, she was by no means a backpacker, and she made it clear that she would never stay in a hostel.

"I'm a little too grown for a bunk bed," she proclaimed.

During our travel, we split the cost of cheap guesthouse rooms that cost us $15-25 each. Succumbing to her Los Angeles stereotypes about the Central American gangs and threats to foreigners, she outwardly refused to travel to countries like Nicaragua or El Salvador with me. She was willing to do a bit of Guatemala, Honduras, and Belize, though.

***

Xaman described the religious rituals fueled by hallucinogenic drugs from the rainforest. Mahogany's eyes grew cartoon-like wide, showcasing her interest and curiosity. It probably it reminded her of her "college hippie" era as a student at Berkeley. Her interest dwindled, as we were informed of the graphic details. During these ceremonies, select Mayans were painted blue and marched to the top of the pyramids to become human sacrifices to the gods. A priest would skin them alive and rip out their beating heart from their chest. Some priests supposedly put on the victim's skin afterwards and performed ritualistic dances. A few Mayans retain a form of blood-sacrifice today. Good thing chickens are used instead of humans in present day rituals, as is common in many religions of the world.

Climbing steep temples built before the eighth century was surprisingly easy. The sturdy gray stones that had stood the test of time thus far and could easily last a few more thousand years. Many of the stones we recently rebuilt, but it was hard to tell the difference. Modern architects still do not understand how the Mayans built these palaces without metal tools. Temple II is the most thoroughly restored structure. Climb the 12-story pyramid, and you'll be rewarded with a sweeping panoramic view from the platform of the summit's shrine. Walk around to admire all 360-degrees of Tikal's magnificence. In one of the most picturesque scenes imaginable, temples of different sizes peep through the dense green jungle and scatter the clouds for miles. It could take decades to build a structure like this. The fact that it has been here for 1,500 years is a testament to its prominence. This prompted one of the first moments on the trip where I paused to take everything in. I was also in no rush to descend the hundreds of ultra-steep stairs, either.

By the end of the 9th century, the majority of Tikal's population had mysteriously deserted these structures that had taken hundreds of years to construct. Royal palaces were then occupied by squatters, as some traditions began to fade. After another century or two, the squatters themselves vanished, as the rainforest began to engulf the ruins. During the jungle hike, Xaman told us that many structures were still buried under the hills we stood on. You could see them from the top of Temple II, looking like small mountains emerging from the sea of trees.

Tikal was not alone. Many Mayan cities were abandoned around the 10th century. Currently, no one can explain why the massive exoduses from these archeological masterpieces occurred. People have hypothesized famine, overpopulation, aliens, and many other theories. Unfortunately, Jersey Jackson didn't have enough time to solve this ancient international mystery. I had five more countries to explore, but only three remaining weeks in Central America. The forest will continue to be the silent guardian of the Mayan's secrets until Jersey Jackson returns.

The natural and cultural awesomeness of Tikal left me eager to experience more of Guatemala. Similarly, Mahogany was itching for a picture with her fearless Mayan warrior with ripped abs. I informed her she may have been 12 or 13 centuries too late, but she remained optimistic. We were excited about doing something that, like most memorable activities, sounded terrifying at first.

"We should hike a live volcano!" proposed Mahogany, a few weeks before our trip.

Remembering my fourth-grade baking soda and vinegar science project, I asked, "Why on earth would I want to do that?"

"Why wouldn't you!?" she responded. "Volcanoes are just glorified mountains on an unpredictable menstrual cycle!"

I silently stared back at her, preparing for the calculated arguments she often gave to encourage me to step outside of my comfort zone.

"You probably don't even know anyone who's tried it before. Be the first!" she said. "And don't worry about an eruption. The volcano we'll hike has only had 23 'major' eruptions in the past few hundred years. So, you're actually more likely to die in an airplane crash."

"Why does every conversation with you seem like an episode of '1,000 Ways to Die?'" I responded.

Unfortunately, one of those rare 23 eruptions had been just a few months before our trip. In May 2010, Volcán de Pacaya fiercely erupted—destroying 800 homes, forcing 2,000 people to evacuate, injuring 59, and taking the life of a Guatemalan TV reporter in its shower of scorching rocks. The international airport in Guatemala had to be closed temporarily. I can imagine the response of airplane passengers seeing flaming lava and rocks launch out of Pacaya like fireworks. One volcanic explosion lasted 45 minutes, and ashes flew over 100 miles away to the Caribbean coast.

"Imagine standing on top of one of the most destructive forces on the planet!" Mahogany exclaimed.

When you're abroad, or in any place you will not see again for a while (Disney World, amusement park, zoo, etc…), all fears must be abandoned. If not, you'll be haunted with eternal regret afterwards. "I should have gotten on that roller coaster," or "If I had only gotten a little bit closer to that lion's cage," may permanently echo in your head, as you wonder what the experience would have been like had you been a bit bolder. Mama didn't raise no chump, so hellz yea I was going to hike this 8,371-foot mountain on PMS!

We used the Spanish colonial city of Antigua as home base for our Volcán de Pacaya adventure. Antigua is rich in character, history, and friendliness. Jagged cobblestone streets separate well-preserved colonial ruins from the faded pastel-colored walls of storefronts. One evening, I stumbled upon what looked like a holy procession through the streets. Hundreds of locals marched solemnly with candles in a ghost-like manner past the rubble of churches from centuries ago. Religion has been deeply embedded in Guatemalan society since the Mayan days. They are still a devout people, and nearly 90% are Christian today. The solemn faith on display in Antigua contrasted sharply with the wildness of the looming volcano.

Antigua had some of the friendliest locals I'd ever encountered. Locals passing by often greet you with a quick "Buenas," which translates to a simple "good" in English—it's short for buenos dias, buenas tardes, or buenas noches. One of the best things you can do in preparation for travel is to try and learn the language. Locals usually sometimes warmer towards you if you attempt to communicate in their language. They appreciate you taking the time to learn their native tongue. The late, great B.B. King—who performed in more than 70 countries—always tried to show respect by learning something in the native language. What I learn in a language depends on my interest in the country. For example, 75% of my Brazilian Portuguese vocabulary involves asking people to join me for a walk, dance, drink, and a few unmentionables that are better off forgotten.

Three enormous volcanoes and an assortment of mountains, hills, and plains surround the city of Antigua. The volcano triplets of Agua, Acatenango, and Fuego are massive shadows in the sky that can be seen from different parts of the city. Predictably, Mahogany insisted on hiking Pacaya, Guatemala's most active volcano. Pacaya's frequent hiccup eruptions are often visible from Guatemala City, an hour's drive away. Magma flow and violent phases of lava fountaining are familiar sights to the locals. Mahogany wanted to see and smell the ash from the recent eruption. She wanted to stand on its surface as she heard the rumble and felt the vibration beneath her feet. Naturally, I was a bit nervous. They don't have these things where I'm from in Jersey. Like most people, I had only seen volcanoes on TV. I was fascinated by the thought of flaming red magma shooting into the sky after traveling 20 miles from the Earth's scorching mantle. The idea of touching and seeing something for myself has always been one of the most alluring parts of travel.

On the morning of the volcano hike, the shriek of roosters served as nature's 4:15 a.m. alarm. We wanted to catch the first shared van to Pacaya and avoid the large crowds that make the hike less serene. On the hour-long ride, I foolishly tried to compensate for the sleep I lost staying up all night in anticipation of the climb. The beauty of the sunrise-lit mountains, combined with the maneuvering of our van around Volcán de Agua's curvy terrain, made sleep impossible.

Arriving at the bottom of Pacaya sent a jolt of adrenaline through my body—instantly overpowered the feelings of restlessness. The adrenaline was catapulted further by the Guatemalan children who greeted us.

"Stick, chico?" a small child offered, holding a stick taller than him.

"Horse?" another asked.

Was Pacaya so steep, a hiking stick or horse—that looked remarkably like a donkey—necessary to climb it? Was I prepared to spend the next few hours climbing the back of one of Mother Nature's most destructive forces?

"Remember, Lord Chocolate," Mahogany teased, "at least it's not Tambora!"

She was referring to the Indonesian volcano she educated me about after I made the mistake of sending her a bold confirmation text for the present trip.

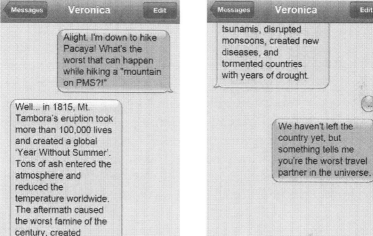

This was the last time I sought her advice on anything. There was no way to prepare to hike something so powerful. Earlier civilizations interpreted the destructive force of volcanos as God's own fury. Pacaya was in deep contrast to Guatemala's nearby natural wonder, Lake Atitlan, which I originally wanted to experience. I could be chillaxin' in its cool crystalline waters, seeing for myself why Aldous Huxley dubbed it "The most beautiful lake in the world." Instead, I was to climb into the clouds on the Earth's preferred method of throwing a temper tantrum.

The sporadically steep ascent up Pacaya that kicked off the journey was the most difficult part of our trek. Our guide led the group of 15 travelers up the volcano in a single-file march. We navigated through more trees and bushes than I imagined could survive on a volcano. Charred black branches emerged from the surface like scars, showcasing their resilience. At times, the density of trees made portions of the hike seem like we were in a forest.

At one point, our guide grabbed a fistful of leaves, wrapped them around the tip of a stick, and stuck it into what looked like a random hole in the ground. A few seconds later, he withdrew the stick with the leaves ignited in a ball of fire. He explained how the lava that flowed a few feet below us could easily rise above 2,000 degrees Fahrenheit. At that point, he explained, you wouldn't even have to touch it to get burned. In preparation for this moment, some of the people on the tour had packed marshmallows to roast on Pacaya.

"See, that's that Crazy-White-People Stuff!" Mahogany whispered. "I'll be damned if I taunt this volcano into erupting by cooking s'mores on it."

As we continued the hike, we felt the heat from steam baths created by the lava. Nearing the top of the volcano, we stopped to enjoy a view. We were literally in the clouds. It made the treacherous climb all worthwhile. I felt like a god on top of an 8,000-foot fire mountain, as I gazed at the three distant volcanoes peeking through the clouds. The view of Agua, Acatenango, and Fuego was much different from when I was in Antigua. Now, I was on equal altitude with the mammoths. It was like standing up to look someone straight in the eye, after bowing at his or her ankles. The Mayans believed God to exist in the sky, mountains, and plants. The power I felt standing atop Pacaya instantly convinced me that they may have been right.

On our descent, we passed caves filled with unbearable heat created by the boiling lava just below the surface. Our guide dared us to enter some of the caves, but cautioned the temperatures were above 500 degrees.

"Don't melt now, Lord Chocolate!" Mahogany joked, as I cautiously approached one.

As soon as I got closer, the air became thick and unbreathable. It smacked me in the face and reminded me of opening a broiling oven in the summertime. I immediately retreated. Simultaneously, a middle-aged guy with his hair in a ponytail took off his jacket, shirt, and undershirt in a single motion. He entered the lava cave.

"CWPS!" Mahogany said. I gave her a look of confusion until she whispered, "Crazy-White-People Stuff."

As the sun began to set, it painted a remarkable horizon—a

light stroke of peach-orange, that faded white, before melting into the purple sky. We continued the descent silently, except for volcanic rumbles and the sound of lava ash crunching beneath our shoes. Sunlight was fading swiftly, and flashlights began to flicker on. When it became nearly pitch-black, I was thankful for the flashlight app I had on my phone. I offered my flashlight to Mahogany, knowing she would proudly refuse. This made it even more enjoyable when she tripped over a rock and tumbled several feet down Pacaya. I slipped a few times myself, but had never fully fallen. Hiking boots would have been helpful, but were not necessary to climb Pacaya's back. I had worn the only sneakers I had packed, a pair of classic Nike Air Maxes. At times, I swore I felt the air bubble in my kicks dwindling beneath my soles, ready to burst from the heat.

***

After getting our volcanic fix, we rested in Antigua for the evening. Tomorrow would be another early morning that included voyaging through mountains, rivers, and forests to get to the small remote town of Livingston. To save money and enhance our experience, I wanted to take a chicken bus, or "camioneta de pollo." There was no possible way for me to convince Mahogany to ride one of these bad boys. Chicken buses are pimped-out American school buses that transport goods and people throughout Central America. Each colorful bus is elaborately decorated, and no two look alike. Reggaetón, salsa, bachata, or any other Latin music can be heard blaring from the bullhorn from blocks away. The word "chicken" could refer to the passengers being crammed in like chickens, or to the fact that locals often transport live animals on these buses. These retired school buses are often driven at top-speed to their destination. The thought of riding one sounded exciting. This, I thought, was traveling in style. Mahogany, however, couldn't envision herself sitting over, under, or next to a chicken. As she put it,

"We too grown to be traveling on a school bus! This ain't a field trip!"

First, we took a more Mahogany-friendly connection of buses to Rio Dulce—a riverfront town in eastern Guatemalan. Rio Dulce, or "Sweet River," was also the name of the 27-mile stream that took us to Livingston. SweetThang River is not very wide until it flows out of Lake Izabal. Here we saw the aging colonial fort, the Castillo de San Felipe de Lara, built by the Spanish in the 1600's to stop pirates from entering the lake from the Caribbean Sea. Livingston was just a few miles' journey from the lake through a narrow channel, surrounded by dense jungle vegetation.

With boat travel being the only way to access Livingston, it made it seem like we were traveling to an island. To the contrary, it is on Guatemala's Caribbean coast in the east. Livingston is secluded by miles of thick forest, rivers, and lakes separating it from any other town. Throughout the thousands of years of Guatemalan civilization, few had the "cojones" to settle in the region. To this day, there is still no road through what is now protected preserve land. This isolates Livingston even more from the rest of the world.

Livingston was founded by the Garifuna, a people possessing one of the most unique shades of black I've ever encountered. Their deep brown skin and almond eyes were familiar. African slaves were first brought to Guatemala in the 1500's, after the disease and brutality of the Spanish conquistadors wiped out two-thirds of Guatemala's indigenous population. The Garifuna didn't come to this region by slave ship, though—they took another type of boat. They are the descendants of West Africans who survived shipwrecked slave ships, and mixed with the indigenous people of the Caribbean island of St. Vincent. When the British took St. Vincent from the French in 1797, they exiled the Garifuna to the islands off of Honduras. Out of the thousands of Garifuna exiled, only half survived the treacherous voyage from St. Vincent. Over the next few decades, the Garifuna diaspora spread throughout Honduras, Belize, Nicaragua, and Guatemala.

One of the greatest benefits of traveling is seeing how your cultural identity translates abroad. There is nothing like finding culture shock from your own diaspora. It creates a feeling of One Love. The overlap of African traditions, Mayan customs, and pirate remnants made the small fishing village of Livingston one of my favorite places. For a long time, Livingston was the only major settlement on Guatemala's Caribbean coast. It was the country's chief Caribbean port, until Puerto Barrios.

As soon as our speedboat docked, we were swarmed by locals trying to get us to stay at specific hotels and eat at certain restaurants. For the first time on the Central American trip, everyone was speaking English or some dialect of it.

"Ayyy, mon! I have the perfect spot for you!" a voice said.

"Come with me, bruhdah!" another said. "I can get you anyt'ing you want!"

We already had a guesthouse booked for 45 quetzales, or roughly $6 each. We didn't need anything else. I let them know that, but unfortunately, it did absolutely nothing to deter their efforts.

"Let me carry your bags and show you around!" another gentleman offered.

"Thanks, but we don't need anything," I said.

Some followed us as we walked down the dock, until they grew weary of us pretending they weren't there.

"Geez, they are THIRSTY!" Mahogany remarked.

We checked into the guesthouse, situated a few feet away from Amatique Bay. The early morning expeditions to climb volcanoes and hike ancient rainforest temples were catching up with Mahogany. She cozied up in the waterfront bungalow and faded into a deep sleep. For the next few hours, I was on my own. Excited to get into the kind of trouble Mahogany was too "grown" for, I headed out.

"I was waiting for you, bruhdah," an unseen voice said.

I was surprised, and relieved that I didn't jump from being startled.

"You want to see Livingston?" he said slowly. "Let a true Rasta man be your tour guide."

This was my formal introduction to Dario. I noticed him earlier among the hustlers who greeted us at the dock. He distinguished himself as being the most relentless. He stalked us like prey all the way to our guesthouse. Now he was moving in for the kill. Dario had long, natty dreadlocks down his back wrapped in a dingy blue scarf. The beads and trinkets dangling from his locks made him resemble Captain Jack Sparrow, Johnny Depp's character in "Pirates of the Caribbean." He had a silver hoop earring, and wore dark, oversized aviator shades. He spoke extremely slow, but with precision.

"I can get you anyt'ing you desire, mon," he said.

"Aren't you the dude I told I didn't need anything a few minutes ago?" I reminded him. I said it in an assertive tone to let him know I was on to his hustle.

"Everyone need somet'ing," he said. "You wouldn't be here if you weren't looking for somet'ing. Where you from, mi bruhdah?"

I kept walking at a steady pace that required him to hustle for his hustle.

"I live in Los Angeles now," I responded "but I'm from Jersey."

"LA!" he said, with excitement. "Wat iz crackin, cuz?!"

I paused in my steps. Did this Guatemalan from a small fishing village just greet me like I was a member of the Crips street gang?

"How do you even know what that means?" I asked.

"I'm a Crip," he said. "I'm one of de founders of Livingston's Crips."

He made a series of swift hand gestures remarkably similar to what I had seen Crips do in LA. He followed it with a graceful Crip-walk around me in a circular, ceremonial fashion. He did it with the same rhythm, cadence, and energy seen in traditional African dance. It made me connect the dots between ancient West African dance and LA street dance traditions. As Dario bounced around, you could hear the trinkets jangling from his dreadlocks. I then noticed that he was wearing all blue, the trademark color of Crips. How could a gang from Los Angeles make its way to a remote town in Guatemala, only accessible by boat? I was intrigued by this Rastafarian-Crip-Pirate-Guatemalan-Hustler. But Jersey Jackson never displays public fascination.

"I don't need a tour guide, 'bruhdah,' but I'll buy you lunch if you help me find the best restaurant," I told him. "Maybe point me in the direction of the beach, a waterfall, and help me find a cheap boat to catch to Belize afterwards."

Because Livingston is only one square mile with a single major street running through town, most of this could be accomplished in one day. The town was so compact, I don't recall seeing a single car while I was there.

"And since you're an O.G.," I added, "you must show me your hood."

Dario withdrew a plastic pint of cheap Caribbean rum from his back pocket and took a swig. He chased it with a pirate-like growl.

"Arrrrrgh!" he said, "No tourist ever come to me hood," he said. "You're not afraid?"

"Fear is not an emotion I pack when I travel," I said softly. "And I'm not an old tourist either, cuz. I promise you, your hood is no worse than mine."

He accepted my proposition as a challenge.

As we moved through town, everyone seemed to know him. Many gave me a "leave that fool alone" look. We eventually stumbled into his favorite "restaurant," the home kitchen of a local Garifuna woman whom I paid 60 quetzales—or less than $8—to prepare a fresh seafood meal for us. Crab and shrimp were scattered in creamy coconut milk, along with an entire grilled fish. Each item had a unique blend of seasonings and spices. Afterwards, we washed it down with a swig of guifitti, a special Garifuna-style rum they distill with tree roots and sixteen different herbs. The bitter, tongue-numbing drink also serves as a homemade medicine capable of cleansing your system, and it's rumored to give "much power" to men.

Throughout lunch, Dario gave me a crash course on Livingston, the Garifuna, Guatemala, and his life as a Rastafarian-Crip-Pirate-Guatemalan-Hustler. I entertained his questions about Los Angeles gang life with gross exaggerations.

"Yea, bruhdah, it's just like the movies," I said. "Last week I saw a drive-by shooting on my way to the supermarket."

At 27-years-old, Dario was only two years older than me at the time. We were able to find many common threads, despite our entirely different lifestyles. Our conversations and chemistry led him to accompany me for hours after lunch had finished. After emptying his first pint of rum in no time, I agreed to buy us a pint to share. Yo-ho-ho and a bottle of rum, I thought.

Holding true to what he believed were his Rastafarian roots, Dario twisted up a marijuana leaf every 90-minutes or so. Brown paper bag was his preferred rolling paper. He'd rip off a piece of the bag, ball it up, and run it through his fingers until the texture was just right. Whenever I pulled out my camera, even if it was to take a picture of something else, Dario went into superstar mode.

"Yea mon! Rastafari!" he'd say. "Legalize it! We 'living stone' in Livingston!"

Some of the most intriguing stories Dario told me involved

pirates. It's a little-known fact that nearly a third of pirates were Black—especially those in the Caribbean. Piracy was one of the first equal opportunity industries for Blacks in the "New World," where slavery dominated. There were infamous Black captains on pirate ships sailing the seas, and cultural crossover were of course inevitable. I can only imagine the clash of language, music, and traditions the global outcasts melded together. Disney's portrayal of pirates was not the most accurate, but at least Captain Sparrow had dreadlocks.

With Dario keeping me company, I was able to see a side of Livingston few have the chance to experience. He showed me sacred waterfalls, and described them as spiritual places for the Garifuna. We stopped to see what he called the "most beautiful beach in the country." It had too much seaweed to appeal to me, but I did enjoy the warm Caribbean water. When I asked to see his hood, he informed me that I already seen it. The "restaurant" we ate at earlier was actually his house, and we had eaten what his mother was already preparing for the day's lunch. I shrugged this off—I couldn't be mad at his hustle. That's what Rastafarian-Crip-Pirate-Guatemalan-Hustler do.

After Guatemala, the rest of the Central America trip was both an adventure and a struggle to stay within my budget of $1,500. Living out of a backpack for a month ended up being one of the most humbling experiences in my life. It showed me how little I actually need in the world. I still remember when I first heard about the idea of backpacking. I responded with one word: DafuqIlooklike? But now, my thinking process has changed so much that I no longer recognize my old self.

Who the hell is Amir? He died so the Street Traveler could survive.

Chapter 3: South Africa, 2007

- Capital City: Pretoria (executive), Bloemfontein (judicial), Cape Town (legislative)
- Population: 54,956,900 Demographic breakdown: Black: 90%, White: 8.4%, Asian: 2.5%
- Currency: South African Rand
- Exchange Rate to dollar: 1 Rand= 0.066 DOLLARS
- Cost of a meal: 55-100 Rand
- Cost of a beer: 12-15 Rand
- Language Name: 11 official languages-Afrikaans, Northern Sotho, English, Southern Ndebele, Southern Sotho, Swazi, Tsonga, Tswana, Venda, Xhosa, Zulu-most SA speak more than one language.
    - Hello [Xhosa]- Molo (sg) Molweni (pl)
    - Hello [Afrikaans]= Hallo
    - Street Slang = "lekker" (leck-kher) used to express that something is good, "babelaas" a hangover
- Must See:
    - Natural Wonders: Table Mountain
    - Architecture: traditional Zulu beehive buildings, Zeitz MOCAA
    - Important Historical Sights: The Cradle of Humankind archaeological site, Robben Island
- Must Do:
    - Festivals: Cape Town Jazz Festival, AfrikaBurn
    - Activities: Safari in Kruger National Park, attend a braai

My host's shower has two settings: cold, and coldazzamutha. I brace myself for the morning ritual of counting to three, before completely submerging my body under the showerhead.

"One... two... threeyooowwwww!"

The frigid water leaves my body numb. The numbness eventually settles to a temporary tingle. After 45 seconds or so, I no longer feel my skin hairs becoming icicles. The cold helps with the looming hangover and body ache that had me paralyzed in bed a few moments earlier.

As I lather my soap, I hear the ceremonial laugh of my host, Joseph.

"Last day here, and you still scream like child!" he cheerfully says.

"A scream you'll miss," I say through uncontrollably chattering teeth.

My arms rapidly lather my body in hopes that the fast movements generate heat. The university told us not to expect hot showers when staying with our host families. Initially, I thought nothing of it because summertime wouldn't require hot showers. I quickly learned that our summer season in the United States is completely opposite the summer season of South Africa (and the rest of the Southern Hemisphere). It's August and more than 90 degrees back in New Jersey. But it's winter here, and some days are in the 50's.

Before the first verse of any shower singing would finish, I'm out of the shower and wrestling a towel around my body. I wipe the icy water off my skin in the critical parts before the chilling air hits me. Full relief comes when I toss on yesterday's jeans and my last clean shirt.

As I step out of the bathroom, I'm greeted with a warm cup of black tea.

"Come, come! We must go! I have a meeting with the teachers," Joseph says, as he shoves the teacup in my path. It's prepared the same way he likes his: two sugars and a dab of milk.

"Is it okay if I walk today?" I ask. "It's my last day in South Africa. I want to take my time and savor the flavor."

His eyebrows rise and wrinkle his forehead. He nearly spits out his tea.

"In a few, I'll be stuck sitting on an airplane for 21 hours," I say. "It'll be good exercise for me."

"Okay," he says reluctantly. "Just be careful. Lock the door and stay away from the wild dogs."

As the headmaster, or principal, Joseph is usually the first to arrive and the last to leave the school. As proof that they have a sense of humor, the gods paired Joseph with me, a 22-year-old who is allergic to early mornings.

"Nice! I'll be there by 7:45," I say. "I'll load my luggage in your car now."

"No, no. You are my guest. Is this all your luggage here by the door?" he asks.

"Yup," I respond.

He drags out the luggage and hurls 55 pounds into his car with ease.

"Still got it, huh?" I say.

"This is nothing. You should have seen me in my rugby days!" he responds, while pointing to a picture of him in his youth hanging on the wall. He looks exactly the same, except his sideburns are now frosted gray, and his brown eyes are hidden by his eternal squint. His reddish-brown skin hadn't wrinkled a bit.

Before I could admire his brawny stature, he knocks the wind out of me with a rugby tackle you would never guess came from a 58-year-old man. He briefly lifts my 6'0," two-hundred-pound frame in the air before converting the tackle into a gentle hug.

"You will be missed," he says, as he pats my back. "Hurry to school. I hear you all have big day today!"

He hustles out the door as I make my bed for the last time. I'm bombarded with thoughts of the many places I've stayed this summer in South Africa. Who would have thought my first 4-star hotel and villa experiences would be in Africa? After all I've done and where I've been, I find it even more surprising that I didn't pay a single dime. This trip is actually $5,000 more than I would have been able to afford as a recent college grad, soon moving across the country to pursue his master's degree. Luckily a group of generous Rutgers University Graduate School of Education alumni saw the significance in sponsoring a student from a disadvantaged background to participate in this South Africa Initiative. I can't wait to do the same one day. I must pay it forward by providing another struggling student an eye-opening experience.

In undergrad, this would have been called a "scholarship," but because I am in graduate school now, it's called a "fellowship." I call it a free ticket to take me back to the continent my ancestors left on slave ships centuries ago. My only regret is that I didn't do another study abroad in my earlier college years. Aside from teaching at an elementary school 40 miles east of Cape Town, this fellowship also allowed me to take a class at the University of Pretoria and volunteer with a Soweto organization serving at-risk youth called Teboho Trust. Eight other eclectic graduate students are staying with hosts like Joseph. Our rambunctiousness is matched by a few quirky professors, to whom we are giving a fair share of hell. They are educating and babysitting overgrown college students who are fresh from undergrad graduations. Professor Clarke and his staff did a lot of work before the trip to maximize our experience.

I say my final farewell and depart from Joseph's house, locking a series of padlocks. The morning dew's moisture on the grass turns my suede Timberland boots dirty brown. Dusty roads paint them a lighter hue. At this point, the South African terrain has toughened the suede to leather.

In the distance, the Western Cape Mountains pierce through a layer of fog. The rising sun reflects orange and purple shades on the mountains' surface, and turns the clouds flamingo pink. An awkward rhythm of animal steps speeds up behind me. The three-legged stray dog I've nicknamed "Trey" hops past, and reminds me of how slow I'm walking.

I cross the street to avoid the trash storage area that often attracts numerous three and four-legged creatures. Further down my path are other universal signs of a slum that remind me of Jersey. A pile of bricks lay concealed under a fading blue tarp. A layer of dust sits atop the construction project waiting to be finished. After a leap to avoid a pothole, my Timbs land thunderously on the ground. A nearby rooster swiftly turns and stares me down out the side of his eye. The impact of the jump reawakens my headache—the remnants of one too many drinks from the evening before. I stride along and enjoy the part of my trip I won't share with my professors and fellow students. Leave it to a KnuckleHead like me to do exactly what they tell me not to do. I can still hear the many warnings I failed to heed.

"Avoid walking around the township areas."

"Never ever walk around alone."

Give me a dollar for every time I broke a rule on this trip, and I wouldn't need the fellowship. Don't get me wrong, I understand the purpose of the warnings and the need to adhere to them—or at least understand them, acknowledge them, and take them into consideration. In most situations, why would anyone think of doing otherwise? The danger is real. Who wants to walk two kilometers with three-legged dogs and territorial roosters weaving in and out of your path? But the answer lies in one of the most important lessons of the trip: when seeking an *exceptional* experience, you have to create *exceptions* to the rules. It is what allows you to smell the pure aromas and taste the raw essence of a country. Not everyone is built for this type of travel, and some places are far too dangerous to explore this way. There are many instances of tourists being harmed, hoodwinked, or even hacked to death during their trips. As cliché as it sounds, being "Street Smart" can help you navigate and explore the world more safely.

What is Street Smarts? It's something that's both simple and complex. It is not in a dictionary, but it's too taboo to define anyway. There is no authority on Street Smarts to tell you what it is or isn't. Nonetheless, if I were forced to articulate a definition, it would be the one below:

Street Smarts: (noun) A rare insight and form of intelligence that encompasses five things: adaptability, confidence, intuition, an awareness of your environment, and a keen ability to read others.

Contrary to popular belief, the streets have no monopoly on Street Smarts. You can see it in ancient books of strategy like "The Art of War" by Sun Zhu, or "The Prince" by Machiavelli—the book that inspired rapper Tupac to change his name to "Makaveli."

"Let your plans be dark and impenetrable as night, and when you move, fall like a thunderbolt."   -Sun Zhu

"The lion cannot protect himself from traps, and the fox cannot defend himself from wolves. One must therefore be a fox to recognize traps, and a lion to frighten wolves."
                                                                        -Niccolò Machiavelli

Indeed, some may be born with Street Smarts, but mastery comes through your experiences and environment. It flourishes in the inner-city because desperation breeds innovation. In street settings, it's absolutely necessary for survival, yet there is no formal teacher. Just the School of Hard Knocks where you're encouraged to "peep game," or get eaten alive.

Street Smarts are helpful for both travel and life experiences. They provide a method of breaking the most sophisticated concepts down into common sense. It empowers you with the wisdom to be both an angel and a scoundrel. It allows you to tightrope-walk with danger, and tempts you to delicately dance with death. Street Smart people can smell bullsh*t buried in the sand… from a mile away…with a runny nose, facemask, and nostrils sewn shut. It's the cool that kept me calm one time despite the cold steel of a 9mm handgun pressed on my forehead during a robbery. It's the poise and audacity to look the gunman in the eye without blinking. It's the stare that said, "I won't be stupid and make a sudden move, but I ain't afraid" (despite being afraid). Street Smarts is the most savage of poker faces—a silent and eternal bluff that no one *dare* call.

Clearly, I haven't reach the pinnacle of my Street Smarts yet. As I walk by myself through a South African slum by my lonesome, I realized that I'm likely carrying a substantial stack amount of money. I'm not even sure how much.

I casually dig my hands into my pants pocket, and discover a cluster of crisp bills of rand—South Africa's currency. Just how much is it? Whatever its amount, it is all the rand I have left. I slide my hand out of my pocket, and wish peace upon the last few minutes of my journey to Amstelhoff Primary School.

From what I recollect, my last night in South Africa began around 9:30 p.m., after I finished packing my suitcase. Joseph's 27-year-old daughter, Sizana, was over for dinner and asked what my plans were for my last night in South Africa. Underwhelmed by my "Just gonna write in my journal" response, she demanded I accompany her for a night out in Cape Town. Being South Africa's second largest city with 3.74 million people in the metro area, I had heard of its flourishing nightlife. I was familiar with the lavish casinos, jasmine-scented beaches, and other attractions that made this South Africa's most visited city. But most of my summer was spent here in Paarl, a small town 40 miles east of Cape Town. Like her father's hospitality, Sizana's invitation was a godsend. I dug through my luggage to find my silk tie and dancing shoes, and prepared for the Boogie.

Sizana blasted Kwaito music, as her compact car bolted across the N1 highway, breaking the speed limit the entire time. We arrived in Cape Town in just under 40 minutes. The Kwaito music increased the anticipation, with its percussion-heavy rhythms and sprinkles of hip-hop, house, and reggae. When the sweeping nighttime skyline entered our view, I felt like I'd returned home. Living in Paarl had been a revitalizing removal from city life.

"Your final night begins," Sizana said, after we parked.

"Zana" is a woman of few words, but extreme energy. In two swift motions, she put on red lipstick in her rearview mirror, before popping the trunk and changing into a pair of scarlet-red high heels. She wanted to "ease" into the night by starting off at a casino. After entering under the flashing marquee, she quickly mumbled something in Afrikaans to the first waitress. I have been here all summer, but I still can't comprehend much of the primary national language. It's a variation of Dutch with faint hints of the Khoisan languages, Malay, the Bantu languages, and German. Luckily a large part of South Africa speaks English. There are 11 official languages in total though, like Xhosa and others spoken by my students.

"Do you gamble any?" she asked, as we stopped at a roulette table.

"I've been known to take a risk or two. Occasionally with money," I responded.

She handed the dealer 100 rand, and she a short stack of chips on the red area of the roulette table. With a swooping thrust, he spun the roulette, and Sizana directed her attention to me.

"What's your budget for tonight Amerikaanse?" she asked.

Good question.

"I could probably splurge 800 rand or so," I said. About 75 US dollars. I had stayed under my spending budget most of the trip, so I had a few rand that I actually needed to blow. Perfect for the last night out in Cape Town.

"Put it all on RED!" she confidently said, as the roulette ball began to slow down. "If you lose it all, the night is on me. If you win, that's sixteen hundred rand!"

The clicks of the roulette wheel grew further apart until the ball leisurely landed on a red 17. A soft chuckle was let out by the dealer as he handed Sizana a sizable stack of chips. At that moment, the waitress magically reappeared wielding two shots of brown liquor, a glass of wine, and a local beer. In what seemed like a single motion, Sizana handed the waitress some chips and me a shot glass.

"Some of the finest brandy in South Africa," she said. "Prost!"

"Prost," I responded to toast with her, in one of the few Afrikaans words I have picked up.

She tossed her head back making the brandy disappear in a single swallow. Keeping her head tilted back, she balanced the shot glass on her voluptuous lips. Her tongue crept through slowly and licked the bottom of the shot glass. Not a single drop escaped. With quick swig, my brandy disappeared as well. With my newly acquired bravery, I pulled 800 rand out of my pocket.

"Swart Asseblief," I assertively said to the dealer before placing a stack of rand on black. Though I know few words, I learned "asseblief," or "please," before the trip to show courtesy and respect to the locals. I picked up "swart," or "black," throughout the summer from my students.

"You speak Afrikaans?! Hoe kom jy nie wed op rooi?" she remarked, while pointing at the red area of the roulette table.

With another swoop, the dealer spun the roulette. I used my logic, and deciphered she was asking me why I didn't bet on red.

"I never bet against Black," I calmly responded.

She handed me a beer and we "prosted."

As we sipped, the roulette wheel slowed down. I was unable to stare at the table as the clicks faded. Of course I didn't tell her, but it was actually my first time in a casino. I slowly ran my hand down the silk peach tie on my chest.

As the ball stopped, the dealer let out the same chuckle. Sizana gasped for air. I hesitantly looked up to discover the ball had stopped on a black 28. I went from 800 rand to 1600 in a matter of seconds. The dealer smiled as he pushed a few stacks of chips towards me.

"Dankie," I said with a half-smirk, thanking him in Afrikaans.

The rest of evening was a blur. All that remains are spotted memories of a few bars, dancing to Kwaito music, and some late-night food before Sizana dropped me off around 4 AM.

The reminiscent episode of the night's victory is cut short after reassessing my current situation. I'm walking through the shanty-side of town by myself with a few hundred rand in my pocket. I pass a row of small houses, as the sounds of screaming schoolchildren amplifies. A half-dozen youth dart past me in navy blue and yellow school uniforms—some with freshly polished shoes, some barefoot. One student turns around briefly and sticks out his tongue to tease me. As I fire my tongue back, I notice a small group of locals in their early 20's sitting on scattered cement blocks near the school. One of their heads turns abruptly as he sees me. We give each other a mutual "who are you" look. I follow with a "what's up" head nod and slightly increase my walking speed as if I am with the group of children. He waves back, welcoming me over to join him and the fellas. I continue on with the kids as if the distance prevented me from receiving his invitation. The undisclosed remains of last night's come-up in my pocket remind me that now is not the time to meet a group of strangers.

I'm soon greeted by the sight of Amstelhoff Primary School, and the distant aroma of smoking wood and barbecue. Rows of metal bars line the doors and windows of the school. Spray-painted steel mesh lines some of the windows providing additional protection.

I make my way to Mr. Isaiah's 6th-grade class for my last day. As I arrive, a sea of smiling children greet me. They stand up and clap for me. I blush through my brown skin. I begin clapping with them, before pointing my fingers around the classroom.

"You are the superstars," I say. "Thank you for teaching me."

Out of nowhere, Mr. Isaiah delivers a rugby tackle that temporarily shoves me out of the classroom door. The students laugh in unison.

"We shall miss you, brother," he says.

A smile creeps through his eternally stern face that looks sullen even in its natural form. He resembled a South African Mr. T. His thick mustache sat atop his mouth like a piece of black electrical tape covering his upper lip.

Mr. Isaiah is the 6th-grade teacher and Rugby coach. He is the only male teacher at Amstelhoff Primary, so he was the perfect match for me, the only male student-teacher at the school. Some of the highlights of my trip were staying after school and practicing with the rugby team and attending their games. I could never understand what exactly Coach "T" was saying, but through his colorful facial expressions, I always got the point of what he was conveying.

Mr. Isaiah frequently left me in the classroom by myself for hours at a time. I assumed he was going home to check on the prized pigeons he raised and raced. Coach took pride in the pedigree of his birds and often boasted about his trophies.

When coach was out feeding birds, I improvised lessons to keep the students engaged. When I ran out of things to teach, I let the students ask me questions about the United States.

"Do you know Michael Jackson?" one asked.

"Of course!" I said. "He lives down the street from me! He taught me how to dance!"

"Wooooow!" they'd say.

I got a kick out of telling them grossly exaggerated stories about America.

"Where I'm from," I said, "cowboys walk around shooting their guns and run from the law." That's not much of an exaggeration actually.

My South African students were just like the students I taught back home in Jersey. They complained about the school lunch—often peanut butter and jelly sandwiches they made for each other in the class. The shy students contrasted with a few friendly chatterboxes. And then there were the inevitable knuckleheads like Dylan, a student Mr. Isaiah had to "pop" quite a few times. Talk about culture shock! I'll never forget the moment Mr. Isaiah first struck Dylan in class. He delivered swift open-palm pops with his wooden ruler. I still hear Dylan counting in Afrikaans between each strike.

"Een," POP!

"Twee," POP!

"Drie..." POP!

One time, Mr. Isaiah popped the entire class. The line of students moved like a caterpillar, as he delivered the licks, one-by-one. I didn't understand what it was for. It was at the beginning of class, after a couple screams in Afrikaans. With the "You want summa dis ruler?" meanmug Coach T gave me after finishing with the students, I didn't bother asking why. I pity the fool who would.

Dylan was the tallest student in the class—13 years old, but just a few inches shorter than me at six feet tall. His large stature in comparison to his peers reinforced his need to exert his Alpha dominance. He started the nickname most of the students eventually called me: Mr. OceanHead. This came from me trying to explain my hairstyle on my first day.

"We call them 'waves' because they go like the ocean," I said, as I brushed my hand over the ripples in my hair.

"We will call you Mr. OceanHead!" Dylan exclaimed, before the class erupted in laughter.

The students' skin tones were a brilliant kaleidoscope of yellow, gold, brown, and red hues. Some were a radiant golden-brown like Dylan. Some were brownish-red like my host, Joseph. One of the biggest moments of culture shock came when learning about how South Africans determine racial groups. It's one of the clearest legacies of the apartheid system. A conversation that revealed this caste system went something like this:

"I live around the corner from Michael Jackson, Beyoncé, and all the other Black people in America" I said.

"Beyoncé is not Black, she is coloured!" a student exclaimed.

"Coloured" is the name for people of mixed ethnicity in South Africa. With ancestry from Asia, Europe, and various ethnic groups of South Africa; genetic studies have found coloureds have the highest levels of mixed ancestry in the world. It began with interracial relations between European males and Khoisan females in the 17th-century Cape Colony. Eventually, apartheid halted the cross-race mingling and used it to divide the population.

In Afrikaans, apartheid translates to "separateness" or "the state of being apart." It was the system of racial segregation written into law by the South African white minority to maintain power. Democracy was destroyed, as all non-white political representation was abolished under the system. After seizing all the land and riches, the descendants of Dutch settlers stripped the natives—who had lived here for thousands of years—of their rights, power, and citizenship. Everyone who wasn't white was removed from their homes and forced to live in segregated neighborhoods.

Like the Jim Crow system of government discrimination in the United States, the apartheid government segregated education, hospitals, beaches, public services, housing, and every other sector of life. At every level, Blacks were given inferior institutions and services. Despite the international boycotts and public outcry, the system survived well into modern history—ending in 1994. I was ten years-old.

The apartheid system imposed arbitrary definitions of race and color to support the oppressive regime. To divide, conquer, and classify human beings, the government; measured body parts, compared people to pictures of skin colors, examined the pigmentation of scrotums, and gave the infamous "pencil test." If your skin color was too close to call, a pencil was pushed through your hair to determine if the texture was "black" or "white." If your hair was thin enough and the pencil fell out, you were considered white and worthy of human rights. Racism became "scientific." Mixed marriages were outlawed, and interracial sex became a crime.

South Africans could be reclassified along racial lines every year. Government tests could change your family structure and living areas at whim. My little sister back in Jersey, who is a few shades lighter than me, would have been taken from my mother at birth and moved to a coloured township. Adults were forced to carry identity cards specifying their racial group. If you were black and in a coloured or white township past a certain hour, you could be arrested. We learned about these and many other policies in our visit to Soweto, a township 900 miles north of Cape Town—15 miles west of Johannesburg.

Soweto is South Africa's largest township, with a population surpassing 1.3 million. It was created under the government-mandated evictions of apartheid. The Black cultural hub of Sophiatown was prime real estate, and was re-zoned for whites only. Waves of bulldozers demolished homes, forcing 60,000 blacks to move to Soweto. One early morning in 1955, over 2,000 heavily armed police officers forced residents to load their possessions onto government trucks and abandon their homes. To add insult to injury, the new white suburb established in place of Sophiatown is called Triomf, or "Triumph."

In 1976, Soweto was home to a mass uprising against apartheid education policies. Blacks received inferior education, could not write or learn in their own languages, and were forced to learn history from a Eurocentric and imperialistic point of view.

During a protest where more than 10,000 students marched from a high school to a stadium, police opened fire on the crowd. Twelve-year-old Hector Pietersen was one of the first of hundreds to die in this struggle for equal education and rights. This complicated history is why some of my students didn't view themselves as belonging to the same race as me—although in America, we'd all be Black.

As part of my goodbye ceremony with my Amstelhoff class, a student named Funi serenaded me with a final violin solo. Mbali, the student whom I had connected with the most in one-on-one sessions, gave me a big hug.

"Hamba kakuhle," she said in Xhosa. "Go...well!" she translated.

South Africa has 11 official languages. Xhosa is one of the most distinctive, with its knocking clicks and complex combination of tongue-sounds. The "Xh" in Xhosa is pronounced by sucking the air through your teeth with the assistance of your tongue. Mbali would try to teach me basic words and laugh as I foolishly tried to mimic her pronunciations.

"Let's go now," Mr. Isaiah said. "We have been preparing the goodbye braai."

I was excited for braai, a South African hybrid of a barbecue and potluck. Guests are encouraged to contribute to the feast. Traditionally, men cook the meat at the braai, and women prepare salads, desserts, vegetables, and other side dishes. The teachers had been talking about our going-away braai since the day we arrived. Professor Clarke raved about it months before we even got on a plane.

We hustled to the playground, where a circle of school staff and study abroad students are gathered around a fire pit. A hickory-like scent of burning wood complements roasting spices and the appetizing smell of meat cooking on an open fire. Mr. Isaiah and I stop at a table a few yards away from the crowd. It's covered in a rainbow of side dishes including pap, a thick porridge that looks like mashed potatoes, but is made from ground corn. He unwraps the aluminum foil off of a tray to reveal his contribution.

"Save room for my sosaties!" he says.

Mr. Isaiah breaks down the ingredients of his delicacies: spicy marinated lamb, peppers, and dried apricots daggered on sharp skewer sticks. After scheming looking from left-to-right, Mr. Isaiah digs deep into a nearby cooler and whips out a silver flask. Grabbing two cups, he pours the milky, tan contents.

"One more taste of Wild Africa for you!" he says. "Prost!"

"Prost!" I echo.

In a single gulp, we swallow the chilled blend of cream, caramel, and alcohol. Mr. Isaiah's blend has an extra bite that burns my throat. The aftertaste numbs my tongue. I wonder what he added to it.

We join our colleagues by the fire pit. Closer inspection reveals two fires burning, cooking separate types of food. Charring on one flame are kebabs, thin cuts of steak, and boerewors—a Dutch sausage of pork, beef, lamb, and spices. On the fire next-door, there's enough potjiekos—or "small pot food"—to feed a village. The black cast-iron pots could easily boil a 30-pound Thanksgiving turkey. Inside the pot is a simmering combination of herbs, lamb, carrots, cabbage, pumpkin, and rice. Steam slowly rises and carries a scent that previews the savory flavor.

As the flames dance under the pot, my mind levitates into a trance. A frenzy of flashbacks from my South African summer ensues. Moments I can't believe happened are reawakened as vivid memories.

***

We are on a minibus headed to Robben Island. Dashing through the Western Cape landscape, we pass pastures of sheep and cows. Greenish brown mountains form a backdrop to the lavish vineyards in the distance. We zoom through scenic Route 62, the world's longest wine route. The South African weather creates fertile conditions nurturing the grapes that make some of the world's finest wines. Traditions have been passed down from the French refugees that arrived in South Africa in the 1600's, after Louis XIV ordered persecution of everyone in France who did not share his faith.

We arrive at a busy waterfront with restaurants, shops, and the occasional seal on its deck. It's reminiscent of San Francisco. From Murray's Bay Harbour, a 35-minute ferry ride transports us 11 kilometers off the coast of Africa. Stubborn waves of the Atlantic Ocean crash against our boat, as a lighthouse and distant island reveal themselves.

Robben Island is one of the world's few prison museums. It allows you to experience life behind the thick concrete walls and rusty barbed wire, where thousands were confined for decades—often lifetimes. The captives at this high-security prison were not criminals though, they were freedom fighters. They risked and lost their liberty so that today's South African citizens could be free.

Following the "Revonia Trial," Nelson Mandela and seven others were sentenced to life in Robben Island for sabotage and treason. Three former prisoners of Robben Island have become some of South Africa's first democratically elected Presidents: Nelson Mandela, Kgalema Motlanthe, and Jacob Zuma. When they entered, the guards welcomed them with the phase, "This is the island. Here you will die!" Mandela would spend 18 of his 27 years in prison here. Despite the years of misery and death experienced here, today it's a symbol of hope and revolution.

I'm greeted by an imposing rising behind the entrance. Large gray stones combine to form the foundation of a wall built by prisoners in the 1960's. Bronze barbed-wire spirals around sunbaked brown poles. The entire prison smells like my grandparents' basement: mildew and ancient funk trapped with no ventilation. We are beyond fortunate to be given a tour by Nkosana, a South African freedom fighter who was imprisoned here for years. He guided us to a 7 X 8 foot room, and rolled a mat out on the ground.

"This is where I slept," he says. "We never let it break our spirt or pride. We gambled our freedom and expected to lose it temporarily." He pauses while a few of us attempt to cram into the cell. Only five or so could fit.

"We knew the atrocities of apartheid could not last forever," he said. "Justice is inevitable. Justice is priceless."

Nkosana shared examples of how daily life on Robben Island was humiliating—how it was designed to break the human spirit. At 5:30 a.m., captives began a day of intense hard labor mining limestone, as armed guards and dogs kept watch. They worked like slaves and the apartheid government was the master, keeping every penny. Family visits were only allowed twice a year—for a half hour—and limited to just one family member. They were only allowed to send two letters a year. Black prisoners were given less food than white and coloured prisoners. Blacks received no bread. This was done to create a divide amongst prisoners and prevent unity.

We peeked into a solitary confinement cell used to torment souls. While trapped inside a space smaller than my closet for days, they had two options: stand up, or kneel and tuck your knees into their chest. The thought of spending an infinite amount of time there converted me to a claustrophobic. Mandela and other prisoners coordinated protests and hunger strikes to challenge the inhumane practices and conditions on Robben Island. They were eventually given the right to study, and manual labor was abolished. Instead of letting the miserable conditions break his spirit, Mandela formed an unofficial university amongst the prisoners. They smuggled books and newspapers, which they hid in toilet areas. They facilitated fierce discussions on freedom and liberation.

Mandela's cell is preserved in the exact form as it was when he was captive. This required little effort. The small space only contains a sleeping mat and an iron bucket, yet it radiates the energy of a mystic shrine. They had no running water in their cells, so they emptied these toilet buckets daily. The thin fleece blanket provided just enough warmth to not freeze to death. I imagined Mandela, a man more than six-feet tall, crammed into the seven-foot space.

Mandela was considered a "Class D Political Prisoner," so he was treated the worst. He was forced to wear shorts year-round, only allowed one 30-minute visit per year, and one letter every 6 months that arrived in pieces. Anything the guards thought "political" was cut out of all letters. He wasn't allowed to attend the funerals of his mother or son. Guards physically abused and mentally tormented Mandela. They urinated on him for further humiliation. He had no rights, he was just a number. Prisoner No. 46664. The apartheid regime did all they could to silence him. During much of his imprisonment, his words and image were banned in the country. When it was discovered he was writing his autobiography, he was not allowed to study for years as punishment.

In his wise and forgiving spirit, Mandela understood no one was born hating another based on race. Love is natural, while hate is taught. Mandela's supernatural strength was rare and came from royalty. His father was a Xhosa Chief, whose property and possessions were taken by the apartheid government. Stripped of their nobility, they were left impoverished and without freedom. In true underdog fashion, Mandela rose to become the first Black president of the country, and the leader of the movement to eradicate apartheid. He received over 250 international awards, including the Nobel Peace Prize, for his heroism and crusade to establish basic human rights for all.

***

From Robben Island, you can see the Cape Town skyline in the distance. Even more imposing is Table Mountain, in all her magnificence. The flat-topped mountain was recently named one of the New Seven Wonders of the World. It stands at more than 3,500 feet high. On top and above clouds, lies Table Mountain National Park. Despite the six million years of erosion, the flourishing botanical kingdom boasts more than 1,470 floral species. Not too far away is an incredibly steep cliff that brings the mountain to an abrupt end. Furry mammals you've never seen before leisurely sit atop rocks, as if they are not inches away from falling thousands of feet.

We took a cable car that crept up the cliff of Table Mountain. We marveled at the panoramic view and could see the exact point where the Atlantic and Indian Oceans collide. The original people called Table Mountain "Hoerikwaggo," or Sea Mountain. On some days, a "tablecloth" of clouds appears over the flat mountain top. Legend has it the clouds are formed by a smoking competition between the devil and a local pirate. Many myths surround this mountain that sits at the foot of the 11 million square-mile African continent. When you are on top, you feel like you are on the edge of the world. In a sense, you are.

***

Africa has some of the most beautiful landscapes, nature, and wildlife in the world. Many of Earth's rarest animals can only be found here. A highlight of the trip—and my life—was our safari through Kruger National Park. Comprised of over 7,500 square-miles of earth and wildlife in its natural habitat, Kruger attracts most first-time visitors of the country. Owls, vultures, storks, and other birds soar above. Black mamba snakes, pythons, and crocodiles lurk below. Elephants, rhinoceroses, buffalo, hippopotamus, and other giants weighing thousands of pounds ignored our safari truck. Close

— 295 —

encounters with lions and leopards made me question the logic of our open-air safari vehicle. Vibrant patterns of giraffes and zebras came to life, as they gracefully galloped across the terrain.

The opportunity to pet a cheetah at Kruger was Dopeness Supreme. Most people on the safari were frightened—with good reason. It's a goddamn cheetah. The trainer calmly stroked the beast and invited us to do the same. He explained how "Acacia" was domesticated to be around humans and open to contact. With reluctance, I approached her. An arm's length away, I reached out and grazed the side of her back. Seeing she was unfazed, I moved two steps closer. As my fingers ran down her spotted coat, she let out a purr that vibrated my hand. I can't wait for people to ask me if I did anything interesting over the summer. I'll nonchalantly respond that I petted a goddamn cheetah. This. Is. Wild.

Africa's rare wildlife is mirrored by its abundant natural resources. More than half of the world's diamonds come from Africa. In 1905, the largest diamond ever discovered was found here in South Africa. This palm-sized, 530-karat rock is worth 400 million dollars. Up until recent history, South Africa alone produced more than 40% of the world's gold. The endless reserves of jewels, precious metals, oil, gas, and other resources make Africa both the richest and poorest continent on earth. In some ways, its richness has been a curse.

The most impactful moment in Africa's history and resource allocation was the Berlin Conference of 1884. This event solidified and legitimized the colonization of Africa. It allowed for 90% of the continent to be placed under European control by 1900. Imperialists drew country borders around the stolen resources and territory with little concern for the hundreds of independent nations—commonly referred to as "tribes"—with their own existing languages, land boundaries, and customs. Imperialism contributed to many African conflicts that have taken place since, like the Rwandan genocide in the 1990s.

Money was the primary motivation for the re-carving of the continent. Trillions of dollars in riches were extracted from Africa, while the world witnessed some of the greatest human rights abuses in history. The best-selling history book, King Leopold's Ghost by Adam Hochschild, documents one of the most egregious stories and reads like horror fiction. The Berlin Conference formalized King

Leopold II's sovereign rule over what is today's Democratic Republic of the Congo. This was an area 76 times larger than Leopold's home country of Belgium.

Up until the 20th century, Leopold's reign tortured the Congolese with forced labor, widespread massacres, beatings, and frequent mutilations when large amounts of rubber were not produced. Entire villages were scorched and exterminated, except for those who were kidnapped and forced to work long hours collecting raw materials. If the Congolese didn't meet their quota, then hands, ears, and genitals were chopped off with no remorse. It's estimated that in just 15 years of these atrocities, the native population was reduced from 20 million to 9 million. More than half of the Congo's inhabitants were slaughtered for the sake of creating wealth for a few Europeans.

The "Scramble for Africa" and the rest of the colonized world was intensified with the introduction of the maxim gun—a destructive machine that could fire 600 bullets in less than a minute. The maxim gun changed war forever, and delivered a significant military advantage: mass slaughter in an instant. In his 1898 poem "The Modern Traveller," Hilaire Belloc provided a concise summary:

Whatever happens, we have got
The Maxim gun, and they have not.

In its battlefield debut, the British South African Police massacred more than 1,600 Matabele soldiers near the Shangani River. One eyewitness claimed they were "mow[ing] them down literally like grass."

"The shooting must have been excellent," said South African forefather and imperialist Cecil Rhodes. Rhodes founded De Beers, today's multi-billion-dollar diamond company, which accumulated much of its wealth through forced prisoner labor in apartheid South Africa. Enslaved on their own land, men were lined up and forced at gunpoint to crawl on their knees and mine diamonds. Rhodes was so wealthy, he established the Rhodes Scholarship in his will—the oldest and most prestigious international fellowship award in the world. The country we know as Zimbabwe was once named after Cecil Rhodes (Rhodesia). The torment and robbery of the region by imperialist has created a deep hatred for whites in the area. Many descendants of the imperialists are still getting rich off of Africa today, while millions of Africans starve and struggle.

***

My reflections on the history, struggle, beauty, nature, and hope of South Africa end, as a vigorous shake by Mr. Isaiah awakens me from the daydream.

"No more Wild Africa for you!" he says.

I come back to Earth feeling like I am a different person in the same body. I came to South Africa to teach, but instead, I was taught. Before this trip, I was a travel-virgin, who had seen very little outside my New Jersey neighborhood. This study abroad trip has rocked my world. This is a thrill that I want to experience for the rest of my life. At 22 years old, I found my first true addiction: travel.

"The world is a book, and those who do not travel read only a page," said Saint Augustine.

If I survived the streets of America, I can survive anywhere. I'm afraid, but curiosity conquers fear. I want to know, explore, see colors, and taste flavors. I've emerged like a phoenix from a place where life is short and limited. Just this year, two of my cousins were shot in the head on separate occasions. I have friends who can't travel 30 miles away from our hometown to New York City, because it violates their parole or probation terms.

Standing on a playground in South Africa made me realize that I may have grown wings. It gives me hope that I might escape one day, after all. My experience in the continent my ancestors left in chains centuries ago has changed me forever. Through my work and volunteering here, Africa may even be a better place because of me. I hope to do a lot more one day, though.

As the embers burn in the braai fire, I realize that something great had just happened. Mandela's words echo in my head.

"Like slavery and apartheid, poverty is not natural. It is man-made and it can be overcome and eradicated by the actions of human beings."

I am awakened.

Chapter 4: England, 2009 and 2012

- Capital City: London
- Population: 65,111,143- Breakdown: White: 85.4%, Asian: 7.8%, Black: 3.5%, mixed: 2.3%, other: 1%
- Currency: Pound Sterling
- Exchange Rate to dollar: 1 pound= 1.28 DOLLARS
- Cost of a meal: 12-20 pounds
- Cost of a beer: 3 pounds
- Language Name: English
  - Hello = Hello ☐
  - Street Slang = "bloody hell" (vulgar expression of anger), "wanker" (a jerk)
- Must See:
  - Natural Wonders: Stonehenge
  - Architecture: Buckingham Palace, Westminster Abbey
  - Important Historical Sights: London Bridge, Tower of London
- Must Do:
  - Festivals: Glastonbury Music Festival
  - Activities: London Eye, British Museum, International Slavery Museum

I recently realized that my favorite Malcolm X quote is actually too long. As noble as it is, the phrase "Education is our passport to the future" can be stripped of three words:

"Education is our passport ~~to the future~~."

It's that simple. Knowledge, or your thirst for it, can take you anywhere in the world. If you are lucky and creative enough, it can take you for free. Education is a gateway to a realm of experiences and discoveries that transform you into a new person. Education is the world, and the world is education.

In the fall of 2011, I discovered an intriguing summer abroad program and scored my second international trip in the pursuit of education. I studied how to make the world a better place, while seeing it first-hand. Through a partnership with the University of Amsterdam, I was able to earn credits towards my law degree. The four credits I could earn in Europe were also more than $1,000 cheaper than my home law school in the United States—the University of Miami. I also avoided paying 1,200 euros in housing fees to the foreign university by couch surfing with my Dutch friend in Amsterdam for the summer. Cutting these two corners provided over a $2,000 excess in my student loan refund, which went towards my flight and educational living expenses. God bless America, and the opportunity for academic come-ups.

By the end of summer 2012, I had visited ten countries in Europe. The experience was both educational and adventurous, as I gained tools to battle for global justice and equality. After spending five weeks studying at the University of Amsterdam, I backpacked through the continent for the remaining three and a half weeks of my summer. Europe is one of the best regions in the world for backpacking. There is a well-established network of buses and trains that quickly transport you between countries. Nearly 20 of the 28 countries in the European Union (EU) also use the same currency: the Euro. Travel burdens are eased when you don't have to worry about exchanging and converting currencies. The division and other math involved with every transaction can become a pain. Backpacking through Europe is also advantageous because the 28 countries in the EU have agreements that make some border crossings effortless. You maneuver through countries' borders without noticing it, often not needing to show your passport.

Despite my love for Amsterdam and the Dutch people, I

aimed to visit a different country every weekend while studying in Europe. The travel addict in me could not resist the cheap flights that take you to another country within a couple of hours. It suddenly became easier to drive to France than it was for me to drive from New Jersey to Virginia (less than 5.5 hours).

In my first excursion, I took a train to Belgium for 29 euros (€) or $32, and spent a weekend in Brussels. There I enjoyed some of the best nightlife in Europe, while couch surfing with the country's reigning pole dancing champion. Next, I flew to England for 86 British pounds ($116) for the 2012 Olympic Games Opening Ceremony in London. After watching more than 200 countries march with their flags behind Queen Elizabeth II, we took the town by storm arrogantly (and correctly) predicting that the United States would dominate the international competition. During a separate weekend, I took another flight to the UK and visited Scotland, Wales, and the city of Liverpool.

After wrapping up studies in Amsterdam, I began my backpacking journey with a 39-euro ($43) bus trip to Germany. In Berlin, I experienced one of Europe's most flourishing art and music scenes, while exploring the remnants of World War II, the Holocaust, and the Cold War. Next, I took a bus from Germany to the Czech Republic for 20 euros ($22) to explore Prague's baroque architecture and castles that inspired fairy tale books. From there, I hopped on a bus to Hungary for 545 korunas ($23) to adore Budapest's blend of Gothic, Renaissance, Roman, and Turkish architecture while partying in ancient caves. I then caught a series of trains and a ferry for 18,827 Hungarian forint ($65) to Zrće, the wildest of Croatia's 1,000+ islands. The endless partying and summertime beach shenanigans were unlike anything I'd ever experienced. With the energy I had left, my trip concluded with a ferry ride across the Adriatic Sea to Italy for 273 Croatian kuna ($40). I spent a few days relaxing and exploring the ancient ruins of the Roman Empire.

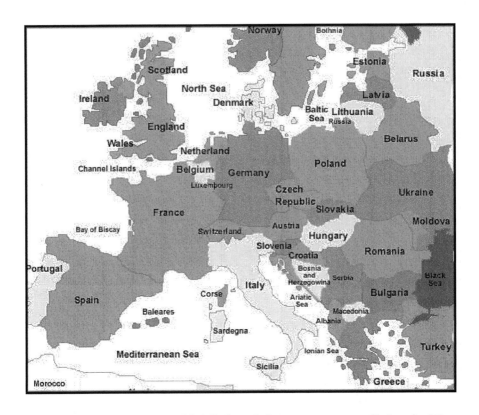

Hands down, the highlight of the summer was living in The Netherlands and studying international human rights at the University of Amsterdam. No, this was not because of the legalized drugs, prostitution, sex shows, etc. (It took weeks to get used to the morning walks through the Red Light District to get to class). Other experiences created timeless memories. I lived with Wally, my Dutch brother from another mother, who made sure I explored every crack and crevice in the city. Wally was one of the few people in Amsterdam whose Afro was larger than mine. I crashed in an extra room in his South Amsterdam apartment, near the university where he was getting his master's degree.

My studies in Amsterdam included four short law classes: International Human Rights, International Criminal Law, Gender Human Rights, and War and Terrorism Law. The Netherlands was the perfect country to study these subjects because it is the globally recognized headquarters for justice and human rights. It is the home of the International Court of Justice and the International Criminal

Court, the primary enforcers of human rights' laws for over 190 countries. The coolest field trip in my 25 years of school occurred when our class went to The Hague to watch the trial of Ratko Mladic, the army commander who was responsible for the deaths of tens of thousands of innocent people during the Bosnian War.

On top of my study-abroad experience and subsidized traveling, another hype moment occurred when a seven-word social media post scored me a free trip to the UK, complete with accommodations in a 650-year-old castle in Wales. I was wrapping up another week of studies at the University of Amsterdam, when I found a round trip flight to Scotland for $158, I seized the opportunity to visit my boy, Nate, who was studying at a university there. Waking up on Nate's dingy dorm room floor before sleeping in a legitimate castle made the experience even more surreal.

Nate and I were roommates at Rutgers University in New Jersey, where we completed our bachelor's degree. He was studying in Scotland as part of his ambitious "Renaissance Man Project." In this feat, Nate would travel the world and explore the skills expected of the proverbial Italian Renaissance Man: poetry, combat, dance, visual art, music, and philosophy. In the 1400's, Leonardo da Vinci became the definition of the true Renaissance Man by becoming an accomplished painter, sculptor, engineer, astronomer, biologist, physicist, architect, musician, and philosopher. Nate wanted to modernize and globalize this tradition. For example: instead of learning to battle with lances on a horse, he went to Thailand and studied Muay Thai—a lethal form of kickboxing. When I met him in Scotland, he had already spent a month in Thailand training in Muay Thai, a month in Italy studying poetry, and a month in Paris studying visual arts. He knew he wouldn't master all of these skills in a month, but aside from challenging himself, Nate's goal was to experience the Renaissance philosophy and enhance his life and perspective. He was seeking wisdom and well-roundedness by casting himself in uncomfortable, difficult, and often painful situations. Indeed, the world will do that to you sometimes—whether you seek it or not. He was also writing a book about the experience.

Because of our thrill-seeking spirits and willingness to sleep on each other's floors, Nate was the friend from Jersey whom I saw most frequently. We've rendezvoused in Scotland, Mexico, Los Angeles, New Orleans, Miami, Alabama, and wherever else one of us was living or studying. Two weeks after I visited him in Scotland, Nate visited me in Amsterdam.

But my weekend in Scotland with the Renaissance Man was cut short when a Facebook post propositioned me with an offer I couldn't refuse.

"Weekend travel to Scotland for $158? Ydafuqnot?" I had posted.

"Funk Scotland!" the post replied. "Take a train down to Liverpool to funk with us, mate! I got your ticket, and you can stay at my castle in Wales!"

It was an invitation from Ace, my favorite Englishman. We met a few years earlier on his musical pilgrimage to my hometown to record an album and tour. When Ace said "castle," I interpreted it as British slang for a house. I soon discovered he meant exactly what he said. The bloody bastard had a centuries-old castle set atop a hill, overlooking the lush green meadowlands of Wales. I couldn't wait to see it.

***

My first taste of the UK came a few years earlier. I spent four days in London during a 12-day Europe trip with my travel companion, Keyshawn. I was a bright-eyed 24-year-old anxious to visit my second country. Keyshawn was an enthusiastic 26-year-old school teacher thirsty to visit his first country.

"Combining flight and everything, it costs us $160 a day to be here," he'd say to remind me. "Let us live like it!"

As rookie travelers, we chased every tourist spectacle in London. Big Ben, Buckingham Palace, London Bridge, the bright red telephone booths, Westminster Abbey—you name it. The highlight of this trip was the British Museum. It's home to more than 13 million artifacts from the ancient world that Britain collected/stolen during its era of conquest. Britain is the most imperial country in history. A recent study found that the British invaded nearly 90% of all countries around the world. Egypt, Australia, India, and many other nations, in all corners of the globe, were colonized or conquered by the British Crown. The British Museum is basically an oversized, expensive trophy case of conquest. I felt like I could spend days exploring its magnificence.

England was also the birthplace of my most treasured travel tradition: Da Jump. Every traveler has a signature photograph pose. For many, it's a simple smile. For others, it's a peace sign, handstand, thumbs up, or one of countless other poses. My boy, Nate, loves to "sprout wings" and fold his arms behind his back, fingers spread like feathers. I wanted mine to be a jump, but not a cliché wild and aimless travel jump. I needed a jump with poise and purpose.

I have always had an uncontrollable urge to jump. It's probably a consequence of coming up in the Air Jordan era. If I could execute a well-timed leap in my travel pictures, it would be a timeless image. The pose would also be symbolic. Being mid-air in a foreign land would signify the fact that not even gravity could keep me down. I was an inner-city kid, who didn't know what a passport was until college. I wanted my pose to capture a moment of me prevailing in a battle against my environment and the Earth's formidable gravitational force. So in England in 2009, I catapulted myself ten-feet in the air in front of the London Eye, beginning a tradition that would be replicated in more than 30 countries (picture in the back of the book).

My second trip to England was prompted by the fact that my summer study abroad in Europe coincided with the most important international event being hosted in London—the Olympic Games.

The original Olympic Games began in Olympia, Greece in 776 BC. It included a series of athletic competitions honoring the sea god Zeus, where each Greek city-state sent its finest men to compete for honor and olive branch crowns to wear on their heads. 1503 years after the original games ended due to change of political control, the modern games began again in Athens, Greece in 1896. Historically, the games take place every four years. The beauty of the tradition of the Olympic Games is in the world coming together in peaceful competition and celebration. A different host city is selected each year, and the productions created for the events are always elaborate feats of artistry.

Luckily, I had packed my throwback Michael Jordan Olympic team jersey from his 1984 rookie year. My boy, Wally, just so happened to have a matching pair of limited-edition Jordan IVs— the "Spizikes"—valued at $200. He said I could borrow them as long as I promised to keep the suede flawless. I tucked the tongue out over my deep indigo 514 Levi's jeans. The cherry on top was my star-spangled flag-print bandana: a three-foot American flag wrapped around my afro in Jimi Hendrix-like fashion. It dangled down my back, and when I moved fast enough, it waved like the Queen of England.

During the Olympic trip to London, I crashed with Rick, my Miami roommate, who was studying abroad there. Rick was a 23-year-old scrappy kid from Chicago. He's only a few hairs taller than five feet, but stacked with enough ripped muscle to be a professional wrestler. Unless something had his undivided attention, Rick chattered uncontrollably. Just about every sentence that came out of his mouth started or ended with the word "bro." He said this regardless of whether he was talking to a male or female.

"Lebron, Kobe, and Kevin Durant are gonna cruuuuush the French, bro!" he said.

We drank warm whiskey from soda bottles as we watched the games on a twenty-foot screen in a park. He trash-talked every non-American who crossed our path.

"Where you from, bro?" he'd ask. And before they responded with the name of their country, "Two words... Michael Phelps!" he'd interrupt.

I pleaded with him to stop perpetuating the stereotype of the loud, obnoxious American—a stereotype I swore on my dead dog's grave I wouldn't sustain.

"Bro," he said, "you're the one walking around London looking like Air Captain America on a flag pole!"

I stepped down off my high-horse, and gave into the moment. Rick's endless facts about how America typically dominates the Olympics continued on and on.

"We've got more Olympic medals than most of the world combined, bro," he boasted. "Bro... Michael Phelps wins more gold medals than entire countries!"

After enough whiskey, I had embraced the stereotype. One time, I almost used the word "bro." Almost.

Before I caught a Sunday evening flight back to Amsterdam, Rick and I hit up the wildest party I'd encountered in all of my travels. It was at a place called The Church, which was notorious for its vicious Sunday afternoon debauchery. In London in 1979, expats from Australia and New Zealand started the tradition that has since entertained millions. They say it was named "The Church" so that patrons could tell their parents they were attending Sunday religious services. Ironically, there was enough sin in this place to make the devil blush.

Around 2:30 p.m., we entered the gothic stone structure. It was packed to capacity. It was so dark inside, we quickly lost track of time and forgot it was the afternoon. The central area had a stage surrounded by a sea of people with their hands in the air. Rick and I had been pregaming since noon. I said an "Amen!" to the blaring house music overpowering his incessant chatter.

As we entered the crowd, the random attire that "churchgoers" are encouraged to wear was revealed. Some groups were dressed in themes. A crew of girls bounced around with every inch of their bodies covered only with paint. Two bearded guys passed us wearing stockings and ballerina tutus. One was tossing confetti in the air like pixie dust, and the other was tiptoeing like a ballerina. Another woman towered over Rick in skin-tight leather and boots to her knees. She petted the shirtless Rick as she passed by.

"Adoooorrable," she said with a deep voice and British accent.

In between a range of music that kept everyone moving, occasional comedians, strippers, musicians, and other performers blessed the stage. It was a sideshow of sorts. One girl, with an accent I was too drunk to decipher, spontaneously showed me her breasts. There was so much madness happening at the moment, I didn't even know how to respond. I just took a look at my drink, slowly placed it on a nearby table, and wondered if I was so drunk that I was only imaging random women flashing me.

***

Escapades, like the antics at The Church and Olympic games, made London great, but the third trip to England revealed Liverpool was really its greatest city. It had soul like New Orleans, hustle like Los Angeles, and attitude like New York. Because of Ace, I was able to venture beneath the surface of the city too.

Before catching my train to Liverpool, Nate and I grabbed breakfast in Scotland and recapped the night's anarchy [chapter in next edition]. A mad-real hangover loomed and combined with the usual sleeping-on-the-flo-aches. Poor self-control was exercised with Scotland's endless options of scotch—one of my favorite drinks. And, of course, I—like all refined gentlemen—prefer to drink my scotch straight. Terrible idea after the third drink. Ruthless idea after the seventh.

For breakfast, Nate suggested I try haggis; a local Scottish dish he said was notorious for curing hangovers.

"I can't tell you what's in it," he said, "but you'll thank me later."

I reluctantly followed one of my most important travel rules: never say no when offered a new experience.

After learning what I had actually eaten, I was both proud and disgusted. Haggis is a pudding-like delicacy made with all the innards of a sheep: lungs, heart, tongue, and liver...you name it, it's probably in there. It's mixed with onions, spices, and oatmeal to improve the taste and consistency. The gooey goodness is sealed in a sheep's bladder and then boiled. The version I ate was in the shape of a hamburger patty. It was like zesty ground beef combined with the dryness of oatmeal. It did absolutely nothing for my hangover. Nate just wanted to get back at me for cutting my Scotland trip a day short, I think. Our scotch-fueled mountain hikes and castle explorations were insufficient.

"Not bad for sheep's sh*t?" he said, after I had eaten the entire portion set on my plate.

With so much to see in the United Kingdom, I couldn't sleep in the same place two nights in a row anyways. The United Kingdom, or "Great Britain" as it is sometimes called, is a sovereign state in Europe comprised of four countries: England, Scotland, Wales, and Northern Ireland. The Kingdoms of England and Scotland first joined together in 1707 to form the United Kingdom. Later, in 1800, Ireland came under its control. Presently, only Northern Ireland remains part of Great Britain, as the rest of the island took its independence back in 1922 and is now a separate country. There have been many struggles within the landmass that is Ireland due to this separation and the political divide created by two governments exerting rule on a once unified people. Smaller than the state of California, the four countries of the UK are home to several unique languages, accents, and distinct cultural traditions.

I headed to Liverpool to link up with Ace—a musician and producer who operates his own studio. He is originally from Cheshire, 36 miles southeast, but came to Liverpool to be part of one of the world's premier music scenes. Throughout his musical career, Ace has worked for dozens of multi-platinum artists and some of the biggest producers in the world.

Before Ace showed me Liverpool, England was still overrated. It didn't help visiting during the Olympics and high tourist season either. It's one of the most expensive countries in the world, and their accents always sounded snobbish and arrogant to me.

"You're the one with the accent, mofo!" Ace would remind me.

Luckily, visiting "The Pool" allowed me to peel back layers of England that I found more desirable. Around 10:00 a.m., I exited the train station fresh from Scotland. Ace was outside waiting, smoking a cigarette while sitting on the hood of his jet-black BMW 3 series. It was a new car, but covered in a layer of dust from the Wales' countryside roads.

"Is Liverpool ready for the funk!?" I screamed.

"Bet your bloody bottom we are!" he responded.

I chuckled at his British vernacular. "Bloody" had to be my absolute favorite word in the English language. It's basically the British version of fu#*%!@, but it's not a curse in the U.S. I used it all the "bloody" time back home, but no one ever got it.

Ace and I embraced each other with huge hugs. Much had changed since we last saw each other six years ago. His musician lifestyle was slowing down now, as he had married and had his third child. College and traveling had changed my world view. But we fell right back into rhythm as if we weren't worlds apart.

I hopped in his car without asking where we were going.

"How come all you European blokes like these small cars?" I asked. "Feelin' like Mr. Bean up in here."

"How come Americans always want so much more than they need?" he responded. Touché.

Ace gave me a rundown of our plan for the day.

"Let's drive around the city a bit, then lay something down at the studio," he said. "We'll check out some live music, museums, and a pub or two."

"Or three," I said. "Who's counting? I simply cannot wait to see this 'stu-e-o,'" I said, poorly mimicking his accent. British accents always sounded like the speakers were allergic to consonants like "d" or "t." Like they were too lazy to pronounce entire words.

We cruised through Liverpool's landscape of 16th-Century Tudor style buildings that look like they were pulled straight from a storybook. They blend with extremely modern glass and metal geometrically designed structures. Many of the buildings date back to the 18th Century Victorian era. Due to the rich variety of historic architecture, many parts of Liverpool have been declared UNESCO World Heritage Sites. The cobblestone streets of the docks are lined with brick warehouses. The decadently detailed facades of the buildings known as the Three Graces stand out as a show of the wealth the port city once attracted during the height of trade. This eclectic blend of architecture makes Liverpool one of the most sought-after port city destinations to visit. Locals were dressed in vintage hipster fashion. Name any bygone era, and you were sure to see someone quite authentically recreating its iconic style. True culture shock, though, was seeing police with no guns.

While driving in through the city, Ace was unable to risk the temptation of stopping by one of the world's most famous places in music history.

"Let's grab a drink and get some inspiration," he said.

We crawled underground into The Cavern, the bar where the Beatles were discovered in 1961. Over their careers, the "Fab Four" from The Pool would revolutionize the music industry in countless ways. Numerous artists over the past 50 years have been influenced by the Beatles. With more than 600 million albums sold, they are the best-selling musical act of all time.

I just so happened to be in Liverpool during the Beatles 50th anniversary. The city had an endless supply of street festivals, exhibits, waterfront concerts, a John Lennon Peace Vigil, and other activities to commemorate the event. The Cavern was jam-packed with wall-to-wall Beatles fans singing along to bands as they covered the classics. The underground structure is a tunnel dug into a cave. The low ceiling is an arch of bricks, and is acoustically perfect for the live music that bounces off the walls.

"The party here starts early," I remarked. "It's barely 11 a.m."

Ace hands me a thick brown Guinness stout beer with a

frothy tan layer of foam covering it.

"Cheers," he says. "To the first of many."

The fourth of many came when we arrived at Ace's studio. It was housed in a massive 200-year-old warehouse, with a most-convenient bar at the bottom. Ace didn't bother closing his tab there either. We ceremonially grabbed a pint during each entrance and exit of the building.

Located in the city's center a few blocks from the docks, Elevator Studios was originally built to store cotton, spices, coffee, and other goods from the New World. Today, it's filled with the music, art, and business ideas of dreamers. The warehouse takes up an entire city block and has been restructured to accommodate 18 studios and 35 offices. Some use Elevator Studios as a rehearsal space. Sounds of bands jamming echoed through the corridors, as Ace and I headed to his studio. The warehouse retained much of the original industrial features like wooden beams, exposed bricks, and chains.

Ace's studio was a musical paradise. A row of vintage guitars worth more than $10,000 lined the left wall. On the right, stood thousands of watts in amplifiers—some older than me. Through a double window was a stellar sixth-floor view of the docks and River Mersey.

Because of Ace's sick skills, I was timid in touching his museum of instruments. Ace and I first jammed on his spiritual voyage to my hometown six years earlier. He and his British band were named "P-Theory" because of the Plainfield Funk influence deep and distinctive in their style. My Uncle Kev was their featured front-man and lead singer. In their eyes, being born in Plainfield and taught by our musicians made me a heralder of the P-Funk torch. Ace was more than happy to spend a few pounds on a train for me to come to Liverpool and lay down some tracks. And I was more than glad to dust off my Funk.

The primary influencers of Plainfield Funk were the groups Parliament and Funkadelic. George Clinton started the movement in the 1950's at a barber shop two blocks from my house on 6th and Liberty Street, across the street from Plainfield's housing projects. Our P-Funk sound inspired entire genres and created legends. Dr. Dre created the sub-genre sound of G-Funk, a West Coast hip-hop version of P-Funk, when he sampled Parliament Funkadelic six times on his classic album "The Chronic." At one point, Parliament Funkadelic was the most sampled band in history, with grooves recycled by Lil Wayne, Tupac, Jay-Z, Daft Punk, OutKast, the Red Hot Chili Peppers, Snoop Dogg, NWA, and hundreds more.

P-Funk was an undiscovered jewel to me until I exchanged crack-cocaine for my first guitar at age 19. The transaction unlocked my soul, and granted me access to a world where I learned from and communicated with local legends. For a long time, I was in denial that the streets that raised me had created Top Ten hits, Rock and Roll Hall of Famers, and inspired musicians from Compton to England. For me, growing up in Plainfield was nothing to be proud of—especially when it came to my neighborhood. The three-block radius that I lived in contained the city's two housing projects—and the highest concentration of government housing. It's the city's poorest and most violent area, and it had claimed the lives of more than a dozen people I came up with. But it also produced some of the world's most influential musicians. This is why my Uncle Twin (R.I.P) called it "Project Funk." I proudly carried on this rare street music tradition with a pure, uncut rhythmic groove.

With the rhythm it takes to dance to what we have to live
through, you can dance underwater and not get wet.
- Parliament, "Aquaboogie" 1978.

For Ace and his bandmates, Plainfield was a sacred land, worthy of a spiritual voyage. Their debut album, "From the Hood to the Wood," represented their world finding a collective groove with ours through music. P-Theory performed in Spain, Italy, England, and all over the United States, but their greatest show was in Plainfield. More than 40 years after classics like "One Nation Under a Groove" and "Flashlight" topped the charts, P-Funk was taking a Plainfield kid around the world. During my visit in Liverpool, I was equally enthusiastic to soak up musical inspiration from the local scene.

"This time," I said to Ace, "I'm the colonial musician coming to conquer!"

Ace and I frequently joked about how much of England's most popular music is rooted in American (often African-American) music.

"Elton John, The Rolling Stones, Adele, the Beatles, Led Zeppelin..." I listed. "They even swap their British accents for American accents when singing!"

There I was again, on that American High Horse. A good number the songs on the Beatles' debut album were covers of African-American Rhythm and Blues classics. The Rolling Stones were named after a song from Chicago bluesman Muddy Waters. In one way, all bands are influenced by American music because the band as we know it (drums, guitar, bass, piano), originated in African-American churches. But like ocean waves, musical influence travels both ways. Groups like The Beatles experimented with and pushed the boundaries of music and songwriting in a manner that changed history. Their classic album, "Sgt. Pepper's Lonely Heart's Club Band," was a pioneer of what's known as the "concept album." These are music albums where songs share a common artistic theme and often tell a story. It shattered records as the first rock album to win an Album of the Year Grammy Award. Time magazine called it "a historic departure in the progress of music." Countless musical acts have been influenced by this album and many other Beatles' tracks. Fifty years later, rapper Kendrick Lamar changed hip hop with his groundbreaking concept album, "To Pimp a Butterfly."

Ace took me to school in a jam session where we exchanged guitar solos. In between earsplitting guitar licks, he'd slow down and show me different techniques. In those moments I could feel myself growing as a musician, and a bit of Liverpool melding into my style. The entire time I was in the studio, I felt proud knowing I had traveled the world to create music. I was one of the only musicians I knew my age who had done so, and I was not even a professional musician. I literally looked to the sky and thanked the P-Funk gods. Ace and I laid down a few vocal tracks over his latest productions and headed back out to the streets of Liverpool.

"I'm going to take you to one of the greatest museums in the world, mate," said Ace.

We walked along the rugged cobblestoned dock area, lined with a collection of warehouses and brick buildings from the 1800's. Like Elevator Studios, they have been repurposed and upgraded, but to house museums and historical artifacts. Along the dock were antique boats and ships of all sizes. Some are a part of the nearby

Maritime Museum. But Ace had a different museum in mind for me—the International Slavery Museum.

If there is one museum that every Black person in the Western Hemisphere should see, it is the International Slavery Museum in Liverpool. It's the only museum of its kind. It documents the greatest forced migration and most profitable trade in history—the transatlantic slave trade. It also highlights current issues with the millions of people presently experiencing slavery around the world today. It's one of the most engaging and enlightening documentations of human rights abuses by one of the greatest perpetrators, England. Having Ace, a white Englishman, give me a tour made it all the more intriguing.

The Liverpool docks are a symbolic place for the museum. The slave trade created immense wealth for Liverpool and laid the foundation for its growth. At the trade's climax, more than 130 slave ships left the Liverpool ports every year, bound for Africa and then the Americas. It's estimated that three quarters of all European slave ships in the late 1700's left from Liverpool. These ships transported more than half of the millions of Africans carried across the Atlantic to the Americas by British slavers. The museum is a few feet away from the dry docks where slave ships were repaired. As we looked at the still waters surrounding the docks, I shared a moment of enlightenment with Ace.

"There is no way to tell," I said to Ace, "but it is very likely the ship that took my ancestors from Africa to America originated from this bloody dock."

"No kidding," said Ace.

Liverpool was a pivotal port in the Triangular Trade that provided three legs of profit for the British Empire. Beginning in the sixteenth century, European traders sailed to Africa's west coast to exchange their goods for people. Next, they embarked on an 8-week voyage across the Atlantic to sell the human cargo in the Americas in exchange for sugar, coffee, tobacco, cotton, and goods produced by slave labor. Finally, the ships returned to places like Liverpool to unload the products in warehouses like the ones that housed the museum and Ace's studio. Each leg of the trade played a key role in creating the trillions of dollars that fueled the Industrial Revolution and solidified European countries as world powers.

The most gruesome leg of the trade is well documented in the

International Slavery Museum. This is the Middle Passage—the journey that shipped more than ten million human bodies from Africa to the Americas. The museum displayed the tools used to brand people like cattle, permanently burning the owner's emblem into their skin. We stood speechless gazing at a replica slave ship inside the museum that showed the bodies packed-in like sardines. The space was so small, captives were forced to crouch or lie on their backs. Torture through physical, mental, and sexual abuse was common on the voyage. Disease spread rapidly in the unsanitary conditions. The foul air was unbreathable. Death was common, and millions of Africans perished on the journey. Dead bodies were tossed overboard so frequently that hungry sharks followed the ships anticipating the meals. It was estimated that at least 20% of the captives were expected to die on the expedition. This is the torture my ancestors endured to come to this country. When I use to give tours at the California African American Museum, I would ask patrons to close their eyes and recreate the experience with me through a 45 second meditation.

Like all great museums, the International Slavery Museum made me feel like I was transported by a time machine. One image in particular haunts me deeply to this day. It was part of an exhibit showcasing the various torture and death techniques used on slaves. There were many: the usual shackles and handcuffs, branding irons, face muzzles, thumbscrews, neck collars, and other devices one could only imagine how they were used on human beings. In the one example I wish I never saw, a man was hanging, but not from his neck by a rope. Instead, the man was dangling from an iron hook impaled through his lower torso. His lifeless body folded over and looked like a worm on a fishing hook. His eyes delivered a frozen gaze back at anyone brave enough to look into them. I pondered questions that had no business in my thoughts: How did they get him on the hook? What did he do to deserve it? Probably just fighting for his freedom and dignity. I stared at it silently, and slightly traumatized.

"And they had to nerve to view Native Americans and Africans as 'savages!" I said to Ace.

I imagined what the natives thought of these white foreigners forcing fellow brethren into a life of labor, and occasionally hanging them from their ribcage.

"That's what they did to your people, mate," Ace said.

"That's what *ya'll* did to *us,* mate!" I said with uncontrollable anger.

"Well, I haven't done a bloody thing except bring you to England, buy you drinks at the Beatles' bar, give you free time in my studio, and take you to one of the best museums you'll ever see!" said Ace in his uncontrollably snobbish British accent. "But I do offer my sincerest apologies for anything my people did to your people. That's what this museum is about, I think."

After the exchange, barriers were taken down and the gloves were taken off. We engaged in an unfiltered dialogue about power, race, history, and music. By the end of the museum and my Liverpool tour, I viewed England as a distant and bitter sweet Motherland. This country is the reason why my native language is English. Of course, it's far from the "Queen's English," but it gets the job done most of the time. My last name "Whitaker" also originates in 12th century England, when the government introduced a personal taxation system. Whitakers usually descended from Wihtgar—a nephew of Cedric, King of the West Saxons in today's South England. On average, 24% of African-Americans' genes and ancestry come from Europe. My European roots are primarily from England. The three other last names of my family—Brown, Anderson, and Lloyd—also originated somewhere across this bloody land.

English last names were given to my ancestors because they were the human property of descendants from England. We were stripped of our birth names, as well as our freedom. This humiliating scar will always limit the amount of pride I have in my last name. It is the reason why people like Malcolm Little became Malcolm X. At times, it makes me feel like a lost, bastard child, unaware of who he is and where he is from. I counter this gloom with an overcompensating amount of African American pride. We've forged our own identity, and the world would not be the same without the contributions of the American "negro." No everyday essentials like Michael Jackson, potato chips, jazz, peanut butter, open-heart surgery, rock and roll, Jack Daniel's whiskey, Maya Angelou, and hip-hop. My apologies for "Soul Plane" and the jigaboo reality show characters. Nobody's perfect.

After the visit to the museum, we walked back to Elevator

Studios to put the finishing touches on our Funk. We then zoomed down the A483 highway for three hours to get to Ace's castle in Wales. The time flew by as we talked music, history, and life. The lush green English landscape was visible at every turn. We stopped briefly to enjoy a cigarette and a view of Sugarloaf Mountain. The sheep looked like distant white dots climbing the slopes.

Eventually, we made a left on a hidden road and drove up a hill. Ace's castle slowly revealed itself on top, majestically, like a medieval movie scene. Stone after stone stacked up to create the two-story structure. A tall peak accommodated the interior's high ceilings. Aside from your typical windows, there were small circular openings that Ace said were for feudal archers with their bow and arrows. There was a courtyard where multiple crosses—taller than me—were engraved into the stone structure. The ground was ancient cobblestone that centuries of grass had begun to grow through. I imagined what people were doing here centuries before.

Out of the diamond-paned window of my guest room, the view was beautifully eternal. For miles, rolling hills of green were all you could see. Various trees speckled the landscape, before randomly giving way to perfectly manicured fields of grass. It was the most peaceful and serene experience of the entire Eurotrip. Breathing was easy—the air felt fresher than in most other places.

Ace's wife, Jamie, made us a delicious shepherd's pie. This dish was composed of ground beef, carrots, peas, and other mixed vegetables settled in savory gravy. This hearty stew of meat and vegetables was layered under a thick cloud of mashed potatoes. The casserole was cooked in the oven to ensure every layer melded together. It was British comfort food at its best.

Early in the morrow when Ace and I exited the castle, we were welcomed by a magnificent sunrise. The gauze-like clouds streaked the sky's shades of red, orange, yellow, and smoky blue. Night had just given way to dawn. Dark, dusky shades faded, then broke into the fiery tones of the sunrise. It made the short trip seem even more fantastic.

I always dreamed of traveling the world through music like a rock star. I'm forever grateful for my musical hometown and that short Facebook post, which scored me a trip to England to play music, be inspired, and embrace the bloody bastard of a Motherland that England is to me. I knew coming from P-Funk would come in

handy one day. I am forever grateful to the Funk.
Cheers.

Chapter 5: Japan, 2010

- Capital City: Tokyo
- Population: 126 ,258,397- Ethnic Japanese- 98.5%, Korean 0.5%, Chinese 0.4%, Other 0.6%
- Currency: Japanese Yen
- Exchange Rate to dollar: 1 Yen = 0.0097 DOLLARS
- Cost of a meal: 1,000-3,000 Yen
- Cost of a beer: 340 Yen
- Language Name: Japanese
    - Hello = Konnichiwa (koh-knee-chee-wah)
    - Street Slang = "shiketeru" (when something sucks)
- Must See:
    - Natural Wonders: Mount Fuji
    - Architecture: Golden Pavilion Buddhist Temple
    - Important Historical Sights: Hiroshima Peace Memorial
- Must Do:
    - Festivals: Sakura Festivals
    - Activities: Japanese cooking class, cycling tour of Tokyo

If you're willing to compromise comfortable sleeping conditions, night travel can save you both time and money when abroad. It also enables you to cover more ground and see what would otherwise go unseen, like the moonlit Japanese countryside yielding to the early morning sun. My boy Keyshawn and I mastered night travel in Japan. We crisscrossed the country on inexpensive buses to explore its distant parts. Other options to navigate Japan included the shinkansen bullet trains—which travel at 200 miles per hour—or short flights between cities. Our night buses were much cheaper, just as comfortable, and only a few hours longer.

Our first bus departed from Tokyo's Shinjuku district at 1:30 a.m. and arrived in Osaka at 8:30 a.m. It cost around 3,500 Yen, or 34 dollars, which was around the same price we would have paid for a hostel in Tokyo if we had stayed the night. Transportation and housing in a one-shot deal—you can't beat that. We spent the day exploring Osaka, before taking an hour-long bus ride to the ancient capital of Kyoto. After spending a few days in Kyoto for some commemorative celebrations, we caught a Friday bus around midnight that arrived back in Tokyo at 7:30 a.m.—just in time for weekend festivals and a taste of the nightlife.

Night buses also made for fascinating cultural experiences. On the way to Osaka, I stepped off the bus in the middle of the evening in a barely lit place with a small-town feel. A little girl was standing there holding her mother's hand, grillin' me like a mofo. I assumed that the adorable little girl had never seen a real-life Black person before. Her eyes grew wide at the sight of me as I hopped off the bus to stretch my legs. She could barely walk or talk, and must've been three or four years-old. She pointed at me, jumped around, and mumbled a few words repeatedly to her mom. Her mom grabbed her arm and tried to calm her down, but the little girl broke free and darted straight towards me. The mother screamed something in Japanese in an attempt to reel the toddler back in.

My first inclination was to run, even though the little girl was no more than 25 pounds. Some street reflexes never die. When she was within arm's reach of me, she paused, gazed at my brown skin in fascination, and swiftly poked me with her finger. After running back to the safety of her mother, she looked at her finger and touched it with the tip of her tongue, as if she expected to taste chocolate.

"Oh god!" Keyshawn said. "It's the return of Lord Chocolate!"

Dammit. Mahogany must have told him about Guatemala. Still, I couldn't help but smirk and admire the universal defiance and curiosity of small children. These types of experiences wouldn't happen in metropolitan cities like Tokyo, where Africans and African-Americans in the military speckled the population.

Keyshawn preferred moments when we were rarities—or as he liked to call them—" Yasuke Moments." Yasuke is the O.G. African Samurai who was one of the first documented Blacks to visit Japan when he arrived in 1579. Originally, he was the servant of an Italian missionary who oversaw the introduction of Catholicism in Japan. When he reached the capital of Kyoto in 1581, the excitement to see him caused a large crowd to crush several people to death. Oda Nobunaga, the powerful feudal lord who helped to unify Japan, heard the commotion from his temple and came to inspect. Believing Yasuke's blackness was the result of paint, Yasuke was stripped of his clothing and forced to scrub his "painted" skin. Ancient Japanese manuscripts later described Yasuke as "looking between the age of 24 or 25, black like an ox, healthy and good looking, and possessing the strength of ten men." Oda Nobunaga was impressed by Yasuke and took him on as his personal bodyguard. As a 25-year-old who was who thought of himself as "black like an ox, healthy and good looking" at the time, I moved through Japan with confidence.

Yasuke quickly rose in status. He was given his own residence and bequeathed an honorable katana sword. He became the first of fewer than ten foreign-born people who rose to the rank of samurai. Eventually, a large army overpowered the feudal lord's reign, forcing Oda Nobunaga to commit ritual suicide. Yasuke fought his way through the forces and fled to a nearby castle. When the invading army came to the castle, Yasuke battled as long as he could. Rather than commit suicide—which is the samurai tradition when facing imminent defeat—Yasuke surrendered his sword over to the opposing army. This curveball prompted the new warlord to spare Yasuke's life. He viewed him as a beast incapable of understanding the honor of ritualistic samurai suicide.

"Shhhheeeiiiid, I woulda done the same thang," said Keyshawn. "Call me a beast all you want, but I'll be a living beast."

Keyshawn was a 28-year-old, easy-going dude, who

disregarded all social norms. This made him controversial back in Los Angeles, but it was an asset when we were abroad. Travelers undoubtedly encounter different norms and cultures on their journeys. This is where culture shock comes from. But according to Keyshawn, there is no such thing as normal. He was open-minded and had enough personality and independence to make traveling with him a lot of fun. He was frugal enough to slum it with me in cheap hostels in London, and daring enough to walk with me in seedy areas in Brazil. He lived in the moment, and as a result, no moment was ever dull. He'd dance anywhere to start the party, even if there was no music playing. He'd foolishly approach women, despite language and communication barriers. According to him, we were taking "Mancations," which strictly prohibited women as travel companions.

"They scare all other women away!" he'd say. "We're not taking sand to the beach!"

Our night bus made it to Osaka a few hours after I failed the little Japanese girl's chocolate taste test. At dawn, rays of the sun rising peeked through tall bamboo trees along the road. This must be why they call Japan the "Land of the Rising Sun." It's represented in their simple and symbolic flag: a large red dot in the middle of a white backdrop.

Osaka was not in our plans originally, but Keyshawn wanted to visit the city to eat their world-famous octopus balls. Osaka is the third largest city in Japan with over 2.5 million people. It is known as the "Nation's Kitchen," or *tenka no daidokoro* (天下の台所). Japanese food has always been one of my favorites. Noodles in their various forms are a reliable, tasty option in many cultures' cuisines. Japan offers two main varieties, differing mainly in thickness. Soba noodles are spaghetti-like, while udon noodles are thicker and chewier. Both can be served hot with broth or chilled with savory dipping sauces. Then there is the ubiquitous and legendary frugal eater's dietary staple: ramen. Cheap ramen noodles with freeze-dried vegetables comprised up to 20% of my diet at times as a college student and struggling bachelor. A more authentic container of this sustenance is available on plenty of corners in Japan, and sometimes in vending machines. They are also served in a more elevated style at ramen-ya, or ramen restaurants. The non-instant versions of this noodle soup come swimming in a delicious broth, topped with various meats and other goodness. Fatty slices of pork belly, crunchy bamboo shoots, zesty rings of green onions, crispy and fresh bean sprouts, a perfectly sliced hard-boiled egg, seaweed, fish cakes, canned corn kernels, and a healthy slab of butter are traditional toppings—and I recommend them all.

Arguably the most famous and popular Japanese food item, sushi comes in an infinite amount of varieties. From sushi rolls to expert cuts of sashimi, the variety is endless. Some may balk at eating uncooked sea creatures, but if you are going to try these artisan creations anywhere, Japan is definitely the best place to get adventurous. Then there's the American favorite: grilled teriyaki—fish and meats glazed with a sweet-tangy-savory-sticky mix of soy sauce, mirin rice wine, and sugar.

If I had to pick a favorite Japanese cuisine, it would be hibachi. The Japanese word for this showy style of cooking is teppanyaki, but Americans refer to it by the name for the hot plates used in this manner of cooking. Eating delicious food prepared by a supremely skilled chef right in front of you would be awesome enough. Throw in some theatrical flair in the form of flaming fire, flipping food, speedy chopping with sharp and shiny knives, and juggling kitchen tools and you've got a gastronomic show that cannot be topped. With this in mind, I was quickly on board with a trip to the Nation's Kitchen.

We stored our backpacks in lockers and began roaming Osaka's bustling Umeda district in search of food. Both of us were starving and unsatisfied with the anpans we had packed for our night bus trip. The sweet rolls baked with red bean paste inside were also losing their texture. With our backpacks in lockers for the day, Keyshawn's short legs hustled swiftly in search of a place to eat.

"Calm down," I said, "Those octopus balls will be melting in your mouth in no time."

"There they go!" he said, while pointing to a street vendor.

We made our way over and Keyshawn did the talking.

"Konichiwa," Keyshawn greeted.

"Konichiwa!" the street vendor responded. He was an older Japanese man with glasses and a chef's headwrap.

"Takoyaki?" Keyshawn whispered.

"Hai! Takoyaki!" the street vendor said, with a quick head nod.

"Ni," Keyshawn said, "Takoyaki." He held up two fingers, pointed to us, then gave a thumbs up.

"Hai!" said the street vendor, as he prepared two orders of takoyaki.

He grabbed a hand-sized carton and used a stick to flip in six balls from a pan molded with rows of circles. He covered them in a syrupy brown Japanese Worcester-type of sauce, before topping them with lines of mayonnaise. Keyshawn and I forked over a few hundred yen in exchange for the gooey goodness.

"You try it first," said Keyshawn.

"Nah ahh!" I responded. "You give those balls a test run."

Takoyaki is a traditional street food from Osaka made with diced octopus (tako), ginger, green onions, and tempura scraps. It's mixed in a batter and cooked on a cast iron griddle. Keyshawn had heard about them on some Travel Channel show. His love for seafood and an apparent novel interest in balls made them a requirement of our trip to Japan, even if we had to take a seven-hour bus trip and be assaulted by curious Japanese toddlers in order to get them.

Keyshawn grabbed a ball with his chopsticks and took a bite.

"Ommmnommnomm," he exaggerated. "Not bad. Could use a lil' hot sauce though."

This is Keyshawn's response to any food we tasted in its original country. He said the same thing after we ate croissants in France.

With our bellies full of takoyaki, we headed to the Hankyu Entertainment Park. This nine-story shopping center is topped off by the Sega Joyopolis. It's a sprawling indoor amusement park on the top two entire floors. Its Ferris wheel erupts up into the sky. The bright red wheel can be seen from much of the city, and allows you to experience a panoramic view of Osaka from nearly 350 feet in the air. Sega Joyopolis was a gamer's paradise, with a multitude of arcade games and other entertainment. There were virtual rides that simulated air gliding, riding down the rapids of a wild river, and a 4-D horror movie.

Video games were my introduction to Japan and Japanese culture. I spent hundreds and hundreds of hours as a youth with a video game controller glued to my hands, seated a few feet from the TV. It allowed me to experience Japan virtually as a ninja, samurai, sumo wrestler, thunder god, martial arts master, teenage android, demon swordsmen, and other mythical characters trying to save the Earth. Japan is the largest video game producer in the world. Sony PlayStation, Nintendo, and Sega became three of Japan's industry giants after the first manufacturing of home video game consoles began.

In 1966, Sega introduced the first video arcade game. It was of submarines shooting ships with lasers, but most of today's youth see it as nothing more than a few dots and lines. America soon entered the field and helped it evolve. Video games became household items after Jerry Lawson invented the technology that allowed game cartridges to be switched on a single system. He was a self-taught African American engineer, who grew up in the projects in Queens, NY. As a kid growing up in Jersey, switching from Street Fighter II to NBA Jam to Mega Man X kept my imagination occupied for months at a time.

After 45 minutes in Sega Joyopolis, Keyshawn and I were overwhelmed by whistles, screeching children, flashing lights, and too-cool teenagers. You couldn't walk three feet without some exclusive game with Japanese text exploding on a screen, asking for your yen. After using machine guns to fight off a few jungle creatures, we were ghost quicker than you could scream "SEGA!"

We caught a subway to Osaka Castle. Built in 1583, the castle grounds spread out over 15 square-acres and contain 13 different structures. The castle has massive gold lions guarding its entrance, and its five layers of gold-plated roof can be seen blinging a mile away. Like all good castles, it sits atop a hill and is protected by a large body of water, or moat. The imposing gate guarding the structure was several feet thick and made you feel minuscule.

Osaka Castle was the battleground of ancient feuds with over 200,000 soldiers. Throughout the centuries, wars have forced the Japanese to rebuild Osaka Castle several times. Each time, it was restored to its original and glorious structure. As late as the 1940s during World War II, the castle was used as one of the largest military armories with 60,000 people working there. This made it a target for enemy bombs, which destroyed part of the castle and killed nearly 400 people. The structure we visited was rebuilt in the 1990's.

After conquering Osaka Castle, we refueled on more takoyaki and other street food. My favorite was the deep-fried goodness of kushikatsu. These were seemingly endless options of meats and veggies cooked golden on a stick.

Our plan for the remainder of the day was to explore Tennōji Park and walk through South Osaka. Language complications nearly stopped us at the gates of Tennōji Park. We couldn't decipher the Japanese text on the ticket machine. Osaka is not as touristy as Tokyo, so English translations were a luxury rarely provided. We spent a few minutes staring at it like lost puppies, until an elderly Japanese man saved us. He pressed a series of buttons and purchased three tickets. I bowed my head in thanks and tried to give him the 300 yen for our tickets.

"No, no," he said. He bowed back, placed his wallet back in his shoulder bag, and walked away. Keyshawn did not mind keeping his measly 150-yen entrance fee, but I was overwhelmed. It was one of the kindest things someone had done for me in a while.

Tennōji Park is a 70-acre oasis that includes a botanical garden, zoo, soccer field, Museum of Fine Arts, and greenhouse. It is sprinkled with ancient shrines and Buddhist temples on its outskirts. The day's weather was finally embracing the spring season, and the sun crawled out through the clouds. We made our way in and saw the man who had purchased our tickets standing in the middle of the walkway.

"Doumo arigatou," I say to thank him again.

"Doumo arigatou *gozaimasu!*" Keyshawn says, to one-up me.

We bow in unison, as we walk past. The gentleman extends his hand and introduces himself.

"Takashi," he says. "My name...is Takashi."

Over a seven-hour period, our new friend Takashi would guide us on a walking tour throughout Tennōji Park and the nearby red light district. We only paused for origami lessons on temple lawns, or snacks and street food on park benches.

Takashi was a 72-year-old retired ice cream factory worker, who now spent his days strolling through Osaka. His eyes shimmered through delicate eyeglass frames. Around his neck was a mask, like doctors wear when they are performing surgery. It's worn by some people in Asia to help prevent diseases from spreading. The bag he carried around his shoulder had an electronic translator, a notebook, snacks, and stacks of origami paper. Takashi didn't speak much. In fact, he said very little, aside from the occasional "Peace. Ok?" when Keyshawn's chattiness interrupted the park's tranquility. He just walked and stared. We mimicked his every movement, from taking off our shoes before entering temples, to quietly observing canary-yellow flowers, to calmly listening to waterfalls trickle, and of course, halfway pretending we didn't notice the women offering sex services in the red light district. The silence was appreciated, and the peace, ok.

Large flower arrangements and sculptures brightly painted Tennōji's landscape. Despite the small crowd of locals, little was heard aside from flowing fountains and twittering birds. The slow and precise movements of silver-haired grandmothers doing Tai Chi added to the serenity of the park. Our path was split by occasional islands of fluorescent flowers. Colossal trees created umbrellas above us with their weeping branches. We paused to admire a couple painting the landscape of a still pond perfectly reflecting the greenery of the surrounding trees. Nature was in her full glory. Lakes were naturally decorated with boulder islands, dressed with trees and delicate flowers. Well-manicured trees in endless shades of green rose out and around a shallow pond. The lily pads and lotus flowers gently floated across the water, undisturbed by the turtles and koi fish. Cranes and other birds, often depicted in ancient Japanese art, flocked in the distance. It was so quiet, I wanted to ask for permission when I exhaled my breath.

Our quest became a spiritual one when Takashi explained the difference between a temple and a shrine. Temples are sacred places of peace for Buddhists. Silent meditation replaces prayer. In Shinto shrines, on the other hand, you clap twice before saying a prayer to one of many kami—a god or spirit. Shrines also have Tori gates—archways that symbolize the transition from the profane world to the sacred sphere. They look like two T's put together, and I remembered them from a few ninja video games. Temples have pagodas instead of gates. These multi-level towers could climb as high as 180 feet into the sky. Before entering a temple, you must also purify yourself by burning incense outside.

We entered a temple where emperors worshiped in the 12th century. It had a mausoleum of Buddha statues made from bones of the deceased. Impeccable restoration techniques revitalized it as if it were built yesterday. The temple was guarded by two monster-like statues of warriors—one green and one red—in attack stances. Just outside the temple, we encountered an authentic sumo wrestler in full robe and hair bun. His massive body imposed on Keyshawn's short, slender frame. Some of these guys weigh up to 600 pounds.

The spiritual cleansing at the temples and shrine was perfect preparation for our visit to Tobita Shinchi, Japan's largest prostitution district. After centuries of legalization, prostitution was outlawed in Japan in 1956. But in Tobita Shinchi, storefronts and restaurants are serving up much more than Osaka's famous food. You'd commonly see two women in a doorless storefront window, barely the size of a closet. One is a young escort, who sits on a raised platform. The other, is an elderly woman seated on a small stool in front of the establishment.

"That is a *mama-san*," Takashi explained.

"That is a *pimp...son!*" Keyshawn translated. "Word on the street...you can get it on in one of these joints for 15,000 yen. That's only a buckfiddy."

"*Only* a buck-fiddy ($150)?" I say. "You know what else is only a buck-fiddy?! Six nights at the hostel we are sleeping in."

"Word," he said. "Between my good looks and with your tall a*s walking around like Yasuke, ladies shouldn't be a problem."

We passed love hotels shamelessly advertising hourly rates in Japanese characters. In front of what might have been a pornography theater, large posters displayed naked women in plain view. They were overdone only by a 15-foot billboard with a topless petite Japanese woman, her hair flowing down her back. Takashi noticed me staring at the billboard a bit too long.

"Ohh hoo!" Takashi said, as he tapped my arm. "Hoo hooooo!" he said again, as he jabbed the side of my leg. "Hoooo!" he said, as he jabbed again, this time aiming for something below my waist and between my legs. I tilted my hips with ninja quickness, barely avoiding what would have become my most awkward travel moment to date.

A few moments later, when I'm walking in front of him and Keyshawn, I heard the same series of sounds.

"Ohh hoo!" Takashi said. "Hoo hooooo! Hoooo!"

"Eeeeeek!" Keyshawn squeaked. I guess he wasn't fast enough.

Peace was certainly "ok" for quite some time after this detour through Osaka's red light district. It's the only part of the Japan trip Keyshawn and I never talked about afterwards.

***

Becoming Takashi's shadow for a day allowed us to taste a rare flavor of Osaka. Who cares if a 72-year old Japanese dude tried to punch us in the junk. We had hoped for the same in Tokyo and Kyoto, but to no avail. Still, the experiences and exposure during the rest of our time in Japan were unforgettable. When we visited the ancient capital of Kyoto, we retraced Yasuke's 16th-century footsteps and visited the castles where he battled. We also followed the path of our favorite legend, Miyamoto Musashi.

Musashi was like Muhammad Ali and Aristotle combined. He was an undefeated samurai, with more than 60 duels ending in death for his opponents. Born into a samurai family, Musashi ran away from an abusive father at the age of eight to live with his uncle. In his first duel as a 13-year-old, he beat a samurai to death with a six-foot staff. He left home completely at the age of 15, traveling and dueling. Musashi also became a deeply philosophical person, leaving behind timeless books and quotes like, "Think lightly of yourself and deeply of the world." His classic <u>The Book of Five Rings</u> is still studied today.

Do not sleep under a roof. Carry no money or food. Go alone to places frightening to the common brand of men. Become a criminal of purpose. Be put in jail, and extricate yourself by your own wisdom.

-Miyamoto Musashi, The 17th Century Street Traveler

Samurai like Musashi were an elite warrior class comprised of the fiercest swordsmen on the planet. Roaming around feudal Japan with impeccable physical and mental discipline, they gambled with death daily in the name of reputation and honor. Their ancient quotes remind us that we can leave our body in battle, but not our honor. Samurai embraced their fate of dying in battle, or else committed ritualistic suicide. Sword was life. Sword was death. In an era before guns, I imagined all the power this had. Samurai culture was the reason why the Japanese were resistant to gun- it's a cowardly and dishonest way to kill someone. We drifted through Kyoto, wishing we could go back to the days where swords were used to handle beef.

In 2013, there were only 13 gun deaths in the entire country of Japan. This was extreme culture shock coming from the United States. In our homeland, there were over 12,000 gun deaths that same year. In Japan, most guns are forbidden. Keyshawn and I would both still have a few friends alive if America subscribed to the way of the samurai. Our lifetimes are tormented by plenty of mass shootings that have killed more children in a day than Japan will experience in a year.

Samurais used their swordsmanship to become ultimate hustlers. They started out as warriors and henchmen for the emperor, busting kneecaps and collecting taxes. The word "samurai" actually means "to serve." By the 14th century, they had come to realize their true power as untouchable masters. They took over the districts they once shook down for the emperors. They became some of the most powerful people in the world, all because of the simple fact that no one could see them with the sword.

On overwhelming days, I begin mornings with an augmented samurai meditation. Some samurai welcomed every day with intense reflections on their imminent deaths. They envisioned their bodies burning in fires, falling from cliffs, or being ripped apart by arrows and swords. In my adapted meditation, I didn't meditate on death, but instead on freedom deprivation. In my routine, I became a slave or prison inmate with no free will or control over his life, never able to see the world or anything outside the plantation or correctional facility, exploited with endless 10-hour workdays for the man instead of working on my dreams. Barred from all opportunities, subjected to inhumane treatment, and told what to do every moment of my day. I cycled through the 250 years my ancestors were enslaved in America, as well as the decades of incarceration my family and friends are giving to the system. When one or both of my brothers are in jail, it hits the hardest. After a few silent minutes with these thoughts, I attack the day with a fearless and appreciative attitude.

Our Sanjusangendo Temple visit allowed us to trace the direct steps of our hero, Musashi. It was the place of his 1604 victory over Yoshioka Denshichirō, leader of the Yoshioka-ryū. Across the street from the Kyoto National Museum, the Sanjusangendo Temple holds many objects categorized as National Treasures by the Japanese Government. Small shrines and cherry blossom trees in full bloom are sprinkled around a pond and garden. In one area, ten rows of 50 life-sized golden statues with hands in prayer are lined up on the left and right walls. Together, they are an army of a thousand statues.

Kyoto has the largest collection of well-preserved temples and ancient structures. We visited Tō-ji, the 1,200-year-old temple with Japan's largest pagoda. Five layers of curvy, intricately-decorated roofs are stacked like top hats. A nearby costume museum allowed us to put on the silk threads of emperors. We played dress-up and snapped pictures inside a replica palace. With no one around to supervise, Keyshawn posed vulgarly with the life-sized mannequins dressed in ancient garb. There was the young emperor, sitting on the floor with his legs crossed in baggy purple silk pants. Not too far from him was a woman dressed in a multi-layered kimono. We were both upset about visiting a costume museum in Japan and not having the opportunity to put on ninja costumes, though. We had both worshiped the mythical characters since we were small boys.

Ninjas were mercenary assassins in feudal Japan. They were viewed as "dishonorable" and "beneath" the samurai caste and their strict code of honor and combat. Some legends say ninjas could turn invisible and dash across water without making a splash. The element of stealth was one of the ninja's greatest assets. They lived in the shadows and walked across wooden floors without causing a creak. I often summoned ninja tactics when hustling as a teen. The inherent danger of selling drugs on street corners makes you creative and cunning. I often wore black or dark blue jeans, hoodies, and skullcap beanies. My black Adidas had white soles and laces, until I customized them with a black marker and new black strings. There was a pitch-black area under a bridge in the hood where I could disappear at a moment's notice. I used ninja agility in every fence I hopped and ninja speed when running from police. During college and graduate school, I would tap into more virtuous qualities associated with ninjas like focus, strength, calmness, skill, and supreme discipline.

The ancient landscape of Kyoto was perfect for Keyshawn

and me to get our ninja on. The picturesque scenery was enhanced by visiting during the peak of cherry blossom or "sakura" season. The beauty of the sakura only lasts for a few days. Shortly after they blossom, the gentlest breeze or rain does away with the delicate petals. Luckily, our trip coincided with the annual sakura festivals and allowed us to enjoy the unique beauty of Kyoto's gardens and parks during this special time. Kyoto was painted in a temporary lavender-pink, which contrasted with the lush green landscape. We participated in festive traditions dating back to the 8th century, where locals gathered to enjoy the rare loveliness of sakura in full-bloom. Hundreds of people congregated around food, family, friends, drinks, and games, as they danced and sang amidst falling fragrant petals. Rows of food and craft vendors lined the paths leading to the temples. Tall sakura on each side spread their branches across, creating heavenly archways. A street performer puppeteer dressed in ancient garb made his dragon dance. After experiencing the festivals, I liked the word "sakura" so much that I declared it the name of my unborn daughter. I often imagine a little brown-skinned girl with afro puffs, who we would call Sa-Sa or Saku for short.

***

The travel gods allowed for another coincidence to occur on our Japan trip in the form of the Kanamara Matsuri Festival. Keyshawn wanted to take a day trip to the city of Kawasaki for this annual jubilee, which translates to the "Festival of the Steel Phallus" (in other words: "erect penis"). Between this and the Osaka octopus balls obsession, I thought Keyshawn might be trying to confess a secret to me on our "Mancation."

Shortly after arriving in Kawasaki by train, we learned that we had just missed the Kanamara Matsuri ceremonial parade. In this spectacle, Japanese women in silk kimonos march a blush-pink five-foot penis through the streets of Kawasaki. They are followed by ten men carrying a shiny, large, black penis housed in a wooden shrine. It is a little taller, but less wide. Crowds of people join the procession behind the revered phallic sculptures, as they are thrusted up and down in the air. Missing it was surely a tragedy.

"Noooooo!" Keyshawn screamed. "That was the main reason why I wanted to come on this trip!"

He was so upset that he wanted to leave Kawasaki and skip the rest of the festival. I tried to sympathize, but a part of me couldn't.

"Lookey here," I said. "I will probably never see Kawasaki or the Kanamara Matsuri again. I probably won't be back in Japan for twenty years." I paused, dramatically. "So I'll be damnnnnnned...if I let oversized weeweeeeees...get in the way of my trip!"

I raised my voice at the end like a basketball coach giving a speech when his team is down by two, with five seconds remaining. I meant business. Nothing, not even a 10-foot penis, could get in the way of my travels.

We continued on with our travel plans, not yet prepared for something that was probably the greatest culture shock I've ever experienced.

Kanamara Matsuri celebrated fertility and life by praising one of the organs that creates it. Penis-shaped memorabilia was for sale on the streets in every form: candles, lollipops, sake glasses, costumes, flower arrangements, and more. Large wooden penises, some hundreds of years old, were on display. People climbed on top of seven-foot penises like they were horses. Small children scattered around as they raised awareness about safe sex and HIV. My prude little American mind exploded with shock. I inevitably took a signature travel picture jumping over a giant black penis statue that erupted from the ground. We enjoyed the festive mood along with some sake and live music.

**

Our last few days in Japan were spent in Tokyo. With 33 million people, Tokyo is the largest city in the world. The city could accommodate the entire population of New York, London, and a few small countries combined. Its sprawling skyline spreads out in front of Mount Fuji, an active stratovolcano that last erupted in the 18th century. Standing over 1,200 feet tall, Fuji is Japan's tallest mountain peak. We maneuvered through all corners of the city on the most confusing subway system I've ever navigated. But nothing else can be expected when you're dealing with 882 interconnected rail stations operated by multiple companies throughout the metropolis.

The trains get so crowded here, railway employees called "pushers" shove and tuck people inside the cars as the doors close.

Tokyo has great nightlife, and it got Keyshawn and me in all sorts of trouble. Futuristic neon lights lined the streets of the Roppongi District and offered an array of options. A combination of J-pop, electronica, and American pop music blared out of bars and clubs. In one small bar that we popped into for a drink, I swore it was about to go down. I was sipping a sake at the bar, while Keyshawn danced to electronica music nearby. I joined him on the floor when some hip-hop classics came on. We boogied down, as I mimicked Michael Jackson and James Brown. Our foreign flyness caught the attention of tourists and locals alike. With little effort, we became a spectacle, as all attention in the bar seemed to focus on us. The groove was on fire until the DJ started playing the Backstreet Boys. Keyshawn showed no sign of slowing down, but I gradually eased up into my two-step. In an attempt to keep us going, a Japanese girl in her early 20's stood up and cheered from the sidelines.

"Iku! Iku! Iku! Iku!" she said, and clapped.

I quickly turned up again, as Keyshawn pulled a few more moves out of his back pocket. He sank low to the ground, while balancing on one arm and splitting his legs. I fired back with a few pop locks. The young woman cheered louder, prompting a guy from her entourage to yank her back to their seats. They were with a group of guys in fitted black suits, some with thick black shades.

"That's the Yakuza, son!" Keyshawn said.

Notorious rulers of the underworld, the Yakuza still exist in Japan today. Their leaders are some of the world's top crime bosses and are blacklisted from countries like the United States. Members turn their bodies into works of art, as they cover themselves in intricate tattoos applied in a most painful method. It's the reason why some of the hostels we stayed at had a "no tattoo" policy. Some city governments also refused to hire citizens with tattoos. Many Yakuza gang members are missing fingers from a samurai-like tradition that forces them to be cut off for wrongdoings. Word on the street is today's Yakuza are usually dressed in full business suits like the entourage among the spectators at the bar we were turning up at in Roppongi. I wondered if the expensive suits were covering colorful tattoos.

Between dance moves, Keyshawn and I snapped a few pictures of each other. During one of my pictures, the young Japanese woman screaming "Iku" earlier jumped in and wrapped her arms around me. A guy who Keyshawn and I had been sharing the dance floor with photobombed the picture as well [picture in back of the book]. After snapping the picture, the suited gentleman returned and once again pulled away my iku-iku girl. He paused and stared at me, speechless and non-blinking. The universal you-bed-not-touch-her look. Keyshawn roared with a taunting laugh. I fired back with a yo-chick-chose-me head nod. We knew better than to stay in there much longer.

***

On our last day in Japan, we melted into Tokyo's Yoyogi Park—one of Japan's most liberated spaces. Japanese society is sometimes viewed as highly regimented, but places like Yoyogi Park flourish with individualized expression and freedom. We fit right in with the city's bohemian and free-spirited souls during their weekly gathering. The vibe reminded me of Los Angeles' Venice Beach at the same exact time of day. Jamming musicians, hustling artists, eccentric cosplayers, athletes, and party people were all in their own universes in separate pockets of the park. The rhythmic thumping of drum circles melded with hip hop break dancers, and a few skinny dippers by the lake. Tokyo's youth jumped around with their heads bouncing to an entirely different rhythm. As the night fell, they added twirling neon lights and glow sticks.

Adjacent to Yoyogi Park was Harajuku Square, a longtime epicenter for Tokyo's vibrant youth culture. The neighborhood is filled with boutique shops, big international fashion chains, thrift stores, and food stands. The people-watching is top-notch. Street fashion is extreme and colorful. You see girls walking around looking like they jumped out of the screen from a Sailor Moon episode. Guys imitate their best anime character's wardrobe. Gwen Stefani brought this look to mainstream American attention when her Harajuku girls with "the wicked style," as she sings, danced and performed back-up at her shows. Sky-high platform shoes, puffy tutu skirts, crazy-patterned tall socks, colorful rainbow weave topped with mammoth hair bows, stuffed animals converted into accessories, touches of punk, and sometimes all-out cosplay attire are common looks on the streets of Harajuku. Nearby, bright pink buses take up half the street they share with a 15-foot Hello Kitty statue. It seems you are in a place straight out of a cartoon, and it is pretty liberating seeing unapologetic self-expression so widely accepted.

After many hours in Harajuku and Yoyogi Park, Keyshawn and I were anxious to finally get some sleep on our 12-hour flight from Tokyo to Los Angeles. Going through customs back in the United States took an hour extra due to suspicion caused by one of my Japanese souvenirs: the twin set of gold and black samurai sword replicas. Samurai swords were lethal works of art that took hours of special techniques to craft. A sharp pair of replicas, that I would later use to slice entire watermelons in a single stroke, were necessary mementos to bring back from this trip. I named one Yasuke and the other Musashi.

"What are those?!" asked the border agent, when examining the oddly shaped box.

"Katana swords," I said.

He stared me in the eye without blinking and raised an eyebrow.

"Kataaaaaana swords?" he said sarcastically. "Why?"

"Why *not*!?" I say. "To chop a muuuhfu-"

"Peace, ok?" Keyshawn interrupted.

- Capital City: Zagreb
- Population: 4,313,707
- Demographics: 90.4% Croat, 4.4% Serb
- Currency: Croatian Kuna
- Exchange Rate to dollar: 1 Kuna= 0.15 DOLLARS
- Cost of a meal: 40-80 Kuna
- Cost of a beer: 15 Kuna
- Language Name: Croatian
  - Hello = Bok (bohk)
  - Street Slang = "Nemoj me jebat" are you serious/don't f*#% with me
- Must See:
  - Natural Wonders: Plitvice Lakes National Park, Zlatni Rat Beach
  - Architecture: Ancient cathedrals, Bokar Fortress
  - Important Historical Sights: Pula Arena, walled city of Dubrovnik
- Must Do:
  - Festivals: Ultra Music Festival
  - Activities: Island cruises, adventure sports
  - Night Life: Zrce Beach pool/beach parties, Dubrovnik cliff bars

"Couchsurfing" in half the countries I visited saved me thousands of dollars. These opportunities to crash with locals also contributed to significant shifts in my world perspective and travel experiences. Still, explaining the concept of couchsurfing is never easy because of two taboos:

1. You are sleeping on a stranger's couch.
2. You are relying on someone you've never met in foreign country.

I was introduced to the underground network of travelers and backpackers known as couchsurfers in 2010. In exchange for (possibly) opening up a couch or spare room, you are granted the opportunity to sleep on the couches of millions of people around the world. Which end of this situation is more risky and/or irresponsible? Letting someone you just met on the internet sleep in your house? Or depending on someone you've never seen before to provide you housing in a foreign land? My experiences have taught me that both situations are worth the risk.

The most popular website for this exchange is www.couchsurfing.org. It's a community of travel addicts, backpackers, hitchhikers, and free-spirits that are perhaps a little too trusting. I fit in perfectly. Through couchsurfing, I have connected with some of the most remarkable people on the planet by way of our couches. Some have become close friends with whom I've created eternal memories. In Budapest, there was my Hungarian homey, László; the Harvard Ph.D. student with a Rasta man spirit. In Port-au-Prince, the was Mirlande; a Haitian artist, working hard to rebuild her community. In Berlin, I met my German soul sister, Hazen; a dentist by day and musician by night. In Amsterdam, I was held down by my Dutch brotha, Wally, an architect and cultural revolutionary. There are plenty of others, and many of my hosts later couchsurfed with me in Los Angeles or in Miami. My couch has been graced by Italian doctors, Japanese hippies, California stragglers, among other characters. By opening my home, I've probably made enough connections to float around the world for months at a time with a guaranteed place to crash. At times, I feel like I'm subconsciously plotting a nomadic retreat from the day-to-day, 9-to-5 hustle.

Staying with a local reframes your travel experience. This is the best part of couchsurfing. Travelers always yearn for an "authentic" experience when visiting another country. Couchsurfing grants you behind-the-scenes access to cultures in all corners of the globe. Some of my hosts have let me tag along with them to work, performances, family meals, gatherings of friends, rehearsals, beach expeditions, and more. Call it good luck, but all of my hosts were people-oriented travelers themselves who appreciate the value of having a free place to stay and a unique experience from an insider's perspective of a country.

"What if they chop you up in your sleep?" my mom asked, after I told her about the movement.

"Well...what if I get hit by a bus?" I said, before she gasped in horror.

You can't ignore the fact that couchsurfing comes with a risk. But as one couchsurfer described, so does crossing the street. If you look both ways and listen out, you are less likely to get hit by a bus. You are actually more likely to be harmed in a traffic accident than hurt by your couchsurfing host. Following a few precautions can also help you limit the drama. Serious hosts have detailed profiles explaining expectations and rules. Their profiles also tell you how long they've been hosting, who their friends are, and compile reviews from previous guests. I also connect with hosts on social media to make sure they are real people. Thorough hosts verify their address via postcards containing confirmation codes sent from couchsurfing.org. Best of all, couchsurfing.org documents each scheduled hosting with the exact address, date, and arrival time.

One of my most unforgettable couchsurfing experiences was in Croatia with my friend, Maja. She had couchsurfed at my place in LA a few years prior. While I was backpacking through Europe in Summer 2012, she invited me to crash with her and seven gorgeous gals on an exotic Croatian island. The dream-like conditions of my accommodations were paralleled by Croatia's many other beautiful natural splendors. Over a thousand islands in crystal waters, calm countrysides between forests, ruins from ancient Rome, waterfall wonderlands cascading into canyons, mysterious caves, luminescent lagoons, and ancient walled towns make it one of the world's top travel destinations. Its picturesque scenery and gothic structures can be seen throughout the "Game of Thrones" TV series. Mediterranean culture blends with Slavic/Eastern European culture, creating a unique cuisine and lifestyle. I'm not sure if I can pick a favorite country in the world, but if I did, Croatia would be one of my top considerations.

After ten hours of travel by bus, train, and boat from Hungary, I finally made it to Croatia's northern coast. The sun was fading from the sky as I boarded the final night ferry across the purple darkness of the Adriatic Sea. The stars illuminated the sky like silver glitter. They were the only light to be seen out on the deck. I couldn't remember the last time I had seen so many stars. The ferry was crowded, but the universe was so still, no one dare disturb her with a single murmur. After we docked, I enjoyed a cevapcici u lepinji sandwich, some golden lager, and the sunrise, until my host, Maja, came to scoop me up.

Maja's apartment was right off what seemed to be the only major street on the island of Pag. A dozen plus pairs of sandals, heels, and sneakers were piled up along the wall by her door. Clothing, beauty products, and hair appliances created an organized clutter all about the two-bedroom loft. There was no room for me. Hell, there was no room for the seven of them living there. Understandably, not all of the roommates were on-board with my couchsurf originally, either. Maja was relentless in convincing them because of her couchsurfing experience with me in LA. So, for three days, I felt like a superhero character trapped on an island with tall Amazonian women. It was a fairy tale, but instead of Snow White and the Seven Dwarves, it was Cocoa Brown and the Seven Croatian Amazons.

Croatian women are well-aware that they are among the world's most beautiful. Many are tall and slender with Mediterranean olive skin. Hair color often falls on two ends of the spectrum: sunshine blonde or midnight brunette. In 2015, Kolinda Grabar-Kitarović, the first female President of Croatia, became the "sexiest President alive," when pictures of her in a swimsuit surfaced on the internet. Maja and her roommates were so foxy, they get paid to hang out at some beach club as professional party girls. They swapped roles as bartenders, hostesses, live pool decorations, and volleyball voyeurs at a club that was open 24 hours. Every morning I crammed into their small European car to hang out with them as they sat pretty by the club's pool [picture in the back]. After a break and evening nap, I'd return with them for their second shifts on the dance floor.

"The owner should pay YOU for those moves!" Maja would say.

Maja and the crew were summer workers on the fabled Zrće Beach (pronounced *zer-chh*). Zrće is one of those places where you constantly ask yourself, "Whose idea was this?" The white-pebbled beach coast is covered with several mega-clubs that never close. World-famous entertainers and DJ's ignite the summer here, with music festivals attracting tens of thousands of people. A combination of international and Croatian visitors adds up to a million people coming through here every summer. I probably experienced Zrće at every hour of the day, and the party literally does not stop. Last call is uncalled for. It's strikingly similar to Spain's Ibiza, but a bit cheaper.

At night, the beach is covered in a purple and blue mist made from smoke machines and laser lights. The daytime is paradise with the mild Mediterranean climate, azure waters, toasty golden sand, and two layers of mountains setting the distant backdrop. A sea of sunbathers between straw tiki huts and palm trees line the beach, even when the sun is down. Slow and steady waves lick the seashore along the lines of coastal clubs, some with decks that allow you to dive into the sea. Party boats circle the island blaring electronic music, as people fist-pump and boogie in the distance. The boats occasionally anchor and allow patrons to dive off the deck and snorkel. I got an adrenaline rush just watching tourists enjoying the various watersports, jet skis, bungee jumping, wakeboarding, and ramps for aqua flips.

Zrće is far from perfect. It's loud, overpriced, overcrowded, and at times, overwhelming. The majority of the visitors are dudes. Far too many drooled thirstily over the women and engaged in cockfights. They come from all over Europe, but Zrće is most popular with people from Italy—Croatia's across-the-sea neighbor. Maja and her crew had jokes for days about the Italians.

"If the Berlin wall had been built by Italians," said Maja, "it would have come down on its own."

***

On my first day, Maja gave me a walking tour of Zrće. It seemed like every club had a pool inside it, despite the beach being a few feet away. As we popped into different spots, she barely had to open her mouth before bartenders she knew slid us drinks on the house. The repetitive and pulsating music blasting in every bar sounded like one long song, with a few variations and breakdowns. I was only 28-years-old, but I felt like an old man as tender sunburned bodies in brightly colored shades grinded on each other. For the first time in my life, I could not keep up with the party.

Maja shared stories of tourists partying their faces off and having sex on the beach, which sounded more cumbersome than comfortable. Her satirical attitude towards the madness made it apparent that the best part of her job was watching tourist make fools of themselves.

"Watch tonight and see," she said with a smirk. "Different Italian guy always try to grab bottle from behind the bar when they think I'm not looking. We fill bottle with water, vinegar, and liquid color for them every time. Surprise!"

Sure enough, every morning we found the fake liquor bottles with half of the red or blue contents still inside. Did they really have to drink that much to figure it was not alcohol?

"Silly Italians!" Maja said as she picked up the bottles, refilled them, and placed them on the bar again.

Zrće's intensity and expensiveness caused me to retreat to quiet pockets of the beach whenever possible. Beach-bumming is one of the easiest ways to spend limited money when traveling. If you pack sandwiches, refreshments, sunblock, and a good book, you could easily spend less than ten dollars a day abroad. Depending on where you are, you might even see a few pairs of boobies flying free. This was a pleasant surprise in Barcelona, Spain, until Keyshawn wrapped his camera in his towel and became a low-key, creep-life paparazzi.

While beach-bumming on Zrće, my self-isolation somehow attracted an outgoing and boisterous Croatian named Vinko.

"The only thing worse than Italian man is American man!" said Vinko.

Vinko was a local hustler and entrepreneur in his mid-40's. His struggle to pronounce my name was real, so he preferred calling me "Stupid American." The vast majority of what he said was vulgar jokes and borderline-offensive wisecracks. The combination of Vinko loving to talk, and me being willing to listen, led to hours of interesting conversations.

Vinko's latest hustle on Zrće was thriving. At the time, he was one of the first people in the world renting flights on flyboards. These devices gave you an experience of a lifetime. After securing your feet to space boots fitted with rocket boosters, water-jet propulsion elevates you up to 45-feet in the air in mere seconds. Advanced riders can do flips, spins, and dive in-and-out of the water like dolphins. Gallons of ocean water gushed out of the boots in streams propelling riders at speeds of nearly 20 miles per hour. People maneuvered like Ironman merged with Aquaman. A long hose attached the device to a jet ski with an operator providing you power to dash across the ocean.

"I spend few thousand on used jet ski," Vinko said, "few thousand on equipment. I make back in two weeks!"

Vinko had that war veteran intensity that made you feel like you needed to walk on eggshells around him. He fought in the Croatian War of Independence in the early 1990s. It was a part of the Yugoslav Wars that lasted until 2001. This is amongst the most gruesome of wars that have taken place in my lifetime. Over 140,000 people perished, and four million were displaced from their homes. While studying at the University of Amsterdam earlier that summer, learning about the Yugoslav Wars added a most regretful term to my vocabulary: Rape Camps. I still remember my professor nonchalantly dropping the term in a lecture. I interrupted a few sentences after:

"Umm...excuse me," I asked, "This is probably a dumb question, but...what's a 'Rape Camp?'"

In an I-thought-you'd-never-ask voice, he explained.

"During the war, Serbian policies urged soldiers to rape Bosnian women and impregnate them. It was a form of ethnic cleansing. Rape was also used to terrorize civilians, force people to flee their homes, and extort money from families. Up to 20,000 women were raped in the first year alone. The United Nations concluded that a 'systematic rape policy' had been implemented. This was considered a Crime Against Humanity—a charge second only to Genocide. Before the semester ends, we will travel to The Hague to observe General Ratko Mladic go to trial for these atrocities."

Ratko Mladić, or "The Butcher of Bosnia," is one of the coldest military leaders the world has seen in a long time. During his reign as leader of the Bosnian-Serb military, he committed some of the most heinous crimes against ethnic minority groups in the former country of Yugoslavia. The list of the atrocities he carried out in the name of ethnic cleansing included the blockade of the city of Sarajevo, cutting off all traffic and aid—not to mention water and electricity. The siege of this city lasted for four years—the longest period of such an attack in modern warfare. Mladic ordered his snipers to target civilians, and used his army to force deportation. This was the kind of environment that Vinko had survived, and it made him the rambunctious watersports hustler he is today.

In 1995, Ratko was indicted by a newly established International Criminal Court for his crimes against humanity, genocide, and other war crimes. His trial had started a month before I arrived in The Netherlands in 2012. The field trip to The Hague to see this trial firsthand was by far the illest field trip I've ever been on. The Hague is home to over 150 international organizations like the International Criminal Court (ICC), the International Court of Justice (ICJ), and the tribunals for the Yugoslavian and Rwandan wars, both of which were rich in mankind's worst behavior: genocide. The Hague is the world's center for justice and human rights. Studying these topics at The Netherland's leading university was a great way to prepare me to become a civil rights lawyer. Throughout that summer, I recognized that the more aware I became of the world's beauty, the more I was also exposed to its horrors.

Yugoslavia broke up into separate countries in the 1990s—Slovenia, Croatia, Bosnia, Herzegovina, the Republic of Macedonia, Montenegro, and Serbia. In this split, Croatia scored most of the southeast coast, arguably the most tropical and desirable portions. The landmass was once a part of the Roman Empire. However, there are islands with names from their ancient Greek era, like Hvar. Places like Rovinj were part of Italy until World War II, and other port cities mirror Venice with canal streets.

"This is why our food the best. It's Mediterranean. It's Italian. It's Greek. It's Turkish, it's Croatian!" Vinko said.

He educated me on history and culture as we guzzled beers well into the sunset and discussed the difference between silence and peace.

To Vinko's dismay, I did not rent his Ironman-Aquaman flyboard for a $150.

"I may be a Stupid American," I said, "but I ain't that stupid!"

A watersport and CWPS (Crazy White People Stuff, remember?) pass time I did indulge in while in Croatia was wakeboarding. I attached myself to a mechanical zipline that zoomed across the Adriatic. It drags you a few hundred feet in a circle as you try to enjoy a view with layers of mountains behind the beach, while being whizzed across the water.

The watersports, war veterans, and infinite Italians of Zrće wore me down by my final night. I wasn't in the mood to pull a double-shift like some of Maja's roommates. Instead, I sat around with them while they pregamed, ate sandwiches, shared jokes about Italians, and enjoyed a purple Croatian sunset over the ocean from their balcony. They rotated like tag-team partners to get dolled-up in the unit's only bathroom. The music and mood were completely different than Zrće. Maja's stereo played only mellow music like Zero 7, Erykah Badu, and Björk. They shared sinister stories of tourists who let the good times get the best of them. They passed around a joint of marijuana—another cultural universal becoming more common around the world. Perhaps it is indicative of the corners I crawl in, but Mary Jane has been openly offered to me in half of the countries I've visited. As the international herbal aroma floated in the air, I praised the heavens for making me a couchsurfer, giving me a break from Zrće, and blessing me with a small army of Croatian beauty queens to keep me company. This, at least for me, was the real Croatia.

"You don't want to go back to Zrće?" Maja asked. "This is last night for you. Peak time for tourist."

"Nah, no Zrće," I said. "And I'm not a tourist, fam. I'm a traveler."

Maja squinted back at me with her deep brown almond-shaped eyes and stern resting face. It was unfriendly, but strikingly foxy. Then she let out one of her rare smiles, which always illuminated the room.

"Zrće is overcrowded, but you come here for crowd!" she explained.

This concludes 1/3rd of Street Traveler. The full book is forthcoming.

Age 15 Arrest/Drug Raid Article

Mom, son among 4 facing drug charges

PLAINFIELD — Four city residents, including a mother and her son, were arrested on drug charges after members of the Plainfield Narcotics Division searched a home at ███ ███ police said.

█████ Whitaker, 34, and her son, Amir, 15, of ███ Fifth St. were charged Wednesday with possession of a controlled dangerous substance, possession of a controlled dangerous substance with intent to distribute and possession of a controlled dangerous substance with intent to distribute within 500 feet of public housing.

████████, 42, of ████████ was charged with possession of drug paraphernalia.

████████, 15, of ████████ Ave. was charged with loitering to commit a controlled dangerous substance offense.

Rutgers Self-Portrait (2007)

"B.A.T.A" Drawing from USC Student (2009)

Guatemala

Hike a Volcano, Jump in the Clouds

Dario: The Rastafarian-Crip-Pirate-Guatemalan-Hustler

Hiking the 2,400-year-old Mayan Ruins of Tikal

South Africa

My South African Students/KnuckleHeads

Petting a Cheetah!

Robben Island After Nelson Mandela Prison Cell Visit

England

The First Jump

2012 Olympics in London

Studio Session in Liverpool

Japan

Sakura (Cherry Blossom) Festival

Tokyo Nightlife (Iku! Iku! Iku! Iku!)

Osaka Garden

Croatia

Pag Island

Wake Boarding (CWPS)

Off to Work!

Actual Journal Entries

2/25/04

Discrimination/Southern 6..4

The day started out normal.
Got to campus then went to accounting II
I missed the last class, but easily
got up to pace. I also found out I had
the highest score on the test. Professor
congratulated me as I walked in class
late as usual, I haven't been on
time yet, and I also missed like
5 out of 12 classes. I'm also sharing my
book with ███████ and ███████ and
because of that, I wasn't even able
to study properly for the test.
Regardless of the circumstances, I still
aced it! Not only that, but most
of class got at least 20 points
under me! I am indeed superior.
At the end of class Professor was
handed out extra credit work sheets
because the class had done so poorly
on the test. When I attempted to
get the she wouldn't let me. She said
you had to have at least lower than 75
on the test to get them. That surprised

Dear Mom   5/14/04

Not a week after mothers day, just inform
Not a week after mother's day and my souls been scorn
As I speak, my moms in a cage,
and ~~were~~ I'm uninformed of her release day
Just a week after mother's day,
and she couldn't maintain,
I guess her felling of unsatisfaction will always remain.
Yesterday I was informed for the umpteenth time
that my mom has been aprehended
for a mysterious crime.
              AND ITs not even a week after mothers day
A designer louie vuitton bag with 5 pair of
matching designer shades
And a card sgen by her 3 children that Hallmart made.
Its what she said she always wanted, she was been telling me for a while
~~She~~ But when I shoved it to her, she didnt even smile.
~~The symptoms could be seen~~
Symptoms that could bee seen by the blind
It was so obvious she was in the danger zone
As a recurring base head who just lost
her job and was forced to move in
a drug infested home.
And it ~~was out~~ even a week after
                                   mothers
                                   day

Who's Who? I'm Me!!
2 grams & A Benjamin with Honors!!
5-23-05

Haunt fell this good in a while. Hasnt
had on one of these graduation caps in 3 years?
I couldnt resist, even though I still got 48 more hours.
The moment I was handed to me I got an
adrenaline rush. Cant believe it finally here!!
After 3 years of night classes, of saturday classes,
Of summer classes, of 3 mile walks, of 4
cars breaking down, of hard grind. Sitting back
reflecting, I went thru alot, but I'm only
half way there. I feel like I can do this
another 10 years!! If I dont have to pay that is.
Totally I'm just coming home from un awards
ceremony. I got two prestigious award plaques.
I gave one to Nana and one to grandma.
I was one of the 20 out of 11,200 UCC
student to recieve the "Who's who among
UCC students." I'm also graduating with gold
on too. Honors!! I remember at my highschool
graduation looking at the hand ful of people with
gold, feeling jealous. Thinking how thier parents force
them to get good grades and my parents didnt even
force me to go to school. Now I wonder how the
700 other students will feel looking at
my gold. BLING BLING ▮▮▮ all

Round 9   8/20/05

Right now I'm at my new job at SOS security.
Been working here for about a month's and shits
going good. The only problem is my porn-greedy
co-workers. It's only on weekends from 12:30am-12pm.
Thats already starting to be a problem. Before I
even get off work a concert will be starting that
I would have died to see 4 months ago (Red hot pepper 50s's Band)
But I didn't even request off or call out. Partly
cuz I need the money & partly cuz I'm not
interested fully (can't even find nobody to go with.
I really got to make some new friends with similar
interest. Hell in less than a week I will be
packing my bag to go away to school. I know Rutgers is
only 20 mins away, but I'll still be on my own
kinda. Think my roommate name is ████████ kid
looking white boy who looks like he knows how to
party. I hope so cuz I sure am ready to hope
I open up and make new friends and find a chick
I can chill with cuz at times it seems like I
don't have either. ████████ are in Va gettin money.
I wasnt even invited to go... but I guess they wouldak
my response. Still coulda asked though ████████
pulled some young girl shit █. She set me up on

6-17-06

Happy Fathers Day

sup Pops, Happy fathers day, know U fell u owe me an eternal apology
Hoth be told the past doesn't bother, But future is on my mind constantly
i don't feel like your day is disregard, Cuz Me, brother & auntie too
struggling right now times is hard,
we had our fair share of mishaps in life, U took me to school (when
I was kick out, I bail you out twice
U left the door unlocked when the cops came for child support,
U kept my bail money when you went to court
U sold me fuck up (cars) damn this gers on, but so does life
and thats why we move on, U to old to be relapsing now gotta stay strong
catchin the ass naked beating of ta pain,

smoking that before I even touch the eulogy think of all the
shit u lost an analyze your worth? Biving Dying to Yeh niggas was the 1st
But there has to be a blessing somewhere in that curse

All you put me thru you cost me only 1992 was the one christmas
thru you wasn't there. It was the best day in my life
Reflecting on those somber days in the shop, Reck tows still
and Fer bros for days non stop
grandpa telling me somethin the wheel right,
my uncle the car or under the hood holding the light
with the tone pumping out of grandpas system
It thats where I got the funk, Thats where I got unk
Rest in peace bo cash, god damn Bishop, just right after you ones
we would go fishing,
wake me the brim for the 5th grade prom straight me you will forever

live on, I know in heaven listing to this song,
I feel your presence on stage every time I perform

I pray to god that im making you proud, I see your face when
look in the clouds, Cant understand why the lord aint allow
you to see your great ur a beautiful great grand child
a her beautiful smile
wish I could jammed with you on the drums, But Im stuck
with far off son who cant keep it on the one
grandpa I appreciate all youve done, we coulda
did alot less, u know it happens to some

Hook: Papa was a rolling stone grandpa aint get to see me make
regardless of the past ya're affect, ya're noble, Don't know how you could take it,
spent more time in jail more than
still the little things are appreciated

9/1/07 Home Sick

Of corse I hate it. My lifestlye has changed
dramaticlly. New friends, new mind-set, ect.
I left everything I know 3 thousand miles away.
So I guess I have to adapt. Either that or
adapt things to me, ha... story of my life.
I guess I'm more of an adapter, huh. Things
can be hard to change. Things like the
world & society, So go ahead & compromise.

But cannot sit by and watch certain things.
I cant be part of that neutral train.
Instead I am willing to be the one willing to
get ran over to taunt down a lil bit.
As long as the people remember us anyway.
I think I've rehedered that. but I have to do
alot more in this physical frame. To Truly my eys
the copycurrent can like change. We all have
potenical to make change but not many of us see it.
so how can I motivate people to see their potenical.
By telling them your story!!

Anyway, LA is not the city for me. I'm sure it needs
change & everything, but I gotta fix my house lot.
So I will soon be returning home.
I can tell that I'm home sick. I talked to
all kind of friends in the past few days. (Almost)
whenever I hang, im mad. I always want
to cry. Ironically I rarely shead tears. But,
maybe things will get better. Always hope.

California Growth

Hard to believe I've been a growing here 4 years. What the fuck... "Unveresse we. Limit the F* bombs. They've grown taller. Emerge from their isolate cocoons. Mature. Knowing I've been a part of that growth. The year we're on our way to the camping trip. 3rd time doing it. The class of 2011 has to be my favorite class though Roll DAWGS. as freshmen & juniors, scholars as 11th graders, young adults now. "We are going to play around the world." Gone at the end of this California journey. I believe Miami is next. Who knows what that holds. The growth I may experience there over the next 1-3 years. Will I transfer to Berkeley? I want to at least try.

So how have I grown here? How am I different?
1. More discipline - The behaviors 3's, absence w/ school.
2. Wiser - From overall experience & maturity
3. Better understanding of relationships - Being forced to start from scratch
4. Better understanding of the world - Travels & cross cultural
5. Somewhat better understanding of education - It's complicated
6. Somewhat better understanding the "system" - Social, political, education. Still conundrums though. Hence law school

9/25/13 Break down

Breath, Slow down, Relax. Indeed there is urgency, but you have always done so well w/ patience. Your success is inevitable. The struggle is secondary. I mean... you're a Dic? Knuckle Head o Mentally Numb. None of that shit matters.

I'm just getting old. Tired. This is not sustainable. I just need to get Oprah-Rich. Everything would be better?? (see "6 Hrys")

—362—

ABOUT THE AUTHOR

Dr. Amir Whitaker Esq.

Amir is an educator and civil rights lawyer on a mission to inspire people with his story. As an author, he aims to foster hope, awareness, and resilience through his writing. His work is a continuation of Project KnuckleHead, a nonprofit organization he started that empowers youth through music, art, and educational programs.

Often referred to as "Dr. KnuckleHead," Amir was introduced to the criminal justice system as a child when he visited both his mother and father in prison. At age 15, Amir himself was arrested and entered the juvenile justice system. Problems at school eventually led to him being expelled. Despite these hardships, Amir went on to complete five college degrees, visit 30 countries before turning 30-years-old, and become one of America's leading social change agents.

As a lawyer referred to as a "civil rights and education stalwart" by the Daytona Times, Amir has negotiated settlements and educational policy changes that have improved the lives of hundreds of thousands of youth across the country. He has also taught all grade levels—from kindergarten to college—in a variety of educational settings for over than a decade, and has held teaching certifications in Florida, California, and New Jersey. He has delivered keynote speeches to thousands, and written for leading publications across the country, including TIME Magazine.

Amir's first book is an autobiographical trilogy entitled *The KnuckleHead's Guide to Escaping the Trap.* This abridged compilation follows Amir's transformational journey through the challenges that have molded him into an agent of change. The first installment, *Origins*, takes place during Amir's adolescence as he is unknowingly engulfed in a war. It chronicles the devastating impacts of poverty, mass incarceration, the War on Drugs, and the School-to-Prison-Pipeline— all through the lens of a youth with an unrelenting desire to overcome the odds.

The second installment—*Million: Money on my Mind*, follows Amir as he pushes himself to double his high school GPA, and dive into a 12-year college career that takes him across the country. In the process, he earns five degrees from some of the nation's leading institutions.

Street Traveler is the final book in the trilogy. It follows Amir's quest to visit 30 countries before his thirtieth birthday. He uses his "street smarts" to escape danger and explore intriguing destinations across Asia, Africa, Europe, Latin America, and the Caribbean. The travels help shape Amir's world view and introduce him to unforgettable characters around the globe.

For book readings and speaking events, contact us at info@projectknucklehead.org.

ABOUT THE PUBLISHER

KnuckleHead Publishing is an initiative that seeks to inspire young and old alike. Each book purchase allows Project KnuckleHead to provide a free book to an incarcerated or "at-risk" youth. KnuckleHead Publishing has provided books and digital libraries to incarcerated youth across the country.

Each One Teaches One!
www.knuckleheadpublishing.com

77448647R00203

Made in the USA
Middletown, DE
22 June 2018